RISING SONS

Also by Bill Yenne

The American Aircraft Factory in World War II

Superfortress: The B-29 and American Air Power in World War II
(with General Curtis E. LeMay)

Indian Wars: The Campaign for the American West

The B-17 at War

Attack of the Drones: A History of Unmanned Aerial Combat

Operation Cobra and the Great Offensive:
60 Days That Changed World War II

Aces: True Stories of Victory and Valor in the Skies of World War II

Black '41: The West Point Class of 1941 and
the American Triumph in World War II

The Go For Broke Monument, located near Little Tokyo in downtown Los Angeles, commemorates the Nisei veterans who served in the United States armed forces during World War II. Designed by Los Angeles architect Roger Yanagita and formally dedicated on June 5, 1999, the forty-foot black granite circle is engraved with the names of 16,126 Nisei men and 37 Nisei women. The architect's inspiration for the circular design originated with descriptions of Nisei soldiers charging upward to capture a hill, which happened frequently during their difficult battles overseas. *(Photo by Bill Yenne)*

RISING
SONS

◆·◆·◆

The Japanese American GIs

Who Fought for the United States

in World War II

BILL YENNE

THOMAS DUNNE BOOKS

St. Martin's Press ≈ New York

THOMAS DUNNE BOOKS.
An imprint of St. Martin's Press.

www.thomasdunnebooks.com

Design by William Ruoto

LIBRARY OF CONGRESS CATALOGING-IN-PUBLICATION DATA

Yenne, Bill, 1949–
    Rising sons : the Japanese American GIs who fought for the United States in
World War II / Bill Yenne. — 1st ed.
        p. cm.
    Includes bibliographical references.
    ISBN-13: 978-0-312-35464-0
    ISBN-10: 0-312-35464-9
    1. United States. Army. Regimental Combat Team, 442nd. 2. World War, 1939–1945—
Participation, Japanese American. 3. World War, 1939–1945—Japanese Americans.
4. World War, 1939–1945—Regimental histories—United States. 5. World War, 1939–1945—
Campaigns—Europe. 6. Japanese Americans—History—20th century. I. Title
    D769.31442nd .Y37 2007
    940.54'1273—dc22

                                                                        2007012901

First Edition: July 2007

10   9   8   7   6   5   4   3   2   1

You fought not only the enemy, but you fought prejudice—and you have won.

—President Harry S Truman, August 1946

From a cautious experiment the Army has received an unexpectedly rich reward. A group of sinewy Oriental soldiers only one generation removed from a nation that was fighting fanatically against the U.S. was fighting just as fanatically for it.

—*Time* magazine, July 1944

As sons set off to war, so many mothers and fathers told them, live if you can, die if you must, but fight always with honor, and never ever bring shame on your family or your country. Rarely has a nation been so well served by a people it so ill-treated.

—President Bill Clinton, June 2000

CONTENTS

One warm spring day not so long ago, I was driving north on California Highway 99, the main freeway through the Golden State's vast Central Valley that links the great agricultural cities such as Bakersfield, Fresno, Merced, Modesto, Stockton, and Sacramento like beads on a chain. Just south of Manteca, a friend from out of state who was riding with me pointed to a large green sign that identified the road as the 442nd Regimental Combat Team Memorial Highway.

"What's that about?" he asked.

I explained that before World War II, many of the people who owned and operated the small truck farms, growing fruits and vegetables here in the Central Valley, and in the rich farm country near the coast from Salinas to Ventura County, were Japanese immigrants and their Japanese American offspring. I went on to say that following the attack on Pearl Harbor, there was a pervasive fear that the West Coast of the United States could be invaded by Imperial Japan, and in the accompanying hysteria, the United States government had ordered the internment of ethnic Japanese living in the West. This included both the Nisei, who were American-born citizens of the United States, and their Issei parents, who had been denied citizenship.

He said that he had heard about this. He knew that people of Japanese ancestry had been rounded up from cities and farms, and that they were confined to internment camps during World War II.

I went on to say that, despite this, thousands of young Japanese American men—and even a few women—had volunteered to serve in the United States armed forces.

"It was their country, and they wanted to serve, just like anyone else their age. The internment camps were especially insulting to them. These young Japanese Americans thought of themselves as Americans, and they wanted to prove it. They too, were part of the Greatest Generation. They just had parents who were Japanese."

"I didn't know that," he replied in amazement. "I don't think that a lot of people realize that this happened. Somebody ought to write a book."

He is right. Too few people know about the Nisei GIs of World War II, and about what they accomplished, both in combat and in proving that they, too, were true Americans—and true members of America's Greatest Generation.

ACKNOWLEDGMENTS

The author is indebted to the many Nisei veterans who shared their time with me and told me their stories, as well as to the many people who helped to facilitate such opportunities for conversations, especially Lawson Sakai of Friends and Family of Nisei Veterans, himself a veteran of the 442nd Regimental Combat Team. Thanks also to my agent, Jake Elwell, without whom this book would not have been possible.

Special thanks go to Teri Kuwahara at the Go For Broke Educational Foundation, who not only arranged for me to meet veterans, but who gave me access to the materials collected by the Foundation. The Go For Broke Educational Foundation was formed in 2000 as the operating organization dedicated to the educational mission of the 100th/442nd/MIS World War II Memorial Foundation that was established in 1989. Their goals include keeping the story of the Nisei soldiers of World War II alive for future generations, and they use the slogan "We must never forget." Our hope in producing this book is to be a part of perpetuating the memory of these courageous veterans.

EXPLANATION OF TERMS

Issei: First-generation Japanese Americans. They were born in Japan and their cultural background was Japanese, but they were in America by choice. Despite a certain nostalgia for the old country, they had made the United States their home. Had they not been prohibited from citizenship, many, if not most, would have become United States citizens. At the time of World War II, they were mostly in the over-fifty-five age group.

Nisei: Second-generation Japanese Americans. They were born, raised, and educated in the United States. Despite having encountered some racial discrimination, they were generally anxious to be considered American. Most of them lived in the ethic melting pot states of the West Coast and Hawaii, so the racial discrimination that they did encounter was much more limited than that experienced in the South by African Americans in the years before the war. As such, they were very patriotic. At the time of World War II, they were mostly under the age of thirty.

Kibei: Like the Nisei, they were second-generation Japanese Americans, but they were distinct from Nisei in that they had been sent to Japan for all or part of their education. Those who had received their early education before traveling to Japan were often as patriotic as the Nisei, because they were treated badly in Japan by native-born Japanese their own age.

Sansei: Third-generation Japanese Americans. At the time of World War II, they were mostly children under the age of ten.

RISING SONS

INTRODUCTION

The date is August 23, 1959, two days after Hawaii was admitted to the Union as the fiftieth state. The scene is the House of Representatives chamber in the United States Capitol in Washington, D.C. Two weeks shy of his thirty-fifth birthday, Daniel Ken Inouye is about to be sworn in as the first congressman to be elected from the new state.

"Raise your right hand," Speaker Sam Rayburn tells the young man, as he routinely told all the freshmen.

The young man cannot.

He has no right hand. He left it near San Terenzo in Italy during World War II.

Lieutenant Inouye had lost his right arm on April 21, 1945, the day that he earned a Distinguished Service Cross that would later be upgraded to the Congressional Medal of Honor.

He cannot raise his right hand, but he proudly raises his left hand, and he proudly takes his oath of office.

It is an abbreviated first term for Dan Inouye. The first session of the 86th Congress is nearly over. Because Hawaii was admitted midterm, he will serve mainly in the second session. However, he will be reelected in 1960, and he will be seated for both sessions of the 87th Congress. He will take his seat for his second term on January 3, 1961, seventeen days before John F. Kennedy will make his oft-recalled inaugural speech, which will contain that stirring admonition "Ask not what your country can do for you, but ask what you can do for your country."

The nation is still stirred and inspired by these words, but it is a sentiment that Dan Inouye and many thousand Nisei men of his generation had heard nearly two decades earlier. Their country had needed them, and they had asked only what they could do. What is most remarkable is that they did so despite the suspicion and animosity that descended upon Japanese Americans during World War II, and the official imposition of a government policy that called for the internment of the families of many of the Nisei men who fought for the United States.

In retrospect, it is amazing that these sons of Japanese immigrants "asked what they could do for their country," and doubly amazing that there were so many. The monument near Little Tokyo in downtown Los Angeles that today commemorates those who asked what they could do contains the names of 16,126 Nisei men and 37 Nisei women. The majority of them, like Dan Inouye, served with the 442nd Regimental Combat Team and its component battalions. This unit was, for its size and its length of service, the most decorated in the history of the U.S. Army, receiving an unprecedented eight Presidential Unit Citations. The 4,000 men who first went overseas with the unit in April 1943 were replaced more than three times over, with many of them killed or wounded. Indeed, there were 9,486 Purple Hearts issued to those men killed or wounded in action. There was an aggregate total of nearly 5,000 Bronze Stars, Silver Stars, and Distinguished Service Crosses (DSC) awarded to the Nisei GIs, and 21 of the men, including Dan Inouye, have been awarded the Medal of Honor, America's highest decoration for valor.

Behind these numbers, there are the stories, individual stories of the men and collective stories of the units with which they fought. This book represents a cross section of the stories of the lives and unselfish heroism of the Nisei GIs who "asked what they could do," and who answered their country's call in the most difficult of times.

CHAPTER 1

Pearl Harbor,
A Cultural Crossroads

ountless accounts of World War II have begun with an
expression of the axiom that both history and everyday
American life changed forever on the morning of Sunday, December 7, 1941. This was true for nearly any American alive at the time, and it was especially true for the people of Japanese ancestry living in Hawaii.

Sunday morning had dawned warm and pleasant, as it almost always does in the mild climate of the Hawaiian Islands, even in December. The mood was relaxed and tranquil, as it almost always was in those days in Hawaii—even in the big city of Honolulu on the island of Oahu, then a sleepy municipality with a population of 137,000 people.

Typical of many people around Honolulu, the Inouye family on Coyne Street were up at 6:30 that morning, and having a leisurely breakfast before church. As Daniel Inouye recalls in his memoir *Journey to Washington,* "It was going to be a beautiful day. Already the sun had burned off the morning haze over Honolulu and, although there were clouds over the mountains, the sky was blue."

About two hundred miles north-northwest of Honolulu, aboard six aircraft carriers of an Imperial Japanese Navy task force, the mood was anything but relaxed and tranquil. Aboard the *Akagi, Hiryu, Kaga,*

Shokaku, Soryu, and *Zuikaku,* armorers scrambled to load ordnance aboard an armada of Aichi Type 99 dive bombers and Nakajima Type 97 torpedo bombers. Crewmen and pilots of these attack aircraft, as well as of the Mitsubishi A6M "Zero" fighters that would escort the bombers, received their final briefings and climbed aboard. The carriers, escorted by two battleships, three cruisers, nine destroyers, and three fleet submarines, had departed Japan's Kuril Islands on November 26, and had made their way to within striking distance of the big American naval base at Pearl Harbor on the western edge of Honolulu.

By 7:00 A.M., 183 Japanese aircraft were airborne, and the only people on Oahu who knew it were a pair of U.S. Army radar technicians at Opana. They weren't sure what the blips on their radar scopes represented. Were they American planes inbound from the West Coast, or something else? Fifteen minutes later, word of the incoming aircraft had reached the duty office of the 14th Naval District, where it was decoded and passed along to Rear Admiral Husband E. Kimmel, commander of American naval forces in Hawaii.

A few miles from Kimmel's headquarters, young Daniel Ken Inouye, two months to the day past his seventeenth birthday on this warm Sunday morning, was finishing his chores. The Imperial Japanese Navy aircraft were seventy miles away and closing.

The snarl of Mitsubishi Kensei and Nakajima Sakae radial aircraft engines was first heard over the sugarcane fields of Oahu's north shore by about 7:40 A.M., and at 7:53, the first bombs fell on the warships anchored near Ford Island within Pearl Harbor.

Dan Inouye had finished his chores and was combing his hair, getting ready for church. Like many people in Honolulu that morning, including a lot of the young sailors at Pearl Harbor, he was listening to Hawaiian music on his radio.

The sailors aboard the ships anchored on Battleship Row near Ford Island were taken completely by surprise. In quick succession, torpedo bombers scored hits on the battleships *Oklahoma, Utah, California, Arizona,* and other vessels. A bomb then penetrated the deck of the *Arizona,* exploding within her forward magazine with devastating results. The bombers kept up their attacks on the ships, as well as Army Air Forces aircraft at nearby airfields.

The musical program that the young McKinley High School senior was listening to stopped abruptly as the announcer suddenly came on the air shouting that Pearl Harbor was under attack. Inouye heard him yell, "Pearl Harbor has been bombed, for real! This is no test!"

Dan and his father walked out of their home and looked in the direction of the big naval base. His younger brothers and sister began to follow them out, but their father told them to stay inside where it was safer. As the eldest son, Dan was considered old enough to witness the unthinkable tragedy unfolding at Pearl Harbor. With his father, he watched the puffs of black smoke as antiaircraft rounds exploded in the sky. When three pearl gray aircraft thundered overhead, they could see that their wings were marked with the red disks of the Imperial Japanese rising sun insignia. Dan Inouye had sensed the Japanese pilots looking down at them as the planes raced overhead. "I felt that my life had come to an end at that point," he recalled as he recognized the insignia of the land of his ancestors. "I wasn't quite certain as to what the future held for us."

As the attacking aircraft disappeared in the smoky haze that now obscured the Koolau Mountains, the phone rang in the little Coyne Street bungalow. Dan Inouye had been volunteering as a first aid instructor at the local Red Cross station, and they were calling to see how soon he could get there. Injured people seemed to be everywhere, and they needed his help. His mother was terrified when he ran to grab his bicycle, but his father told her that it was his duty, that he must go.

The second wave of 168 Japanese aircraft swept in around 8:40, attacking the surviving American ships as they attempted to get under way and steam toward the open water of the Pacific Ocean. By this time, young Dan Inouye had reached the Red Cross first aid station. "We worked all night and into the next day," he recalled. "There was so much to be done—broken bodies to be mended, shelter to be found for bombed-out families, food for the hungry. We continued the following night and through the day after that, sleeping in snatches whenever we could."

Although greatly overshadowed by the air attack, Imperial Japan also attacked Hawaii from the sea. Five 46-ton Type A one-man, midget submarines were also intended to take part in the attack. Launched by larger I-Class fleet submarines the night before, they were not nearly as successful as the aircraft. Except for unconfirmed speculation that one may have entered the harbor and fired torpedoes, the submarine attack failed.

One of the five was confirmed sunk by the destroyer *Monaghan,* and one was attacked and probably sunk by another destroyer, the *Ward.* Two disappeared completely, and the fifth, the Ha-19, suffered a failed gyrocompass and went aground at Waimanalo on the east coast of Oahu on December 8. The sub and its pilot, Ensign Kazuo Saka-maki, were promptly captured by the Hawaii National Guard. Among those involved were the first Japanese American soldiers to see action in World War II, notably young Thomas Tsubota, who would later be in combat in the Far East with Merrill's Marauders.

In 1941, the Hawaii National Guard included the 298th Infantry Regiment, composed of men from Oahu, and the 299th Infantry Regiment, composed of men from the outer islands. The pool of young men who made up the Guard in Hawaii naturally included Japanese Americans, including Tsubota. In fact, while they comprised a third of Hawaii's population, Japanese Americans accounted for half of the approximately three thousand troops in the Hawaii National Guard.

The two waves of bombers that attacked Oahu had struck in the space of just ninety minutes, leaving 2,335 American service personnel and 68 civilians dead, and 1,178 Americans badly injured. All eight battleships at Pearl Harbor were damaged or destroyed, as were three cruisers, four destroyers, and four other vessels. The sinking of the *Arizona* alone had cost the lives of more than 1,100 men. Like no other incident before September 11, 2001, the attack stunned and infuriated the American people and galvanized the nation.

On December 8, as Thomas Tsubota and the 298th Infantry Regiment were taking the Ha-19 into custody, President Franklin D. Roosevelt went before a joint session of Congress to ask for a declaration of war.

"Yesterday, December 7, 1941—a date which will live in infamy—the United States of America was suddenly and deliberately attacked by naval and air forces of the Empire of Japan," he began. He discussed the Pearl Harbor attack, and the Imperial Japanese attacks on Malaya, Hong Kong, Guam, the Philippines, and Wake Island that had occurred in the hours immediately following the initial bombing of the naval base in Hawaii. He concluded by asking Congress to "declare that since the unprovoked and dastardly attack by Japan on Sunday, December seventh, a state of war has existed between the United States and the Japanese Empire."

The United States was at war.

For the Japanese Americans in Hawaii, and for those living on the mainland, the Pearl Harbor attack had come as a devastating clash of cultures, and as a most ominous milestone on what had been a long and difficult road.

CHAPTER 2

Coming to America

The first immigrants from the Far East to arrive in the United States in large numbers were Chinese. The first major wave of immigration had reached Hawaii—not yet part of the United States—and the West Coast of the mainland in the middle of the nineteenth century. As with the European immigrants arriving on the eastern shore of the United States during this period, they saw opportunities in the rapidly expanding economy of a robust and growing nation. Many Chinese immigrants tried their hand in the California gold fields, while still others started small businesses. A sizable number of Chinese were employed in the construction of the Central Pacific Railroad in the 1860s.

Immigration from Japan was a slim trickle compared to that from China, because Japan remained a closed society until the latter half of the nineteenth century. Japan had begun actively trading with Europeans around the middle of the sixteenth century, but with the beginning of the seventeenth century, her emperors had deliberately cut Japan off from outsiders. They were anxious to eliminate the influence of European Christian missionaries as well as that of other Asian cultures. The pendulum swung, and this policy began to change again during the reign of Mutsuhito, the Meiji ("Enlightened Rule") emperor, who reigned over Japan for forty-five years, from 1867 to 1912. During this time, he initiated a complete reversal of earlier policies, transforming Japan from an isolated feudal society into a modern, industrialized nation. Mutsohito gradually embraced the industrial revolution as a means toward economic progress, while opening Japan to outside cultural influences. This change of course would also gradually open the door to Japanese people emigrating abroad, although this would remain a mere trickle until later in the Meiji period.

A handful of Japanese immigrant workers had reached the sugarcane fields of Hawaii and the gold fields of California as early as the 1860s. One of the first large groups of Japanese settlers to reach the mainland came to Gold Hill in California's El Dorado County in 1869 as part of a venture known as the Wakamatsu Tea and Silk Farm Colony. In 1884, the Meiji government reached an official agreement with sugar plantation owners in Hawaii to permit the emigration of contract laborers, but few Japanese immigrants continued eastward to the mainland.

In contrast to the large numbers of Chinese, the Japanese population of the United States remained tiny. In 1870, when the Chinese population was numbered in the tens of thousands, there were just 55 Japanese in the United States, of whom 33 lived in California. A decade later, the United States Census counted only 148, with 86 in California. By 1890, however, there were 2,038 Japanese in the mainland United States, with 1,114 in the Golden State. In Hawaii, which was not yet a territory of the United States, there were twice that many.

A backlash against Asian immigration to the United States gathered momentum in the 1870s, leading to passage of the Chinese Exclusion Act of 1882, which effectively banned Chinese immigration. The act did not mention Japanese immigration, and did not affect immigration to Hawaii, which would not be formally annexed by the United States until 1898. In the final decades of the century, most Japanese nationals who emigrated eastward went to Hawaii, but a sizable number began setting their sights on the West Coast of the mainland. The Japanese population increased quickly after 1894, when a treaty between the governments of Japan and the United States endorsed open immigration.

Among those who came to Hawaii to earn money cutting sugarcane was Asakichi Inouye, the grandfather of future U.S. senator Daniel Inouye, who grew up in the tiny rural village Yokoyama, on the southern island of Kyushu. Asakichi's father, Wasaburo Inouye, was a rice farmer, and Asakichi would have lived out his life as a rice farmer, too, had it not been for a fire that started one night in Wasaburo's house. The fire destroyed another man's house, and because it had originated in Wasaburo's home, honor dictated that he would be liable for the damage. However, there was no way that Wasaburo could earn enough to reimburse his neighbor, so he came up with a plan. He would send his son to Hawaii, where wages were higher in the cane fields than anyone could possibly earn in the Kyushu hills. To honor his father's wishes, Asakichi packed up his wife and his four-year-old son, Hyotaro, and headed into the unknown. In September 1899, they set out across nearly four thousand miles of Pacific Ocean to a new and very different life. Slowly and methodically, Asakichi would send money home until the debt was finally paid—in 1929.

As Daniel Inouye, Hyotaro's oldest son, recalls in his autobiography, *Journey to Washington,* "If it had not been for a fire one night in the home of my great-grandfather, I might have been a Japanese soldier myself, fighting on the other side [in World War II]."

As with Asakichi Inouye, the Japanese laborers recruited by agricultural interests in Hawaii came mainly from the rural areas of the prefectures of Fukushima, Hiroshima, and Yamaguchi on the main island of Honshu, and Kumamoto on the island of Kyushu. They came as farm laborers, but gradually they entered skilled trades or became commercial fishermen, and the more ambitious entrepreneurs among them started small businesses, including retail stores.

As the numbers of Japanese increased, especially on the mainland, and as they became more visible within mainstream American society, they faced increased prejudice. As with the Chinese a generation earlier, the Japanese were perceived as a threat, especially by organized labor, as their numbers grew.

Some jingoist editorial pages screamed "Yellow Peril," and the

Japanese Exclusion League—originally formed in 1905 as the Asiatic Exclusion League—specifically targeted the Japanese. Supported by unions, the League issued anti-Japanese propaganda and lobbied for a curtailment of Japanese immigration. San Francisco's school board, whose racial policies are still controversial, attempted to impose the segregation of Asian students. This was significant because at the time San Francisco had a Japanese population of 1,781, the highest concentration of Japanese anywhere on the mainland.

By comparison, there were 1,209 in Sacramento County, 1,149 in Alameda County, and only about 500 in Southern California. At the time, the north and central California agricultural counties of Fresno, Monterey, San Joaquin, Santa Clara, and Santa Cruz had an aggregate Japanese population of 2,140. Meanwhile, the Japanese had begun to acquire acreage and had started farms and orchards. There were thriving Japanese agricultural settlements at Florin in Sacramento County and Bowles in Fresno County, as well as the Yamato Colony in Merced County.

After the 1906 San Francisco earthquake and the school board effrontery, the center of the Japanese population within California shifted south. By 1910, the United States Census listed Los Angeles County with 8,461 Japanese, compared to 4,518 in San Francisco and 3,874 in Sacramento County. This trend continued in the ensuing decade, and by 1920, 19,911 of the 71,952 Japanese living in California were in Los Angeles County. Sacramento County now contained 5,800, while San Francisco's *nihonmachi* (Japanese neighborhood) had a population of 5,358.

In 1907, to head off support for a Japanese Exclusion Act similar to the Chinese Exclusion Act, the governments of Japan and the United States entered into the so-called Gentlemen's Agreement, under which Japan would no longer issue passports to Japanese citizens aspiring for employment in the United States. However, wives and families of men already in the United States would be allowed to enter. As wives—often by arranged marriages to men they had not actually met—continued to arrive in the United States, the proportion of

Japanese women to men increased from about 2 percent to about 33 percent. Because they had seen the objects of their matrimony only in photographs, the Japanese women who married the workers in Hawaii were called picture brides. It is common, even to this day, to hear someone speak of a grandmother, or a great-grandmother, as having been a picture bride.

Despite the Gentlemen's Agreement, anti-Asian sentiment continued to simmer on the mainland. In 1913, California enacted the Alien Land Law, which prohibited aliens who were ineligible for citizenship from owning land in California. This included the Issei, Japanese residents born in Japan, but *not* their children, the Nisei, who were born in United States or Hawaii, and who therefore were American citizens by birth.

Many of the Issei, who already owned nearly 13,000 acres of farmland in the state, put the property in the names of their Nisei children, or entered into lease-back arrangements with white farmers. The latter arrangement was permitted under a stipulation of the 1913 act, but the lease provision was terminated in 1920. Within a few years, similar restrictive legislation was on the books in Arizona, Oregon, Washington, and other western states.

In 1920, a strike by Japanese sugar plantation employees in Hawaii increased racial tensions that led to an exclusionary clause for Japanese immigrants in the Immigration Act of 1924, which is also referred to as the National Origins Act. Sponsored in part by Senator Hiram Johnson of California, it called for immigration quotas based on the percentages of the population from a particular area already present in the United States. The law is often referred to as the Japanese Exclusion Act, although it was also designed to restrict immigration from Southern and Eastern Europe, which had been sizable since the 1890s.

In Hawaii, Asakichi Inouye, who had immigrated in 1899, was typical of the first-generation Issei laborers. He worked twelve-hour days on the McBryde plantation on the island of Kauai, and sent a sliver of his salary home to Japan each month. The enterprising Asakichi, and his wife, Moyo, set up side businesses, running a bathhouse in the small hamlet of Wahiawa and baking tofu. They worked hard, and gradually things improved. As with most Japanese parents in Kauai, they sent their son to the Japanese school. However, they realized that if their family was going to have a future in this American territory, he would need to learn English, so, as with many Japanese parents in Hawaii, they enrolled Hyotaro in a regular grammar school.

Despite the animosity that flowed from the 1920 strike, the Japanese living in Hawaii were making steady progress toward integration into the cultural and economic mainstream within the territory. There was no ban on Japanese owning agricultural property as there was in the mainland. Most significantly, by the 1920s, the Japanese had eclipsed the Chinese and Filipinos—as well as whites and native Hawaiians—to become the most populous ethnic group in Hawaii.

Hyotaro Inouye, the small boy who had come to Hawaii in 1899, had learned English and had grown to manhood against the backdrop of a growing Japanese population in the Islands. When he finished grade school, he left rural Kauai to attend Mills High School in the big city of Honolulu. It was there that he met and married a Nisei girl named Kame Imanaga in a courtship and wedding that was not arranged by elders, nor facilitated by photographs sent over long distances. In 1924, the same year the Immigration Act was passed, their first son, Daniel, was born in Honolulu.

On the mainland, relatively few Japanese immigrants ventured farther inland than the Pacific Coast. One of these adventurous souls was Tsuneji Fujita. The son of a prominent family from a village near Nagasaki, he had learned English in school and decided to seek his fortune in the land across the sea. He arranged to be sent to the United States as a student, to study agricultural methods. The Gentlemen's Agreement had prohibited laborers, but not students. According to his son's memoirs, Fujita had no intention of studying anything, nor of returning to Japan. He arrived in California in 1914, changed his name to Frank, and joined the Salvation Army in Los Angeles. Meanwhile, he was befriended by a society matron, who sent him to culinary school.

Frank Fujita managed to work his way into a job as an executive chef for the Chicago, Rock Island & Pacific Railway, and while working at the company headquarters in 1919, he met and married a young Caucasian waitress named Ida Pearl Elliot. By the time that Frank Fujita settled down in Fort Worth, Texas, in 1925—operating a restaurant that he won in a poker game—he and Ida had two sons. The younger of these, Frank Fujita Jr., was destined to have one of the most amazing, and harrowing, World War II adventures of any of the Nisei GIs.

On the mainland, the Immigration Act of 1924 had the possibly unintended result of shifting the demographics within the Japanese community from a majority of Issei to a majority of Nisei. Whereas the Issei were "aliens ineligible to citizenship," the Nisei were citizens. As is typical of American-born children of immigrants, the Nisei grew up speaking English and readily embracing American culture. As they reached their teens in the late 1930s, they danced to Benny Goodman and Glenn Miller, they snacked on hamburgers and milk shakes, and they followed major-league baseball. Much to the chagrin of the Issei, many young Nisei were becoming more culturally American than Japanese. Though many parents sent their kids to Japanese language schools, and some of them learned to speak Japanese, they preferred English—and they spoke it with the same accent as their white classmates at school. The vast majority pointedly identified themselves as Japanese Americans, rather than as "Japanese living in America."

While most Japanese Americans still lived in Japanese neighborhoods, Nisei were just as likely to seek employment or entertainment in other parts of their cites and towns. On the West Coast and in Hawaii, schools were generally integrated, although on the island of Oahu, home to half of Hawaii's population and the largest concentration of ethnic Japanese living under the American flag, most of the Nisei attended McKinley High School, nicknamed Tokyo High, while most whites—known in Hawaiian as haoles—went to Roosevelt High School. If they went on to college, as most young Nisei in Honolulu were encouraged to do, they crossed paths with the Caucasians of their generation at the University of Hawaii. At the university, many of the male students—both Nisei and haole—enrolled in the ROTC program, and by 1941 a number of these young men were junior officers in the Hawaii National Guard.

The Nisei were just as likely to be as strongly patriotic as their Caucasian neighbors. On the mainland, the Japanese American Citizens League was a respected organization of Nisei professionals, with a strong pro-American outlook. Their credo, penned by University of Utah professor Masaji "Mike" Masaoka in 1940, was unabashedly patriotic: "I am proud that I am an American citizen of Japanese ancestry, for my very background makes me appreciate more fully the wonderful advantages of this nation. I believe in her institutions, ideals and traditions; I glory in her heritage; I boast of her history; I trust in her future. She has granted me liberties and opportunities such as no individual enjoys in this world today. She has given me an education befitting kings. She has entrusted me with the responsibilities of the franchise. She has permitted me to build a home, to earn a livelihood, to worship, think, speak and act as I please—as a free man equal to every other man.

"Although some individuals may discriminate against me, I shall never become bitter or lose faith, for I know that such persons are not representative of the majority of the American people. True, I shall do all in my power to discourage such practices, but I shall do it in the American way—above board, in the open, through courts of law, by education, by proving myself to be worthy of equal treatment and consideration. I am firm in my belief that American sportsmanship and attitude of fair play will judge citizenship and patriotism on the basis of action and achievement, and not on the basis of physical characteristics. Because I believe in America, and I trust she believes in me, and because I have received innumerable benefits from her, I pledge myself to do honor to her at all times and all places; to support her constitution; to obey her laws; to respect her flag; to defend her against all enemies, foreign and domestic; to actively assume my duties and obligations as a citizen, cheerfully and without any reservations whatsoever, in the hope that I may become a better American in a greater America."

By 1940, when Masaoka expressed this sentiment, there were 157,905 Japanese in the Territory of Hawaii and 93,717 in California. Elsewhere on the mainland, mainly in Oregon and Washington, there were another 33,493, including 263 in the Territory of Alaska. More than six in ten were Nisei rather than Issei.

During the 1930s, the American people had become more preoccupied with the Great Depression than with the animosities that had consumed earlier generations. On the West Coast, much of the anti-Asian racial tension that had prevailed earlier in the century was fading. In California and Hawaii, where most Asian Americans lived, schools were integrated. The Nisei thought of themselves as American, and their classmates thought of them that way. In California and Hawaii, it was not uncommon to see the shingle of an Asian American dentist, or to see white Americans shopping at an Asian American grocery store or eating at an Asian American restaurant. By this time, nearly every town in the West that had a main street had a Chinese eatery on that main street.

As Imperial Japan began flexing its military muscle in the Far East, second-generation Asian Americans watched with the eyes of Americans. In 1937, when Japan launched its brutal invasion of China, committing atrocities such as the abhorrent Rape of Nanking, the Issei saw the culprit as being the land of their birth. The Nisei saw it as the land of distant ancestors.

In September 1940, one year after Adolf Hitler lit the fires of World War II, Japan signed the Tripartite Treaty, formally becoming a partner with Nazi Germany and Fascist Italy in the Rome-Berlin-Tokyo Axis. It was understood that if—most people assumed it was *when*—the United States became involved in World War II, the country would be at war with Japan. Most Nisei still saw Japan as a foreign country. Like most Americans of European descent, they gave no second thought to the notion that they were American.

Beginning in the summer of 1941, Japan and the United States had been locked in a diplomatic crisis. The issue was continued Japanese aggression in China, and their recent incursions into French Indochina. The United States had retaliated by cutting off exports, and Japan was angry. Despite the growing friction during the latter part of 1941, few people predicted that the war would begin for the United States in the way that it did on that warm Sunday morning in Hawaii.

When Imperial Japan brought the war to America on December 7, 1941, the Nisei reacted like Americans. They looked on Pearl Harbor as an attack on *their* country, rather than as an attack *by* the nation of their ancestors. The Nisei thought of themselves as being no less American than the person down the street whose grandparents had immigrated from Germany or Italy. Until December 7, most Caucasian Americans regarded them that way as well.

Things would soon change.

CHAPTER 3

The Morning After

For all Americans, things were much different on the Monday morning of December 8, 1941, than they had been when the weekend began. For Japanese Americans of all ages, the theoretical notion that the United States might some-day be at war with an Axis that included Japan was theoretical no longer. For the young people in the eighteen to twenty-four age group all across the United States—and that included most of the Nisei—the happy-go-lucky postadolescents of Friday afternoon were now sober adults facing an entirely new reality.

Lawson Sakai was a typical young Nisei man who had grown up in Montebello in Southern California. In December 1941, he was a student at nearby Compton Junior College. On that fateful Sunday when everything changed, he was doing homework and listening to his radio around 10:00 A.M. Pacific Time when the news of the Pearl Harbor attack reached California. For him, because Hawaii was so far way, the attack also seemed far away at first, and very abstract. He called his friend, Roy Kentner, and they discussed the situation at length.

Because Lawson had a car, a 1932 Ford, and Roy did not, it was his typical Sunday afternoon routine to drive Roy over to Loyola University, where he attended school and lived in the dorm during the week. As they were driving across town, the two men decided to go in to see the naval recruiter the following day. Like so many young Americans on that fateful day, they thought of themselves first and foremost as citizens of a nation that had been attacked. They saw no distinction between Lawson, whose parents were born in Japan, and Roy, whose father was from Nebraska, and whose mother was from Samoa.

"We realized that we were at war," Sakai recalls. "And we were very gung ho. We decided to go down tomorrow and join the navy!" They picked the navy because Kentner's father was a navy veteran.

Monday morning found the two men from Montebello, and two other friends, at the recruiting office.

"Roy was accepted right away," Sakai explained. "But with me, they kept mumbling around. Finally, they said, 'You're out.' I asked why, and they told me I was an enemy alien! The others told the recruiter, 'If he doesn't go, we're not going,' and we all left and went back to school. That was my first experience with a situation that had gone haywire."

Sakai remembers that the news of the Pearl Harbor attack upset his Issei parents very much. "They were caught in the middle. They realized that the country where they were born was fighting our country."

For Lawson himself, it was just the opposite. It was obvious to others that he looked Japanese, but he didn't think of himself as a foreign enemy of the country of his birth. "I had no connection to Japan," he explained. "I was different from a lot of others whose families wanted them to keep their Japanese traditions. I hadn't gone to a Japanese language school. I hadn't learned martial arts or anything. I would have gone to fight in the Pacific as soon as Europe. It didn't make any difference to me."

Robert Ichikawa, who later served in Company E of the 442nd Regimental Combat Team, was in the tenth grade at the Manual Arts High School in Los Angeles. He recalls that the full impact of the Pearl Harbor attack really began to sink in on Monday morning, when the principal called the student body together on the football field to listen to President Roosevelt's "Day of Infamy" speech on the loudspeakers.

In the immediate wake of Pearl Harbor, the backlash of animosity against anything and anyone who was Japanese quickly spread. In northern California, at the University of California in Berkeley, Victor Abe was a civil engineering student scheduled to graduate in 1942. He lived in an apartment with his brother and an electrical engineering student named Tug Tamaru. Victor was on his way to the library that Sunday morning when he heard on the radio that Imperial Japan had attacked the United States.

"I wondered what was going to happen to us," he said. "The first week after Pearl Harbor, we both dropped out of school and took the Greyhound bus home to Los Angeles. My brother's mineralogy professor told him that if he needed any money, he would be glad to lend it to him. He was really nice, but my brother said he could manage."

Across campus, Charles Kikuchi, another Nisei student at the University of California, wrote in his diary on Sunday night: "We are at war! Jesus Christ, the Japs bombed Hawaii and the entire fleet has been sunk. I just can't believe it. I don't know what in the hell is going to happen to us, but we will all be into the army right away . . . I think of the Japs coming to bomb us, but I will go and fight even if I think I am a coward and I don't believe in wars but this time it has to be. I am selfish about it. I think not of California and America, but I wonder what is going to happen to the Nisei and to our parents. They may lock up the aliens. How can one think of the future?"

Like many Nisei of his generation, he saw the American entry into World War II as an opportunity for the Nisei to prove that they were Americans first. "The next five years will determine the future of the Nisei," he wrote prophetically. "They are now at the crossroads. Will they be able to take it or will they go under? If we are ever going to prove our Americanism, this is the time."

Though Kikuchi would not go on to serve in the U.S. Army, his sentiments were echoed by many other Nisei of his generation, including Lawson Sakai, Robert Ichikawa, Victor Abe, and Dan Inouye, who would.

As Dan Inouye would recall in his memoirs, "Like all Nisei, I was driven by an insidious sense of guilt from the instant the first Japanese plane appeared over Pearl Harbor. Of course we had nothing to feel guilty about, but we all carried this special burden. We felt it in the streets, where white men would sneer as we passed. We felt it in school when we heard our friends and neighbors called 'Jap-lovers.'"

When young Charles Kikuchi had speculated that the United States government might "lock up the aliens," he was thinking of the Alien Registration Act, passed a year earlier, which had mandated that all aliens over the age of fourteen register with the government. The Issei had registered, but the Nisei were citizens, not aliens. In his comments that terrible Sunday, he didn't even consider the possibility that the *Nisei* could also soon be locked up.

In retrospect, it seems entirely counterintuitive that the United States government should have feared the Nisei. President Roosevelt knew better. In 1941, as tensions had increased between the United States and members of the Rome-Berlin-Tokyo Axis, Roosevelt had designated Chicago businessman Curtis B. Munson as a State Department special representative with orders to look into the issue of Japanese American loyalty in California. Munson had concluded that "there is no Japanese 'problem' on the Coast. There will be no armed uprising of Japanese. . . . There is far more danger from Communists . . . than there is from Japanese. The Japanese here is almost exclusively a farmer, a fisherman or a small businessman."

Munson went so far as to note that the Nisei were eager to show their loyalty, and added that the Japanese American Citizens League "should be encouraged." If there was to be an official dread of what the Issei might do, he recommended putting their assets under the control of the intensely loyal Nisei. He suggested that the government could "squeeze control [of Issei property] from the hands of the Japanese Nationals into the hands of the loyal Nisei *who are American citi-*

zens [our italics]." His recommendation would be ignored. The government would go much farther.

With the population fearing a Japanese military invasion of the mainland, and mainly just fearful of the unknown, civilian and military leaders felt pressured to do *something*, but what?

As Charles Kikuchi had feared, there was a sudden groundswell of public pressure with regard to citizens of the Axis powers, especially those of the nation that had bombed Pearl Harbor. However, both state and federal government officials couldn't decide how far to go, nor in which direction. Only the FBI had moved quickly, selectively rounding up relatively small numbers of enemy aliens that were on their watch lists. The Justice Department had about three thousand people, including German and Italian, as well as Japanese, nationals on their watch list as possible spies and saboteurs—and many of these were arrested immediately after Pearl Harbor. Subversion was a real fear, not an irrational paranoia, especially after what had occurred in Europe. Indigenous fascist and pro-Nazi elements, especially men such as Vidkun Quisling in Norway, had facilitated the Nazi victories. After Pearl Harbor, people in the Pacific Coast states genuinely feared—and many expected—Imperial Japanese attacks, and even an invasion. Japanese submarines shelled several locations along the West Coast, but not until the spring of 1942. Still, after the Munson report, Roosevelt should have known that he could trust the Nisei just as he could trust most second-generation German Americans.

Beyond the initial arrests of possible subversives, there was official confusion. Beyond the people on the FBI's watch list, should all the German, Italian, and Japanese aliens be rounded up and jailed? Or should they simply be relocated away from the coastline and proximity to important military and industrial locations?

In the three West Coast states, there were 58,000 Italian aliens and 22,000 German aliens, but many of these were refugees from Nazi or Italian Fascist oppression in Europe and assumed not to be a danger. In the same area, there were 112,353 persons of Japanese decent, but 71,484 were Nisei and therefore American citizens—and also probably not a danger. As for the Issei, they were legally not permitted to become citizens, so they were technically aliens whether they had wanted to remain aliens or not. They were still aliens whether they had lived in the United States for three months or thirty years. To fear these people really did border on paranoia.

At the top of the military chain of command on the West Coast was Lieutenant General John L. DeWitt, who commanded both the Western Defense Command and the United States Fourth Army from his headquarters at the Presidio of San Francisco. The man responsible for defending the West Coast against foreign military attack, DeWitt is often portrayed as a racist who was single-mindedly frothing at the mouth to jail Japanese Americans. However, by his actions in the immediate aftermath of Pearl Harbor, he actually appears to have been mainly jittery and indecisive with regard to Japanese Americans.

On December 19, DeWitt had discussed the removal of all *aliens* who were citizens of the Axis powers from the West Coast, but a week later, he complained to Provost Marshal General Allen W. Gullion that he was doubtful whether it would be feasible to intern all of the Japanese American living there. He added that he was apprehensive about interning Nisei, because they were citizens and "an American citizen, after all, is an American citizen."

With his characteristic inconsistency, DeWitt also told reporters, in an infamous statement that is still widely quoted, "A Jap is a Jap," implying that anyone who was ethnically Japanese would be automatically predisposed to want to work on behalf of the Imperial Japanese war effort.

Despite a groundswell of anxiety about Japanese attacks within his area of responsibility, it was not until January 5, 1942, that DeWitt even set the deadline for Axis aliens to surrender ham radio transmitters and shortwave radios.

In Hawaii, however, where the incoming attackers of Pearl Harbor had used commercial radio broadcasts to home in on their target, radios had been seen immediately as a potential problem, especially in Japanese American hands. Within a week of the attack, the authorities were beginning to imagine that even radio receivers with shortwave band capability were somehow a danger, and people who owned such radios were ordered to report them. Hyotaro Inouye reported his, and was soon visited by agents from the Office of Naval Intelligence. Having ordered Inouye to produce his radio, one of the federal agents proceeded to remove and destroy the vacuum tubes by smashing them on the ground. Hyotaro angrily pulled out his own ax and smashed the radio. The agents went for their concealed sidearms when they saw him grab the ax, but he told them that he was only doing his duty by destroying a Japanese American radio set.

Don Seki, who later served in Company L of the 442nd Regimental Combat Team, watched his neighbor's radio being destroyed. On December 7, he had been waking up at a friend's house in Manoa Valley, north of Honolulu, after an all-night poker game when the attack occurred, and he hadn't heard a thing. "We couldn't see Pearl Harbor from where we were," Seki recalled. "But a guy came by and told us that it had been bombed, so we headed home. At home, my neighbor, Mr. Satoshi, had an amateur shortwave radio. The FBI came that same day and smashed it. They busted all of his equipment. He went crazy."

Seki soon felt the wrath of the nervous authorities himself.

"I worked at Pearl Harbor for McKay Construction, a big contractor from the mainland," he said. "About three days after the attack, here came the marines. They said 'Out you go. You're the enemy, y'know.' They told us that we couldn't work inside any U.S. Navy installation, so I took a job building machine-gun emplacements at Kahuku on the north shore of Oahu."

While DeWitt fussed and tried to make up his mind about the issue of the Japanese Americans, the FBI continued its policy of selective arrests of possible subversives. Often, they got it wrong. Tets Asato was born and raised in El Monte, California, where his family operated a small farm, and he was enrolled at El Monte High School in December 1941.

"When I got home from school the day after Pearl Harbor, I discovered that the FBI had turned the place upside down," he recalls. "My sister and two brothers were there, but my father was not. They told me that dad was gone."

A widower since 1939, Tokusuke Asato had been placed in custody by the FBI and taken to a facility in Tujunga Canyon, north of Los Angeles. The reason, as the family was told, was that he had ties to a Japanese language school. This, of course, was not unusual. Many Issei were involved with institutions whose activities were related to Japanese language or culture. When the family went out to visit Tokusuke, they had to speak to him through a barbed wire fence. He was later transferred to the Department of Justice Internment Camp at Santa Fe, New Mexico, when it opened in February 1942.

Meanwhile, as it often does when a tragedy befalls the United States, the government empaneled a commission to analyze the failings that had caused the Pearl Harbor attack to have been such a surprise. On January 23, 1942, when the Roberts Commission Report on Pearl Harbor blamed the senior U.S. Navy and U.S. Army leadership in Hawaii—Admiral Kimmel and General Walter Short—for failing to appropriately safeguard the Islands, DeWitt became increasingly nervous that he'd be criticized for not doing enough, so he finally took initial steps to move aliens, but not yet citizens, away from sensitive areas. At last, DeWitt was moved to action. It wasn't so much that the general had a job to *do*, it was that he realized he had a job to *save*.

He had reason to be nervous. He had yet to act, and if there *was* an enemy attack, he would be following Kimmel and Short out the door. Amazingly, it was not until the middle of February that the San Francisco waterfront and the port area at Los Angeles were finally declared restricted zones by the military. DeWitt had waited for more than two months to secure the two major ports under his jurisdiction. The fact that nothing had happened, no sabotage and no invasion, should have been a clue.

While DeWitt had dithered, both California's Democratic Governor Culbert Olson and State Attorney General Earl Warren—who later made a name for himself as a liberal chief justice of the United

States—vehemently championed the removal of *all* Japanese Americans from all the state's coastal counties. In Washington, D.C., congressmen from California and other Pacific Coast states directly lobbied President Roosevelt to remove Japanese Americans.

On February 19, the president bowed to pressure from the politicians and signed the controversial Executive Order 9066, authorizing Henry L. Stimson, the secretary of war, to "prescribe military areas in such places and of such extent as he or the appropriate Military Commander may determine, from which any or all persons may be excluded, and with respect to which, the right of any person to enter, remain in, or leave shall be subject to whatever restrictions the Secretary of War or the appropriate Military Commander may impose in his discretion."

Executive Order 9066 was vague on the issue of whether all persons of Japanese ancestry should be interned. In fact, it specifically mentioned only aliens. It also did not delineate the areas from which they should be removed, nor where they should be taken. In typical Roosevelt style, he left such decisions up to those in the field.

At last, Executive Order 9066 gave DeWitt the authority that he needed to appear more decisive than he actually was. Under his new 9066 powers, the general initially went only so far as to order the removal of Japanese Americans from a narrow strip of land near the coast. On March 2, DeWitt issued a public proclamation demanding that Japanese Americans leave a "prohibited zone" along the coastline, and many left voluntarily. The relocation process was complicated by the fact that Japanese Americans often received a frosty reception when they tried to relocate to inland states.

In many places along the coast, the prohibited zone created the bizarre situation of neighbors on one side of a street being compelled to leave, while those across the road could stay. By the end of the month the Japanese Americans in all of the West Coast states were ordered out.

Lawson Sakai, the Nisei student at Compton Junior College who had tried to enlist on the morning after Pearl Harbor, first heard about the exclusion order from several classmates. They lived on Terminal Island at the mouth of the Port of Los Angeles, and they had been given twenty-four hours to move out. Soon the Sakai family was also ordered to leave Montebello, so they went north to California Hot Springs, near Porterville in Tulare County, leaving their property in the care of a neighbor, who was also in the greenhouse business. They had a house and five acres that had originally been purchased by an aunt who came to the United States in the early twentieth century before Japanese Americans were forbidden to own real estate.

"We thought that we'd be safe there, and in two or three months we'd go home," he explained. "Then the order came that the *whole state* of California would be evacuated."

In the meantime, the Sakais had already begun looking beyond the Golden State for a safer refuge. They were members of the Seventh-Day Adventist church, and had already made inquiries with out-of-state congregations. They knew they might face a general evacuation order, but they hadn't yet been ordered to report to a specific place, so they wanted to stay ahead of the evacuations.

The War Relocation Authority (WRA) was created on March 19 to oversee the removal of Japanese Americans. The first head of this new agency was Milton Eisenhower, the brother of an obscure and newly made brigadier general (later president), Dwight D. Eisenhower. He favored resettling the Nisei in civilian areas away from the coast, but in a meeting with western governors, it became apparent that there was no place that would welcome a mass influx of Japanese Americans, and the decision was made to incarcerate them all in government-run camps. The Japanese Americans would be forced to give up homes, businesses, and farms. Though it was not an officially articulated goal, many would never be able to return.

In California, the Nisei leadership of the Japanese American Citizens League naturally opposed removal and internment, but they finally chose to cooperate with authorities in order to demonstrate that they were loyal Americans. Only three Nisei challenged the relocation orders in court, and all three lost. In Hawaii, there would be no general internment.

By the end of the March 1942, civilian exclusion orders for the whole West Coast were issued, and Japanese American civilians were being ordered to report to a number of temporary assembly centers, which included the Tanforan and Santa Anita racetracks in California, and the Pacific International Livestock Exposition Pavilion in Portland, Oregon. In many cases, people found themselves being housed temporarily in filthy stables. In general, these temporary facilities opened between March and May of 1942, and were closed in the fall of the same year as the internees were sent to ten large, long-term relocation centers, or internment camps, that were located on federal land in very isolated locations.

The ten relocation centers were Gila River and Poston in Arizona, Jerome and Rohwer in Arkansas, Manzanar and Tule Lake in California, Granada in Colorado, Minidoka in Idaho, Topaz in Utah, and Heart Mountain in Wyoming. Most of the Japanese Americans uprooted from the Western states spent the duration of the war at the ten camps. However, those who were suspected of crimes and those determined to be "troublemakers" because they incited protests or disobedience of the rules were housed in locations that included U.S. Army and Justice Department facilities.

"Everything was taken from us," recalled Tets Asato, whose father had been arrested and taken away to a Department of Justice facility in December 1941. On their farm near El Monte, California, the Asato family raised typical truck farm crops, such as carrots, lettuce, and strawberries. The crops were in the ground when the evacuation order came, and there they remained as the rest of the family was hauled off to the Assembly Center at the Los Angeles County Fairgrounds in Pomona. Later they received some money from a neighbor family who had harvested the crops.

"If someone had a car, a truck, or a tractor, they took it," he said. "I don't know what they did with them. They just took everything. At Pomona, we were luckier than the people who were sent to Santa Anita. We didn't have to sleep in horse stalls. We were in barracks at

Pomona until they shipped us to Heart Mountain a couple of months later."

George Katagiri was just fifteen years old when his family was ordered to leave their Portland home and report to the Pacific International Livestock Exposition Pavilion. As they arrived in the facility, manure was being swept up and a wooden floor laid.

He later recalled in an interview with the Go For Broke Educational Foundation that he looked at internment as a challenge. "Having been a Boy Scout, loving the outdoors, I loved to improvise," he said. "And so this adjustment to the Assembly Center for me, was kind of challenging and kind of intriguing. I wasn't minding it very much. I was adapting to it quite well. I played a lot of ball, but most of all, just horsing around with friends. I was just a happy-go-lucky kid in there, not really understanding what was going on. But one hot day, it became so hot in the assembly center that the only way to cool off was to go outside. And so I went out the north side of the building and I just sat down on the ground with my back against the building in the shade. Right along side of the building on the north side is a busy street. Before I realized it, someone said, 'Hey, George.' I looked up. Here was this car going by, and from the back window, it was my old friend, Evan. He and I went through eight years of elementary school together. All I had time to say was 'Hi, Evan,' and he was gone. But it was at that moment that my eyes focused on the fence between us and the barbed wire that was on top. And, all of a sudden, in an instant, this happy-go-lucky kid kind of sobered up. I thought, wow, there is something amiss here. Here, Evan, my friend, who I grew up with, is riding in a car with his parents out there twenty feet away from me, and I'm on this side of the fence. . . . For the first time, I realized the seriousness of the whole situation."

By the time the Portland Assembly Center closed on September 10, 1942, the Katagiri family had been sent to Tule Lake. George was later recruited for the Military Intelligence Service, and he returned to Oregon after the war to build a career as an educator.

A sense of despondency settled over the Japanese American community. Mas Tsuda, a high school senior at Watsonville, California, north of Monterey, just quit going to school. In a peculiar irony that is amusing only in retrospect, the school district sent truant officers to locate him. Even after his family was relocated to Poston, he refused to attend high school classes. Finally, the high school advisor at Poston arranged for him to receive his diploma from Watsonville.

"The government gave us thirty days to pack up and get ready to move out," recalled Robert Ichikawa, the tenth-grader from Los Angeles. "We sold everything in the house, all of the furniture and the stove, for $21. The teachers knew we were going to be moving out and they volunteered to send me class papers so that I could graduate, but I said no. . . . I didn't know where we were going. We all gathered at the Methodist Episcopal Church on Normandie Avenue and we boarded the busses to the racetrack at Santa Anita. They had built tar paper barracks at the track, and there was a barbed wire fence all around, with fifty-foot guard towers and machine guns."

Provisions had been made within the Santa Anita complex for a grammar school and junior high school, but there was no high school, so Robert Ichikawa was put to work. He was called down to the labor pool at Santa Anita, where the Japanese American clerk who was staffing the assignment desk told him: "You're going to clean toilets."

"I am not going to clean toilets," he replied.

"You have to clean toilets."

"No, I *don't* have to clean toilets."

"Well, okay," the clerk said at last. "Come back tomorrow."

The next day he went back and was sent to work in the nursery that took care of the plants and trees around Santa Anita. When the Santa Anita facility closed on October 27, 1942, the Ichikawa family was sent to the Granada relocation camp near the town of Amache, Colorado, where they arrived in their California clothes in the midst of a blizzard.

The reality of the camps was probably not what Milton Eisenhower or any of the other WRA bureaucrats in Washington imagined.

According to an official description in a WRA document published in 1942, the typical internment camp was a "pioneer community, with basic housing and protective services provided by the Federal government, for the occupancy by evacuees for the duration of the war."

This description made the camps seem benign, and almost inviting in a rustic sort of way. However, conditions at the camps were spartan at best, with people housed in drafty, tar paper barracks that were cold in the winter, and stifling during the summer. Worst of all, the camps were enclosed by humiliating barbed wire. Of course, even if an internee had escaped, the camps were so isolated that there was nowhere to go. Nevertheless, the internees made the best of things, planting gardens and organizing activities in an effort to recapture a sense of normality amid the degradation of being put in a cage because of the color of their skin.

For most of the Japanese Americans the change of environment was disagreeable at best. It was deplorable that they had been forcibly uprooted, but here they were in an alien land in a climate they had never experienced. "It was miserable," Shig Kizuka recalled. Along with his parents and two younger siblings, he had been uprooted from Watsonville on the California coast and sent to Poston, near Parker, Arizona. "I was used to the cool, foggy weather at the coast, but it was 120 degrees out in the desert."

Meanwhile, Canada declared war against Japan shortly after Pearl Harbor because of the simultaneous Japanese attack on the British Crown Colony of Hong Kong. As a dominion of the British Empire, Canada had been at war with Germany and Italy since 1939. At the same time that the United States made the decision to evacuate persons of Japanese ancestry from its West Coast, Canada followed suit. In March 1942, the Canadian government undertook to move more than 21,000 Japanese Canadians from British Columbia to work camps in central Canada. While the United States allowed most ethnic Japanese to leave the internment camps by the time the war ended, the Canadians did not let Japanese Canadians back into British Columbia until 1949, four years after the United States had reversed its policy. Mexico also removed persons of Japanese ancestry from the Pacific Coast to inland locations.

Strangely, the exclusion and evacuation orders issued in the United States under the authority of Executive Order 9066 *did not* apply to the small number of Japanese Americans who lived in the central or eastern part of the country away from the region under DeWitt's command. For instance, despite the fact that the Granada Relocation Center was located at Amache, Colorado, it contained people from California—including Los Angeles, San Diego, and Santa Clara counties, the northern California coast, the western Sacramento Valley, and the northern San Joaquin Valley—but not people from Colorado.

One of the most outspoken opponents of the relocation was Ralph Lawrence Carr, the Republican governor of Colorado. "If you harm them, you must harm me," he said in August 1942, speaking to an angry crowd of people who were vociferously objecting to the influx of Japanese Americans coming to Amache.

"I was brought up in a small town where I knew the shame and dishonor of race hatred," he continued in this speech, whose text is preserved in the Colorado State Archives. "I grew to despise it because it threatened the happiness of you and you and you."

With Governor Carr's sentiments well publicized, the Sakai family from Montebello had already made arrangements with the Seventh-Day Adventist community in Delta, Colorado, to take them in. They had done this when they reached Porterville, before the exclusion order was issued, and had applied to the FBI for permission to go there.

"The day before we were supposed to leave Porterville for evacuation, we got a card in the mail from the FBI," Lawson Sakai recalls. "It said that we were officially allowed to drive from California to Colorado."

There was an immense sense of relief that they would be leaving the following morning for a distant haven, and not a relocation camp. As they headed south through Bakersfield and west on U.S. Highway

466 toward Barstow, the Sakais were relaxed and cheerful. For them, the tension surrounding the evacuation had abruptly vanished.

They were so certain that their troubles were over, that they made the rash and impulsive decision to take a detour up U.S. Highway 6 and *stop at Manzanar to visit friends.*

"Quite a few of our friends from Montebello were in Manzanar," Lawson Sakai explained. "So we just dropped in. At the gate was a soldier with a rifle. I guess he was surprised to see somebody wanting to come *in* on their own."

The Sakais had their FBI pass, so they were confident that the man with the gun would let them *out.* Not many people came into Manzanar voluntarily and simply left. In fact, probably *nobody* did. Nevertheless, the Sakais were confident that the FBI pass that permitted them to travel to Colorado would also permit them to drive back out through the big, ominous gate at Manzanar.

They were skating on very thin ice.

The Sakais drove over to the administration building, where they announced that they had stopped by to visit their friends. Among them was their neighbor, Mr. Negoro, a ham radio enthusiast who had built a primitive television receiver in his garage before the war. As they were reunited with their neighbors, they chatted with them as though it was over the backyard fence in Montebello. At last, someone whispered that the Sakai family had better leave, and quickly. Calmly, they decided that maybe they would. They said their good-byes and climbed back into the family car.

At the gate, the guards were there to keep Japanese Americans *in*, not to let them leave. The Sakais were halted there at the closed portal, while an armed soldier studied their papers. Though the documents seemed to be in order, he was not posted there to facilitate Japanese Americans *leaving* the camp.

Officially, it probably shouldn't have happened, but at last the guard opened the gate and permitted the Sakais to simply drive away.

They were probably the only family to arrive at Manzanar voluntarily and to leave the same way on the same day.

CHAPTER 4

We Need You After All

I ronically, even as West Coast Japanese Americans of all ages were being earmarked for concentration in internment camps, a number of the sons of Japanese immigrants were already serving in the U.S. Army. Some Nisei men, like their contemporaries in other ethnic groups, had joined the armed forces voluntarily and others had gotten into the service after having enrolled in college programs of the Reserve Officers Training Corps. Many had also been drafted.

In 1940, with World War II already raging in Europe, the United States Congress had passed the Selective Service Act, authorizing the nation's first peacetime draft. Selective Service numbers were then issued to young men between the ages of 21 and 30, an age range that was expanded to 18 to 45 a year later.

As Lawson Sakai and many other Nisei men of his generation discovered on the morning of December 8, 1941, nearly all armed forces induction centers started to refuse to enlist Japanese Americans immediately after Pearl Harbor, although, technically, the men were still eligible. Nisei men who had already registered for the Selective Service but had not yet been inducted would soon be reclassified 4-C, "enemy aliens"—but not until January 1942. Despite this classification, they were, of course, neither the enemy nor aliens.

As the Nisei men received their new draft classifications, the U.S.

Army was in a quandary over what should be done with those who had already been inducted. On the mainland, the army eventually made an effort to consolidate the Nisei draftees at bases in the South, mainly at Camp Robinson in Arkansas. In Hawaii, where half the National Guard was Nisei, the dilemma came to a head more quickly. Shortly after the Pearl Harbor attack, a decision was made to disarm 600 new recruits, mainly Nisei men, who were billeted at Schofield Barracks on Oahu.

One of the Nisei men from the 298th Infantry Regiment of the Hawaii National Guard who was disarmed was Yeiki "Lefty" Kobashigawa, who would later receive the Medal of Honor for his heroism in World War II. Born in Hilo, he had earned his nickname as a left-handed pitcher for several baseball teams in Hawaii, including the one sponsored by the Waianae Plantation Company.

On the morning of December 7, Lefty had been getting ready for a game on the west side of Oahu when he heard the news of the attack. "I caught an Army truck which took us through Kolekole Pass back to Schofield," he told the *Honolulu Star-Bulletin* in a 2000 interview. "But shortly after that, they took away our rifles. I don't know what they thought we would do."

On December 11, with the Hawaii National Guard already on alert, the territory of Hawaii had organized the ROTC cadets at the University of Hawaii, as well as volunteers from Honolulu high schools, into a new and parallel organization known as the Hawaii Territorial Guard. Most of these men, 317 in all, were Nisei. On January 19, 1942, however, the Nisei men were suddenly discharged and given their 4-C draft classifications. The Hawaii-born Nisei student soldiers were now officially enemy aliens.

In another twist of bureaucratic irony, the War Department would not *officially* cease inducting Japanese American draftees into the army until the end of March, more than two months *after* they officially became enemy aliens!

Victor Abe, the former engineering student who had dropped out of the University of California the week after Pearl Harbor, recalls that "guys were getting called into the service, and my number was called on February 25, 1942. We took the red car [the Pacific Electric Railway streetcar] down to the induction center at Fort MacArthur in San Pedro. Burgess Meredith, the movie actor, was being inducted there at the same time, and he was wearing a floppy blue fatigue cap that sure looked weird to me at the time. Right after I got in, they stopped inducting Japanese Americans, but I was one of a few that slipped by."

Abe was shipped to Camp Robinson for basic training. At the time, he was the only Japanese American in his group. He was later sent on to Fort Warren, Wyoming, where the army discovered his civil engineering background. He was assigned to the engineers and found himself at a drafting table next to another Nisei inductee, Hisashi "Sash" Horita from San Francisco.

At the time that Pearl Harbor changed everything, there were not only Japanese Americans in the armed forces in Hawaii and on the mainland, but at least one Nisei soldier had already been sent overseas. Sergeant Frank "Foo" Fujita was the son of Tsuneji Fujita, who had emigrated from Nagasaki in 1914 and who had become a successful entrepreneur in Texas and Oklahoma. Born in Lawton, Oklahoma, in 1921, the younger Fujita graduated from high school in Abilene, Texas, where he acquired his nickname as the cartoonist for his school paper. His father had put Japan firmly in his past, and young Frank grew up as American in his outlook as any of his classmates. The elder Fujita and his American-born Caucasian wife had two sons and three daughters, to whom they specifically did *not* teach the Japanese language. As Mrs. Fujita later wrote of her husband, "He wanted them to always speak American."

In 1938, looking for adventure, Foo Fujita had joined the Texas National Guard and became part of the 2nd Field Artillery Battalion of the 131st Field Artillery Regiment in the 36th Infantry Division. The division was mobilized in November 1940, and a year later it was ordered to contribute units for overseas deployment.

Across the world, Japan had been swallowing large slices of China since 1937, and spreading its empire across Asia with apparent impunity. The United States had been strongly critical of the Japanese invasion of China, and the U.S. Navy gunboat *Panay* had been attacked by Japanese aircraft while in Chinese waters. When Japan's Axis partner, Nazi Germany, conquered France, Japan lusted for French Indochina, and rattled the imperial saber over the Commonwealth of the Philippines. To counter Japanese ambitions in the Far East and to safeguard the Philippines—already scheduled for independence in 1946—the United States undertook to reinforce the Philippine garrison.

They sent Fujita's battalion. Though most of the men would not know it until after they shipped out from San Francisco on November 21, they had been earmarked for the defense of the Philippines in the event of a Japanese attack. Two weeks later, their ship was in the western Pacific when the men heard the news that Pearl Harbor had been bombed. Simultaneously, the Philippines were also under attack by a superior force, and the ship carrying the 2nd Field Artillery Battalion was diverted to Australia.

By the time Sergeant Fujita and his fellow Texans arrived in Australia on December 22, the Imperial Japanese Army was moving into the Netherlands East Indies (now Indonesia). To help stem the tide of their advance, the Allies sent whatever forces they could spare from the defense of Australia, and this included the men of the 2nd Field Artillery Battalion. Fujita and the others arrived in the large port city of Surabaya (then called Soerabaja) on the island of Java on January 11, 1942. From there they were deployed westward to defend the island.

On February 19, the same date (albeit a day earlier because of the International Dateline) that President Roosevelt signed Executive Order 9066, Foo was writing in his diary about his unit being attacked and strafed by Japanese warplanes.

On March 1, the Imperial Japanese Army landed on Java, having just captured the British fortress city of Singapore, as well as Sumatra, the large Netherlands East Indies island northwest of Java. Fujita's unit was pulled back to help in the defense of Surabaya, and on March 7, he had his first contact with the enemy. The Texans managed to slow the Japanese advance, but they were vastly outnumbered and forced to withdraw into the city. The Dutch colonial government formally surrendered the Indies to the Japanese on March 8. Fujita and several others managed to elude the enemy for a time, but on March 10, he became the first Japanese American soldier to become a prisoner of Imperial Japan during World War II.

As he was fighting bravely in Java—he killed several Japanese troops with his rifle during the fighting at Surabaya—the Fujita family in Texas was starting to feel the animosity that was sweeping the United States. Foo's sister Naomi, who worked at the Woolworth's novelty counter in Abilene, became the target of customer complaints. The manager said that she could continue to work at Woolworth's, but that she would have to remain out of sight in the stock room. Their younger sister, Patricia Ruth, suddenly found herself being referred to as a "Jap" by high school classmates. Their brother Herbert Lee Fujita, who was a corporal in the U.S. Army Air Forces, wanted to sign up for pilot training, but he was denied because of his race even as Frank was becoming a prisoner of war despite his race.

As the anti–Japanese American hysteria was still howling on the mainland, cooler—and more pragmatic—points of view were beginning to prevail in Hawaii. In the wake of the Roberts Commission Report on Pearl Harbor, General Delos Emmons arrived in Hawaii as commander of U.S. Army troops in the islands. He was sent to replace General Walter Short, who was discredited by—and blamed for—the disastrous unpreparedness on the day of the attack.

As he arrived, Emmons was so taken aback by the sight of so many Japanese troops in American uniforms that he briefly considered following General DeWitt's lead by ordering them to be interned. Luckily, he was convinced by Colonel Kendall Fielder, his G-2 (intelligence officer), that the Nisei were at least as loyal and enthusiastic as the other troops if not *more* loyal. If Emmons had been so foolish as to lock up half his command, there is no telling what sort of backlash might have rippled through Hawaii.

One of the first items that landed on Emmons's desk after he took over in Hawaii was a letter of protest from more than half of the

Nisei men who had been drummed out of the Hawaii Territorial Guard. In this document, today preserved in the National Archives, the men explained to Emmons that "Hawaii is our home, the United States is our country. We know but one loyalty, and that is to the Stars and Stripes. We wish to do our part as loyal Americans in every way possible and we hereby present ourselves for whatever service you may see fit to use us."

To help him make up his mind, Emmons also had access to a secret report prepared by Lieutenant Gero Iwai, a deep-cover counterintelligence officer who had served with the Office of the Assistant Chief of Staff for G-2 in Hawaii for more than a decade. The Honolulu-born Iwai was one of the first Nisei to take ROTC at the University of Hawaii, and upon his graduation in 1931, he was assigned to the G-2 section in the islands, the unit later headed by Colonel Fielder. As war clouds began to gather over the Far East, Iwai was assigned to go under cover to conduct surveillance of the Japanese consulate general. After the Pearl Harbor attack, he undertook a comprehensive investigation of Hawaii's Japanese American community, which concluded that the United States had nothing to fear from them. Armed with Iwai's report, Emmons was able to report to Washington—in a classified document—within weeks of Pearl Harbor that "no American citizens or alien Japanese residents of Hawaii was involved in any acts of hostility against the U.S. Forces."

This was, in fact, true. The Imperial Japanese Navy did have a spy in Hawaii, but after the war he complained that he had found the local Japanese Americans too loyal to the United States to be trustworthy in his espionage efforts. Ensign Takeo Yoshikawa had arrived in Honolulu in October 1941, and operated out of the Japanese consulate on Nuuana Avenue. Friendly and congenial, the English-speaking secret agent exploited the lax sense of security at the military facilities to gather information for transmission to Japan. He drove around Oahu, observing all of the U.S. Army, Navy, and Marine Corps installations, and he spent long hours at a Japanese tea house in Alewa Heights that had an exceptional view of Pearl Harbor. He snooped, eavesdropped on barroom chatter, and read details of the comings and goings of navy ships in the local newspapers. After the December 7 attack, he was among the Japanese officials rounded up at the consulate. These people would be repatriated in 1942 in an exchange of diplomatic personnel. Yoshikawa returned to Japan without his cover having been blown and continued to work for naval intelligence. After the war, he kept his activities at Pearl Harbor secret until 1960.

Placated by Iwai's report, Emmons turned his attention to the bigger fish he had to fry. Short had lost his job for being unprepared, and Emmons turned his attention to getting his house in order. There was more to be accomplished by building Hawaii's defenses than by chasing a nonexistent threat.

Curtis Munson, Colonel Fielder, and Gero Iwai were right. The Nisei in Hawaii, like those on the mainland, really *were* enthusiastically loyal. While Japanese Americans were suddenly pariahs on the mainland, Hawaiian society generally remained color-blind, with the exceptions being mainly among military officers like Emmons, and other federal officials from outside who were unfamiliar with island culture. Just as they made up half of the territory's National Guard, Japanese Americans were an integral part of all Hawaiian society. Indeed, when World War II began, Masaji Marumoto, a Harvard-educated Honolulu attorney, became a prominent member of Hawaii's Emergency Service Committee.

Moved by the memo from the young Nisei men, and nudged by Colonel Fielder, Iwai's secret report, and community leaders such as Masaji Marumoto, Emmons agreed to let the young men reorganize. On February 23, they officially formed themselves into a group that would be optimistically called the Varsity Victory Volunteers (VVV). Assigned as an auxiliary of the Hawaiian Department of the U.S. Army Corps of Engineers, the Varsity Victory Volunteers worked on various military construction projects, especially roads, throughout the islands during 1942, and briefly into 1943.

As he gradually came around to accepting the loyalty of the hardworking Nisei under his command, Emmons went so far as to propose in May 1942 that the Nisei troops in the two Hawaii National Guard regiments be organized into a single battalion and sent to the mainland to be integrated into the regular U.S. Army.

Amazingly, considering the hysteria still prevailing on the West Coast, Emmons's proposal was well received in Washington. On May 26 Army Chief of Staff General George Catlett Marshall issued an order establishing what would temporarily be called the Hawaii Provisional Infantry Battalion, a unit to be made up of 1,432 Japanese Americans from the Hawaii National Guard. Of the 29 officers in the newly created outfit, 16 were Nisei and 14 were graduates of the University of Hawaii ROTC program.

The unit commander, as would be the case with the battalion commanders and higher under whom the Nisei would serve during World War II, was a haole. Lieutenant Colonel Farrant Turner was an old National Guard officer who had lived in Hawaii for many years, and who had gotten to know the Nisei GIs personally when he served as executive officer of the 298th Infantry Regiment. His second in command, Major James Lovell, had been a baseball and football coach at McKinley High School in Honolulu and had coached many of the young Nisei whom he now commanded. Lovell also played on the National Guard football team. The team had missed its final game of the 1941 season. It was to have been played on the afternoon of December 7. By that afternoon, the men had put on a different uniform and had rushed to other duty.

Amid a great deal of secrecy, the new battalion shipped out on June 5 aboard the transport vessel SS *Maui*, arriving in Oakland seven days later. During the voyage, the men naturally speculated about where they were headed. Wartime secrecy was in force, so about all they knew was that they were going to the mainland, a mysterious place that almost nobody aboard had ever seen. They didn't know what to expect, so rumors were rife. They had heard that Japanese Americans—including Nisei like themselves—were being caged in relocation centers, and some of the soldiers speculated that this might be their own fate.

As soon as they disembarked at Oakland, the men of the Hawaii Provisional Infantry Battalion were quickly and quietly loaded aboard trains and shipped eastward, many of them still fearing that they were heading into captivity. This was not to be. On June 16, they arrived at Camp McCoy, amid the rolling hills and dairy farms of Wisconsin's Monroe County about half way between Stevens Point, Wisconsin, and Rochester, Minnesota.

Their quick movement through the exclusion zone on the Pacific Coast was kept secret at the urging of DeWitt. He didn't want anyone to see them. In a handwritten memo preserved in the National Archives, within the files of the Office of the Chief of Staff, DeWitt snivelled that any news about their being in California, or even at Camp McCoy, might create a "public fuss."

The man who had said, "A Jap is a Jap," didn't want anybody to know that he had permitted a group of armed "Japs" to pass through *his* jurisdiction.

By the time they settled in at McCoy, the Hawaiian battalion was officially designated as the 100th Infantry Battalion (Separate) of the U.S. Army. The term "Separate" identified the unit as not being assigned to a regiment, as was the case with most battalions. The men quickly had a nickname of their own for the outfit. They called it "One-Puka-Puka," with the word "puka" being a Hawaiian word that was a double entendre for both "zero" and "hole." The latter described their initial impression of Camp McCoy. That impression would soon change.

When the Nisei men were first seen by local people as they were marching near the camp, they were reported to the sheriff as enemy paratroopers, but as folks in the nearby towns got to know the Nisei, relations quickly improved. The young Hawaiians were polite and friendly, bringing a ready smile and an *"Aloha"* to their encounters with the Wisconsonians. This "Aloha spirit" was reciprocal, and many locals invited the Japanese Americans to their homes for meals. The Nisei also formed a baseball team, and later played teams all across the state, from Madison to Green Bay. They stenciled the word "Aloha" on their shirts and billed themselves as "that team from Hawaii."

One of the most memorable games pitted the Nisei against a highly regarded minor-league team at Green Bay. The star Aloha player that day was Shigeo "Joe" Takata, who had earlier played with the Asahis of the Hawaii Baseball League, which had been the premier amateur league in Hawaii before the war. Born in Waialua, on Oahu's north shore, Joe was a natural athlete with a very good arm, who played shortstop and center field. He batted left-handed, but threw right-handed.

In an interview with journalist Steve Lum that appeared in the July 4, 2003, issue of the *Hawaii Herald*, the game was recalled by Takashi "Ted" Hirayama, who was then the Aloha team's manager, and who went on to serve overseas with Takata in Company B of the 100th Infantry Battalion. As Hirayama recalls, "An opposing batter hit a towering drive over our right fielder's head. After Kenneth Kaneko retrieved the ball, he threw it to Joe, who was playing center field. Joe relayed it on a line to our second baseman, 'Mushie' Miyagi, who then turned and threw the ball on one skip to Yozo Yamamoto, who tagged the surprised runner out. What the runner thought was going to be an easy, stand-up triple turned out to be just another out. Joe's throw to Miyagi was outstanding. I still remember the announcer saying that it would take a major-league team to make a play like that, and these little guys from Hawaii just did it. They play like pros."

For Joe Takata, he had put his dream of one day trying out for a pro team on hold in order to serve his country.

The situation at Camp McCoy was not entirely without negative incidents. When the men of the 2nd Infantry Division were briefly stationed at the base, there were some angry encounters between the Nisei and Caucasian soldiers who took exception to sharing the same parade ground with men whom they were quick to deride as "little Japs." Name-calling devolved to physical violence that mushroomed into a brawl. The white solders, being larger in stature than the men from Hawaii, assumed that they could pummel the "little Japs" with impunity. Unfortunately for them, many of the Nisei were adept in martial arts, and things didn't go as the bullies had planned.

The Nisei men also put the larger soldiers in their place during training. They demonstrated that they could cover ten miles in a three-hour march, while the average for the other troops was less than eight. They also demonstrated that they could set up a heavy machine gun in less than a third of the time officially specified by their instructors.

The history of official racial profiling in the United States includes examples that are often odious and occasionally benign. Sometimes, they are simply bizarre. One such incident came in October 1942. Somewhere in the chain of command, someone had suggested that Nisei soldiers could be used to train dogs to attack Japanese troops! This was 1942, and the war was not going as well as hoped. The United States armed forces were willing to try anything, no matter how unconventional.

Lieutenant Ernest Tanaka of the 100th Infantry Battalion's Company B was given secret orders to take two dozen men to an undisclosed location. They left abruptly and none of the other men in the battalion were briefed either on their departure or their destination. They had just disappeared. In fact, the men of Company B spent those months on Cat Island and West Ship Island in the Gulf of Mexico, due south of Biloxi, Mississippi.

When they arrived, their home was Fort Massachusetts, an aging fortification on West Ship Island that had been under construction when the Civil War started and which had been unused, except by a lighthouse keeper, since 1866. At first, the twenty-six Nisei relished their new assignment. The warm waters of the Gulf reminded them of Hawaii, a welcome change from the woods of Wisconsin. They found good fishing in the waters off the islands, and oysters in its estuary. They even struck up a trade with the men on the shrimp boats that passed by. The men were also allotted a substantial ration of beer.

Soon, they were moved across to Cat Island, where the training was done. Among the Nisei, only Tanaka had been briefed beforehand on the actual nature of this training. As they began, the soldiers got along well with the dogs, which included German shepherds, Dobermans, and even Labrador retrievers. As the strange experiment proceeded, the men were ordered to be progressively more cruel to the dogs, beating them with sacks while they were chained up. The idea, as offensive and weird as it seems in retrospect, was to associate Japanese body odor with something that should be attacked. Gradually, the dogs became more aggressive and conditioned to attack the Nisei men. Whether it was because Japanese body odor is somehow distinctive, or because the dogs simply recognized men who beat them, will never be known, because the strange experiment was abruptly terminated, having been deemed a failure for reasons that were never explained to the Nisei men. The twenty-six Nisei participants were rotated back to the 100th Infantry Battalion.

As the first full year of America's involvement in World War II gave way to 1943, and as the winter snow blanketed Wisconsin, the men of the 100th Infantry Battalion departed Camp McCoy for sunnier climes. After seven months in the north and a two-day train trip, the Nisei arrived at the larger all-weather training facility at Camp Shelby, a few miles south of Hattiesburg, Mississippi, on January 8.

Shortly thereafter, Lieutenant Young Oak Kim, a twenty-four-year-old recent graduate of Officer Candidate School, arrived at Camp Shelby to take command of the 2nd Platoon of the 100th's Company B. Kim was a Korean American, and the War Department had apparently assigned him to the unit because they thought he was a *Japanese American*! Lieutenant Colonel Farrant Turner, the commander of the 100th, offered him the opportunity to transfer to another unit, citing the traditional animosity between Korean Americans and Japanese Americans.

In an interview with the Go For Broke Educational Foundation many decades later, Kim recalled that Turner told him, "I don't think you realize that this is a Japanese unit. And of course you're Korean. . . . I'll have you transferred."

"Sir, they're Americans and I'm an American," Kim replied. "And we're going to fight for America. So I want to stay."

Kim recalled that the colonel looked kind of startled.

"I can have you transferred first thing in the morning," Turner promised.

"No, sir." Kim replied.

"Well, you can stay," Turner said with a smile. "But you are going to be on probation. See how well you can get along with the men."

With that Kim saluted, turned around and left. In 2003, he told Joyce Caoile of the Asians in America Project, "We're all Americans and we're all fighting for the same cause."

Apparently Kim passed his probation. He would remain with the battalion throughout the war, serving as its operations officer for most of its last year in combat, and would stay in the U.S. Army until 1972, when he retired as a full colonel. Throughout World War II, he identified with his Japanese American comrades and was a staunch advocate of what the Nisei men sought most—acceptance.

As Kim later told the Go For Broke Educational Foundation, "We had to do well in combat in order to rectify all these conditions. . . . If the stigma that the Japanese Americans were living under was to be removed, then we had to do well in combat. And everybody recognized that. . . . By doing well, it meant that we had to . . . make a good record, but we had to shed blood. And that some . . . of us were never going to return. But that was a price we had to pay."

As the 100th Infantry Battalion relocated to Camp Shelby, plans were already in play for the number of Nisei in the U.S. Army to increase dramatically. Though the interment camps would remain, the army needed their inmates.

CHAPTER 5

Linguists on the Horns
of a Paradox

As their mainland parents were being relocated, and as their contemporaries were training with the new 100th Infantry Battalion, other Nisei and Kibei men were being instructed as linguists with the U.S. Army's Military Intelligence Service (MIS). The importance of having linguists conversant in the Japanese language was obvious to some officers within the U.S. Army even before the war as Imperial Japan was rattling its sabers across the Far East, and as relations between the United States and Japan deteriorated.

A pair of intelligence officers, Lieutenant Colonel John Weckerling and Captain Kai Rasmussen, conceived the idea of a language school early in 1941 and fought against official War Department indifference to get the project started. At last, the brass in Washington accepted their proposal, and they were able to establish a clandestine language school on November 1, 1941, just a few weeks prior to Pearl Harbor. Born in Denmark, Rasmussen had graduated from the United States Military Academy at West Point in 1929 and had served for four years at the American embassy in Tokyo. The new school was quietly set up in San Francisco in a disused hangar at the Presidio's Crissy Field, and had fifty-eight Japanese Americans and two Caucasians enrolled by the first of December 1941.

The attack on Hawaii and the United States entry into World War II brought a burst of energy into the American intelligence community and a major reorganization of the army's intelligence apparatus. From August 1918 until March 1942, the service's intelligence function was under the direction of the Military Intelligence Division (MID) of the War Department General Staff. Analogous to the U.S. Navy's separate Office of Naval Intelligence (ONI), it was more an administrative organization than an operational unit. In March 1942, the U.S. Army decided to peel off the operational intelligence functions and place them in the newly created Military Intelligence Service, which was charged with the active collection, analysis, and dissemination of intelligence.

John Patrick Finnegan, in his Center of Military History study of military intelligence, states, that "Perhaps the most important organizational change within the MID/MIS organization was the development of an element charged with exploiting sensitive communications intelligence. This occurred as a result of the weaknesses in handling such sources at Pearl Harbor."

The new service also took over the language school at the Presidio, which was now officially designated the Military Intelligence Service Language School (MISLS), with Rasmussen as its commandant. The importance of the school grew as army commanders throughout the Pacific Theater were now begging for more Japanese-speaking linguists. In another one of those bewildering ironies that were so much a part of officialdom's relations with Japanese Americans in 1942, just as the young Nisei were needed more than ever, they were becoming pariahs in California—the state that most had called home all their lives, and the state where the MISLS was located.

In the autumn of 1941, it had made a great deal of sense logistically to locate a Japanese language school at the Presidio in San Francisco. The huge base served as headquarters of the Fourth Army and it was in the heart of a major West Coast city with a large Japanese American population from which recruits could be conveniently drawn. By the spring of 1942, however, with the exclusion ordered by

Executive Order 9066, maintaining such an institution within California was simply impossible. The Japanese-speaking students, who were a majority of the student body, could no longer walk down the street. It was about a fifteen-minute stroll across the landscaped grounds of the Presidio from the MISLS to General DeWitt's office in the headquarters building—yet men wearing the same uniform as DeWitt and saluting the same flag could not make that walk, thanks to the orders he had promulgated.

Just as San Francisco had been a good choice to locate the language school in terms of attracting students, so, too, was the school close to a rich pool of potential instructors. One of the best remembered among the founding faculty at Crissy Field was a man named Shigeya Kihara.

A native Californian, Shig Kihara was born in the Solano County farming town of Fairfield, and grew up in Oakland. He enrolled at the University of California in Berkeley, earning his bachelor's degree in political science in 1937 and his master's degree in international relations two years later. He had then decided to go to Japan for further study. What he found in the country of his forefathers both surprised and dismayed him. Already at war in China, Japan had adopted a national policy of aggressively absorbing much of the Far East into its empire. He left as soon as he could.

Around the time that Kihara returned to the United States, the Military Intelligence Service was in the midst of planning its language school, and they had contacted Florence Walne, his former Japanese-language instructor at the University of California. She recommended him, so he applied and was invited to join the MISLS faculty in October 1941.

In order to help get the school off the ground, Kihara and another faculty member, Akira Oshida, brought in their own Japanese-language books for use in the classroom. When Pearl Harbor was attacked, and the authorities started to confiscate Japanese-language materials, Kihara went to his brother's house to grab armloads of Japanese periodicals to get them to Crissy Field before the FBI could seize them!

As his son Ron Kihara said in an interview with Charles Burress of the *San Francisco Chronicle* on the occasion of Shig Kihara's death in January 2005, "He was extremely loyal. He never wavered in his commitment to the American side, even though his parents, brother, sister, and wife's family were sent during the war to the Topaz, Utah, internment camp."

Another important faculty member was John Fujio Aiso. Born in Burbank, California, Aiso was the 1926 class valedictorian and the captain of a debating team at Hollywood High School. He then traveled to Japan and studied the Japanese language at Seijo Gakuen University in Tokyo. Upon his return to the States, he attended Brown University, graduating with honors as the valedictorian of the Class of 1931. Three years later he graduated from Harvard Law School and went to work for a New York firm, specializing in Japanese banking law. He then spent several years in Japan, working in the world of international finance. Returning to the United States in 1940, he was drafted into the U.S. Army, which, in its infinite wisdom, assigned him to work in the motor pool at Camp Hahn near Riverside, California! Fortunately, when Private Aiso met Captain Rasmussen in the fall of 1941, he received an immediate transfer to the Presidio. He soon became the school's chief instructor.

While plans were being made to relocate the MISLS away from California, the first class of forty-five Japanese Americans and two Caucasians graduated in May 1942, and the second class, double the size of the first, graduated in June. The new home for the school would be at Camp Savage, a former Civilian Conservation Corps facility in Minnesota, a state where Republican Governor Harold Stassen had a more even-handed view of Japanese American civil rights than his West Coast counterparts.

Although the Japanese Americans recruited for the MISLS understood the Japanese language, the purpose of the school was to instruct them in "heigo," Imperial Japanese Army and Navy terminology. This included the words and phrases describing the nuances of military organization and weapons systems. As anyone close to government or military bureaucracy in any country knows, the insiders within such organizations have a "buzz-word" dialect of their own, regardless of the country and its primary language. Robert "Rusty" Kimura, in an interview with the Go For Broke Educational Foundation, described the MISLS curriculum as including heigo, as well as "the probable attitude of Japanese soldiers if [or] when they're captured. And how to talk to them, how to interrogate them."

The MISLS grads entered active duty at a critical time in World War II. Since the attack on Pearl Harbor, the Japanese armed forces had run over much of the Far East in what seemed to be a juggernaut. Within a month, they had captured Guam, Wake Island, Manila, and Hong Kong. Their forces were on the offensive throughout Southeast Asia, from Burma to Malaya. When the huge British fortress at Singapore fell in February 1942, it was seen as a disaster for the United Kingdom. Next, Japan swallowed the colonies of German-occupied France and the Netherlands, the latter including Java, where Frank Fujita was captured in March 1942. The Japanese also landed on New Guinea and occupied islands across the South Pacific, such as Guadalcanal, of which few Americans had heard, but which would soon become household words. As they went, the Japanese forces seemed to be surrounding Australia and preparing to pluck it like low-hanging fruit.

In June 1942, in a bold new offensive that was blunted only by a decisive U.S. Navy victory in the Battle of Midway, the Japanese occupied United States territory for the first—and only—time during World War II. Located in the Aleutian island chain that stretches west of mainland Alaska, the islands of Attu and Kiska were captured by Japanese troops during the first week of June at the same time that the Japanese were attempting unsuccessfully to invade and occupy Midway Island.

These numerous actions, taking place across the vast expanse of the Pacific, formed the backdrop for the work that was to be done by the Nisei GIs of the MIS. Members of the first MISLS class were assigned to the Alaskan Defense Command to help monitor Japanese radio traffic in and out of the occupied Aleutian Islands, while others traveled to the South Pacific, where the United States would soon be mounting its first major offensive ground actions of the war.

While the upper echelons of the War Department debated whether to use the Nisei infantrymen of the 100th Infantry Battalion in combat, there were no such qualms about the Nisei linguists. Their value was obvious, even as their very existence remained secret. General George V. Strong, the War Department's assistant chief of staff for intelligence, wrote a memorandum to Chief of Staff Marshall on August 31, 1942, which said in part that "Americans of Japanese Ancestry must be used because no non-Japanese with the necessary qualifications are available."

In May and June 1942, Nisei MIS linguists set up shop in New Caledonia, the headquarters of the South Pacific Command, and immediately began to scrutinize the massive volume of enemy communications. Over the coming months and years, they would be a crucial part of battles fought at Bougainville, Guadalcanal, and New Guinea. When U.S. troops began their campaign to recapture Guadalcanal in August 1942, the Nisei MIS troops were on the ground, interrogating captured enemy troops.

Meanwhile, the first of an eventual three thousand Nisei MIS men arrived in Melbourne, Australia, to staff the Allied Translator and Interpreter Section (ATIS). Later relocated to a racetrack in Indooroopilly, a suburb of Brisbane, the ATIS would be used to translate mountains of enemy documents that would be captured over the next several years.

By the end of 1942, as the 100th Infantry Battalion was still in training, Nisei GIs were already at war. In fact, as a third MISLS class was forming, mainly from volunteers from relocation centers, ninety-two men were recruited out of the 100th Infantry Battalion.

Victor Abe, the former engineering student who had been drafted before the ban on Japanese Americans fully took effect, was recruited by the MIS while he was posted to Fort Warren, Wyoming, in December 1942. He traded the bitter cold of the Wyoming winter for even colder weather in Minnesota. The mercury dipped to 32 below zero, something that Abe had never experienced in Los Angeles.

He was eventually assigned to ATIS in Australia, where he went to work translating diaries and other personal effects found on dead or captured Japanese troops. "I couldn't speak Japanese very well," he recalled. "Because after I had started going out for basketball, I didn't have time to continue with Japanese school—but I could read the language very well."

On his way overseas, Victor Abe visited his parents, who were interned at the Heart Mountain relocation camp. By now, his father, who had once owned a successful Nash automobile dealership at San Pedro and Tenth in Los Angeles, had lost everything.

"Here I was, an American soldier," he recalls sadly, "and my folks were behind barbed wire with guns pointed inward! I was shocked, but, as we often said, *Shikata ga nai*, it can't be helped. My dad told me, 'You've got to do your best for your country.'"

Among the men recruited from the relocation camps were Kenjiro and Harry Akune from Turlock, California. They were interned at Amache in Colorado when the MIS recruiters came calling in December 1942.

"It was by accident that I found out about it," Ken Akune recalled. "My older brother Harry came by when I was playing football and said that he was going to see the recruiters. I asked him, 'What recruiters?' He told me that the army was looking for linguists. I decided to go with him to take the test, which consisted of reading and writing Japanese, which we had learned in Japan. When our mother had passed away in 1933, our family decided to send us to live with relatives in Kagoshima until 1938, when I was fifteen. We both passed the test and were accepted."

"The Nisei had wanted to serve, but we had been denied, and now a door was open," Ken Akune said emphatically, describing why joining the MIS was so important to him. "What had bothered me more than going into the internment camp was the fact that all of my high school buddies were being accepted into the service, and I wasn't. When the war began, all the guys I used to play basketball with were going into the air force and the marines, and we couldn't. We used to brag to the first-generation Japanese Americans that we were *American,* and now they were telling us that we were no different than they were. It sounds crazy today, but we were excited to be able to volunteer. I felt like I was American again!"

CHAPTER 6

Expanding Their Numbers

On February 1, 1943, less than a year after he signed Executive Order 9066, President Franklin D. Roosevelt finally admitted, "No loyal citizen of the United States should be denied the democratic right to exercise the responsibilities of his citizenship, regardless of his ancestry. The principle on which this country was founded and by which it has always been governed is that Americanism is a matter of the mind and heart; Americanism is not, and never was, a matter of race or ancestry. A good American is one who is loyal to this country and to our creed of liberty and democracy."

In those fifty weeks, the president and many others at the apex of the United States government had come to realize that, to quote Roosevelt, "Every loyal American should be given the opportunity to serve this country wherever his skills will make the greatest contribution— whether it be in the ranks of our armed forces, war production, agriculture, government service, or other work essential to the war effort."

The occasion of Roosevelt's remarks was the formation of the 442nd Regimental Combat Team, a military unit *triple the size* of the 100th Infantry Battalion that, like the 100th, would be composed entirely of Japanese American enlisted men and noncoms in which many of the junior officers would also be Nisei. By now, it had also been decided that the U.S. Army would actually use the Nisei GIs and this unit in combat. Such a notion had not been a foregone conclusion when the 100th Infantry Battalion was formed, but it was now an understood part of the doctrine for the utilization of the Japanese American troops.

The idea for this larger unit had been percolating in official Washington throughout the summer and fall of 1942. As the MIS Language School was training its third class of linguists, and as the Nisei men of the 100th Infantry Battalion drilled and trained in Wisconsin, the U.S. Army had been pondering whether to incorporate even more Nisei soldiers into their organization.

The original battalion had been formed almost as an expedient to get the Nisei men out of Hawaii, and it was formed even before the army had made a firm decision to actually send its Nisei GIs overseas to fight as an integral unit. On June 26, just ten days after the 100th Infantry Battalion arrived at Camp McCoy, the army had empowered a committee to study the notion of whether to create the larger Japanese American unit, whether to include men from the mainland as well as from Hawaii, and whether to use these troops in combat.

A major proponent of giving the mainland Nisei an opportunity to serve was Mike Masaoka, of the Japanese American Citizens League. He had unsuccessfully recommended such a unit early in 1942 as an alternative to the internment of draft-age mainland Nisei. The men were anxious to prove their loyalty, and permitting them to volunteer would be an excellent way for them to do so.

Nevertheless, the idea of permitting Nisei to openly volunteer for army units other than the Military Intelligence Service continued to meet opposition at all levels within the War Department, including Secretary of War Henry Stimson himself. Those who did not agree with Stimson's arbitrary attitude included Colonel Moses Pettigrew, a former military attaché at the United States embassy in Tokyo, and now head of Far Eastern Division of Military Intelligence. He thought it to be counterproductive, and a bad use of available manpower to deny Nisei—or any other able-bodied draft-age man—an opportunity to serve.

On September 14, the committee, which included five army officers and Dillon Myer—who had succeeded Milton Eisenhower as head of the War Relocation Administration—recommended *against* deploying a Japanese American unit. However, by this time, the once-adamant opposition within the army was crumbling. This was due in no small part to the apparent success that the army was having in the Pacific with the Nisei linguists of the Military Intelligence Service. The men of the 100th Infantry Battalion were also setting an excellent example during their training. One by one, the critics were reversing their thinking. Stimson's influential assistant secretary, John J. McCloy, changed his mind when he observed the Varsity Victory Volunteers men at work while he was on an inspection tour to Hawaii. In turn, he nudged his boss on the issue.

One of the most important converts to the notion of a Japanese American unit in the U.S. Army was the chief of staff. In May 1942, Marshall had authorized the creation of the unit that became the 100th Infantry Battalion, and in a memo now in the Chief of Staff files in the National Archives, Marshall succinctly stated, "I don't think you can permanently proscribe a lot of American citizens because of their racial origin."

On October 15, 1942, Elmer Davis, the director of the Office of War Information, took the matter to the top, recommending to President Roosevelt that Japanese Americans be allowed to enlist for military service in an all–Japanese American combat unit.

Even Dillon Myer soon changed his tune. The more he looked at the situation, the more he became convinced that the camps were a bad idea. In fact, he felt they were so bad an idea that he undertook to develop a way to process people *out* of internment. He decided that he would administer a loyalty oath. If someone answered correctly, that would give him an excuse to release that person. Unfortunately, he borrowed the wording from the loyalty questionnaires administered to potential draftees, and some of the wording was grossly inapplicable to the internees. Two questions in particular on a questionnaire were problematic:

Number 27 asked, "Are you willing to serve in the armed forces of the United States on combat duty wherever ordered?" Number 28 posed the question: "Will you swear unqualified allegiance to the United States of America and faithfully defend the United States from any or all attack by foreign or domestic forces, and forswear any form of allegiance or obedience to the Japanese emperor, to any other foreign government, power or organization?"

Elderly women usually answered no when asked if they'd be willing to serve in the armed forces, and none of the Issei were willing to answer yes to forswearing allegiance to the Japanese government. Since they were not permitted to become United States citizens, such a renunciation would leave them precariously stateless. The questions were also troubling for many people who feared that Issei parents would be separated from their Nisei children on the basis of their answers. Then there were those who interpreted the whole idea of the loyalty questionnaire as an insult. For Nisei men of draft age, there were usually no qualms, although the latter query seemed to many like a trick question. Since they were United States citizens, they had no allegiance to the Japanese government to renounce!

A number of Japanese Americans—including a few Nisei—answered no to both questions in protest against the camp system. The draft-age Nisei among them became known as the No-No Boys because they had answered no twice.

While most draft-age Nisei answered yes to both questions, there were also a few Yes-No men. Henry Ikemoto, whose family was interned at the Rohwer Relocation Camp in Arkansas, answered Yes-Yes and served with the 442nd Regimental Combat Team, but he recalls that his brother was a Yes-No man. He answered yes to Number 28, but he did not want to serve overseas.

With the decision for the larger Japanese American unit having been made, the U.S. Army worked at designing it. The idea was to create a regiment-sized organization composed entirely of Japanese American enlisted personnel, just as the 100th Infantry Battalion had been a battalion composed entirely of Japanese Americans. (Essentially, a World War II–era regiment was three times the size of a battalion—and contained three battalions.)

Under the army's triangular organizational design, the basic building block of the service was a roughly 14,000-man infantry division, composed of three 3,000-man infantry regiments, plus additional support units, including artillery, medical personnel, and so on. In turn, each regiment was composed of three battalions of about 900 men, plus their support personnel. The 100th Infantry Battalion, which had been created as a separate battalion that was unassigned to any regiment, contained over 1,400 men. It was larger than a typical battalion because it contained people to provide support functions normally handled at the regimental level.

The organizational plan for the 442nd was completed on January 22, 1943, by which time the 100th Infantry Battalion had relocated to Camp Shelby in Mississippi. The 442nd would also be formed at Camp Shelby. The plan called for the new regiment to comprise three infantry battalions, plus the 522nd Field Artillery Battalion and the 232nd Engineer Company. The infantry battalions were numbered 1st, 2nd, and 3rd, each containing four companies, except the 3rd, which had five. The adding of the additional units to the three infantry battalions made the regiment a "regimental combat team." Technically, the three infantry battalions constituted a 442nd *Infantry Regiment* that was contained *within* the 442nd *Regimental Combat Team*, but for the sake of clarity, the unit was and is almost always referred to as the 442nd Regimental Combat Team.

The regimental combat team concept was a new idea that had just emerged. The notion was to augment a basic three-battalion regiment with a small support staff such as one would find at the division level. This would make the regiment more autonomous and self-sustaining. A regimental combat team would be assigned to a division just as a regiment was, but it would have an organizational structure that allowed it to take care of itself, with less dependence on the division-level support units.

A week later, on February 1, President Roosevelt formally activated the 442nd Regimental Combat Team. Roosevelt had tested the political winds, and they seemed to have changed direction with regard to the Nisei since he had authorized Executive Order 9066. Thanks to the example of the 100th Infantry Battalion, a great deal of progress had been made.

Unlike the all-Hawaiian 100th Infantry Battalion, however, the new regiment would be comprised of Japanese American soldiers from both the Islands and from the mainland. It would be the first opportunity that mainland Nisei had to get into the service since they were declared enemy aliens.

Within the Japanese American community, the response to the formation of the 442nd was overwhelming. The plan had been to recruit 1,500 men from the mainland, and 1,500 from Hawaii—and there had been some concern that the unit wouldn't get enough volunteers. Nothing could have been farther from the truth! In fact, so many men volunteered in the islands that the size of the contingent had to be nearly doubled. Among those who volunteered were the men of the Varsity Victory Volunteers. Indeed, the VVV was officially inactivated in February 1943 after so many of its members joined the 442nd Regimental Combat Team.

Daniel Inouye recalls in his memoirs the day in January 1943 when the colonel in charge of the University of Hawaii ROTC unit called the men together to announce that the 442nd was being formed and that the draft board was ready to take enlistments. "As soon as his words were out, the room exploded with excited shouts. We burst out of there and ran—literally ran—the three miles to the draft board, stringing back over the streets and sidewalks, jostling for position, like a bunch of marathoners gone berserk. The scene was repeated all over the islands."

"I had been really devastated," Honolulu construction worker

Don Seki said, recalling the shock of Pearl Harbor and why he was excited about the 442nd. "I don't care who it was, Japanese or foreign elements, they bombed our island. I was so disgusted with Japan, so I was thinking, we got to do something about this. . . . That's the thing that made me volunteer."

In contrast to the secretive way in which the 100th Infantry Battalion had departed from Honolulu in May 1942, the new volunteers received a huge send-off by their families and the Japanese American community. The Honolulu Chamber of Commerce threw a huge farewell bash for them on March 28. Estimates of the size of the crowd ranged as high as 17,000. The proud families bade them aloha on the streets of Honolulu, and at smaller, tear-filled moments in private homes.

Two days later, the *Honolulu Star-Bulletin* reported: "No scene in Honolulu during World War II has been more striking, more significant, than that at the territorial capitol grounds on Sunday." The paper went on to cite "the evident pride of the families and friends of these young Americans—their pride that the youths are entrusted with the patriotic mission of fighting for their country and the Allied nations."

On the mainland, the response to the formation of the 442nd was not nearly as exuberant. Many of the young draft-age Nisei men were anxious to be a part of it and to prove that they were loyal Americans. However, many of their parents, still embittered by internment and by the loyalty oaths, were skeptical. Shigeru "Shig" Kizuka from Watsonville, California, whose family was at the Poston Relocation Center in Arizona, wanted to volunteer for the 442nd, but his Issei father, a community activist at Poston, would not have approved. By this time, though, Kizuka was living in Detroit, having been allowed to leave Poston to attend Wayne State University, so he signed up and told his parents that he had been drafted.

After boot camp, as he was preparing to go overseas, Shig Kizuka returned to Poston to visit his family. His father refused to speak with him, so Shig responded by ignoring his father. Finally, as he was getting ready to board the bus that would take him away, perhaps for the last time, Shig's mother intervened, chiding her son for his stubbornness, and asking him to say goodbye to his father. She told him that this would be the way to break the impasse. At first Shig resisted, telling his mother that he wouldn't be the first to say goodbye, but finally he relented. He spoke first, and his father bade him farewell. Mrs. Kizuka absolutely did not want these words to go unsaid, and they weren't.

Robert Ichikawa, who had been in the tenth grade at the Manual Arts High School in Los Angeles when the war started, finished his high school career behind the barbed wire at the Amache relocation camp in Colorado as part of the camp's first high school graduating class. As soon as he graduated, he volunteered for the 442nd Regimental Combat Team, and on May 18, 1943, as he turned eighteen, he was inducted into the U.S. Army at Fort Lupton, Colorado.

"They put us on a train, and sent us south to Camp Shelby. It was night as the train slowly passed the camp. I could see the lights of the building where I used to live. I wanted to get out and say goodbye to my folks, but the train wasn't stopping. It just kept on going. My friend Roy Sato said later that he thought I was going to cry."

Of course, a handful of West Coast Japanese American families had managed to avoid the camps entirely. In March 1942, after being permitted to simply drive out the Manzanar main gate with their FBI pass, Lawson Sakai's family had driven eastward to Delta, Colorado, a small town about forty miles south of Grand Junction on U.S. Highway 50. Young Lawson, who had been attending school at Compton Junior College in California when his college career was interrupted by war and dislocation, had enrolled at Mesa College in Grand Junction.

Though he was of draft age and not living in a relocation camp, being Japanese American had made him a pariah as far as the armed forces were concerned. That is, until the formation of the 442nd Regimental Combat Team was announced. He read about it in the newspaper and signed up as quickly as he could. He went on to serve in every campaign in which the 442nd saw action.

George "Joe" Sakato's family, meanwhile, had moved voluntarily from Colton, in California's San Bernardino County, to Phoenix, Arizona. The family was operating a grocery store in Colton when Pearl Harbor was attacked, and in fact, Joe had just opened the store that Sunday morning when he heard the news on the radio. Sakato had then tried unsuccessfully to volunteer for the U.S. Army Air Forces. When the Nisei men were reclassified in order to form the 442nd, Sakato volunteered for the USAAF again, but the air service eluded him, and he found himself in the infantry.

To command the new 442nd Regimental Combat Team, the army picked Colonel Charles W. Pence, a career soldier who had served with the U.S. Army mission in China during the early 1930s, when the Japanese had invaded and occupied Manchuria. As such, he was considered something of an expert on the cultures of the Far East, and this was why the army had picked him to lead a Japanese American regiment. The irony was that he had spent more time in Asia than most of the Nisei soldiers under his command.

Like the regimental commander, the battalion commanders and most of the company commanders within the 442nd, as with those within the 100th Infantry Battalion, would be Caucasian. However, like Lieutenant Colonel Turner and Major Lovell in the 100th, most—albeit not all—were men who had confidence in the Nisei soldiers under their command, and who inspired confidence in themselves. Dan Inouye recalls that Captain Ralph Burnell Ensminger, the Company E commander, "was a haole who had gone to Roosevelt High in Honolulu, and from the start there wasn't a man of us who wouldn't have followed him right into [German Field Marshal Erwin] Rommel's command post."

When the 442nd joined the 100th Infantry Battalion at Camp Shelby on April 13, they were in a much different type of unit than the 100th had been at Camp McCoy ten months earlier. Whereas the men of the 100th had all been Hawaiian, and most knew one another, the men of the 442nd came not only from the Islands, but from many mainland states as well. Within the 442nd, the Hawaiians differed from the mainlanders in that they were volunteers, while many mainlanders had been draftees.

The men from the mainland had much different life experiences than the Hawaiians. For one thing, in Hawaii, Japanese Americans were the largest single ethnic group, while the mainlanders had grown up in a culture where they were a distinct minority. For this reason, the mainlanders had become more attuned to American mass culture. They were more in the American mainstream, and were more likely to speak English with an accent that was indistinguishable from that of a Caucasian from the West Coast. The mainlanders were also much more likely to have immediate family members who were incarcerated at the relocation camps. In fact, most of the mainlanders had been in the camps themselves.

To the men, there would always be a difference, and in the beginning, this delineation often boiled over into animosity and even brawls. The Hawaiians derided the mainlanders, referring to them as "kotonks," meaning that they were empty-headed. "Kotonk" is said to be the sound that an empty coconut makes hitting the ground.

The mainlanders, meanwhile, called the Hawaiians "Buddhaheads," while ridiculing them for being crude and unsophisticated. The Nisei from major West Coast cities thought of themselves as urbane and cosmopolitan. Certainly they were better versed in popular culture, which is the yardstick that people in the eighteen-to-twenty-five age group have always used to measure sophistication. On the other hand, the Hawaiians had so many experiences in common that they formed a much more cohesive group as the two sides frequently squared off.

As different as the Kotonks were from the Buddhaheads, they were all Japanese American. Outside the gates of Camp Shelby, the differences faded by comparison to the realities of the racial dichotomy of the mid-twentieth-century Deep South. Most of the Nisei had come from Hawaii or the West Coast, where racial discrimination certainly existed, but where it was subtle. In Mississippi, it was not only overt, it was mandated by the law.

The Nisei men found themselves riding buses in which whites

were required to sit in the front, while African Americans were told to step to the back and wait until a white person needed their seat. The Nisei men, being neither black nor white, wondered where they should sit. There were "whites only" drinking fountains and public bathrooms, and there were those designated for "coloreds." Where would a Japanese American person get a drink of water in public?

It was made known to the Nisei soldiers that they would be treated as "honorary whites," which should have been a good thing, because naturally the better drinking fountains were those reserved for the sons and daughters of the Confederacy. However, many Nisei took exception to being treated as honorary whites. They weren't white, and they were not ashamed of being of Japanese ancestry. In one instance, when some Nisei GIs sat in the colored section of a city bus, the driver refused to move until they changed seats. When other Nisei men drank at a colored drinking fountain, they were reported to the police!

"As we went out to the town, we noticed that the drinking fountains were marked 'colored only' or 'white only,'" Robert Ichikawa recalled. "We had heard about this before, but only vaguely. We'd never seen it. The government declared that all of the Japanese Americans in Camp Shelby were 'white,' and that we would use only 'white' facilities from then on. It didn't make that much difference to most of us. By then we were used to being pushed around anyway. On the busses, blacks were supposed to sit in the back, so we'd ask the bus driver where to sit. Some drivers would tell us to sit in the back, others would tell us to sit in the front. After a while, the guys would just sit anyplace there was room."

Many of the Japanese Americans were confronting a dark side of institutional racism that they had never seen before. Especially for those coming from Hawaii, the idea of separate drinking fountains was unfathomable. Soon, however, they would be in a more deadly environment. German bullets had no regard for the color of one's skin, nor for the birthplace of a grandmother.

The men of the 442nd Regimental Combat Team were out to prove themselves, not only as soldiers, but as representatives of the Japanese American community. They adopted the slogan "Go For Broke," meaning that they were giving it all they had, and that they were laying it all on the line.

CHAPTER 7

Going Overseas

T he men of the 100th Infantry Battalion already had nine months of training under their belts when the 442nd Regimental Combat Team arrived at Camp Shelby in April 1943. The two units would continue to train simultaneously for four months, although the 100th had reached a much more advanced stage of their training, so there was little overlap. Indeed, the 100th would be ready to go overseas nine months ahead of the larger 442nd.

In August 1943, the 100th traveled to New York by way of Camp Kilmer, New Jersey, and from there, they shipped out aboard the troop ship *James Parker*. The Nisei men arrived overseas in Oran, Algeria, on September 2, after nearly two weeks at sea. The Japanese American combat unit, whose capabilities were still doubted by some leaders in Washington, as well as many field commanders, had finally arrived in an operational theater of the war.

Three days after their arrival, the Nisei battalion received its first regimental assignment. Whereas most battalions were created as a component of a regiment and sent overseas as such, the 100th had remained independent of a regimental "parent" for more than a year. In anticipation of the upcoming Allied landings in Italy, they were attached to the 133rd Infantry Regiment of the 34th Infantry Division, commanded by Major General Charles Ryder.

Typically, battalions within regiments were numbered 1 through

3. Within the 133rd Infantry Regiment, the 100th Infantry Battalion would function as the de facto 2nd battalion, with the others being the 1st and 3rd. The 133rd's original 2nd Battalion had been detached in the fall of 1942 to serve as a guard detail at Allied headquarters, and it would remain as such until March 1944. The Nisei soldiers of the 100th, meanwhile, would remain attached to the 133rd until May 1944.

Known as the Red Bull Division because of the image on its insignia, the 34th was a National Guard division originally formed of Guard units from Minnesota, Iowa, and the Dakotas. The Red Bulls had gone ashore with the first Allied landings in North Africa in November 1942, and had fought numerous engagements across Algeria and Tunisia. By the summer of 1943, they had been pulled out of the line to train for Operation Avalanche, the Allied invasion near Salerno, just south of Naples.

As it went into combat, the 34th Infantry Division would be part of the American VI Corps, commanded by Major General Ernest Dawley. The VI Corps was in turn part of the Allied Fifth Army, commanded by General Mark Clark. Clark's command also included the British X Corps. Along with the British Eighth Army, the Fifth was a component of the 15th Army Group, the principal Allied land warfare organization within the Mediterranean Theater. It was commanded by Britain's General Sir Harold Alexander.

Allied strategy in the Mediterranean Theater had involved first securing Axis-controlled North Africa, and next, taking the war to Italy. When the United States had entered the war a year and a half earlier, the European Axis partners, Germany and Italy, controlled all of nonneutral continental Europe and most of North Africa. Adolf Hitler's blitzkrieg had swept up all the countries from Scandinavia to the Balkans. His armies were deep inside the Soviet Union, and his troops were present in nations such as Hungary and Romania, which were Axis junior partners. In North Africa, Italy had controlled Libya since before the war, and the pro-Axis Vichy French government controlled Morocco, Algeria, and Tunisia.

The only toehold that the Allies had retained in North Africa was provided by the British armies in Egypt and in the eastern part of Libya. These forces were all that stood between the Axis and the twin prizes of the Suez Canal and the Mideast oil fields beyond. The Italians had been taking a beating from the British, so in order that the Axis might finish the task of conquering all of North Africa, Hitler had sent the brilliant German Field Marshal Erwin Rommel to Africa in early 1941 to take charge. Rommel organized his Afrika Korps and launched an offensive against the British that nearly succeeded.

In the autumn of 1942, however, the tide of battle had finally turned. On November 3, after a bitter eleven-day battle at El Alamein in Egypt, the British decisively defeated Rommel, putting him on the defensive. Less than a week later, the Allies, mainly American troops— who had not yet faced the German armies during World War II— made simultaneous amphibious landings around Casablanca in Morocco and at Oran and Algiers in Algeria. Bitter fighting ensued throughout the winter as the Allies pushed Rommel from both sides. Though the Afrika Korps put up a tremendous holding action, lack of supplies and superior Allied numbers gradually pushed the Germans and Italians into a corner in northern Tunisia. On May 13, 1943, the Axis finally surrendered in North Africa.

During the third week of January 1943, President Franklin Roosevelt and British Prime Minister Winston Churchill, together with their key military leaders, had held a summit conference in Casablanca to discuss global strategy. Among other key decisions, they agreed that they would accept nothing short of unconditional surrender from the Axis powers.

In terms of strategy, they wanted to take the war to Germany as soon as possible. In order to do this, they would have liked to have landed their troops in northern France, which was closer to the heart of the Third Reich, but they did not yet have sufficient forces available in England to overwhelm the Germans. They decided to postpone the invasion of northern France until the middle of 1944 and to take the war to Italy instead. In terms of logistics and strategy, Italy was a logical next step. It was a short distance from North Africa, which is where the recently victorious Allied armies were already operating. Italy was also the weakest of the three primary Axis nations, and therefore it was potentially the easiest to defeat. An Italy strategy was operationally obvious, and it was the best shot at a quick elimination of one of the three main Axis enemy nations.

As decided at Casablanca, the next Allied operation would be an assault on the Italian island of Sicily, which lay in the Mediterranean as a stepping-stone between North Africa and Italy. Operation Husky, the Anglo-American invasion of Sicily, went ashore on July 10, 1943. As in North Africa, the Axis forces, mainly the Germans, put up a vicious defense, but again the Allies, with their superior numbers and robust supply lines, prevailed. The Axis forces were defeated, formally surrendering on August 17, although most of their troops had managed to withdraw from Sicily to Italy.

Having stepped on their stepping-stone, the Allies stepped into Europe. On September 3, the British launched Operation Baytown, crossing the narrow Strait of Messina that separates Sicily from the rest of Italy. Five days later, the Italian government formally surrendered and withdrew from the Axis. King Victor Emmanuel had sacked Fascist dictator Benito Mussolini as head of the government six weeks earlier, and replaced him with General Pietro Badoglio, who secretly negotiated a surrender with the Allies.

One Axis nation was down, but this made little difference to the actual battle, because the Italian armies had largely imploded after the defeat in Tunisia, and the Germans were already doing most of the fighting. Hitler simply ordered his armies to treat Italy as an occupied country rather than as an Axis partner and to carry on as before. Hitler set Mussolini up as a puppet head of government in German-controlled Italy, but aside from a few diehard Italian Fascists, most of the battlefield opposition that would be faced by the Allies from now on in Italy would be German.

On September 9, the day after the Italian capitulation, the British landed troops at Taranto in Italy in Operation Slapstick, and a large Allied force went ashore at Salerno in the operation code-named

Avalanche. General Mark Clark, the commander of Operation Avalanche, planned that his troops would encircle and capture the huge Italian port of Naples inside of two weeks.

The estimated 450 Allied ships taking part in the operation had sailed from Sicily, as well as from the North African ports of Tripoli, Oran, and Bizerte. The American spearhead for the Salerno invasion was the 36th Infantry Division, mainly a Texas National Guard unit commanded by Major General Fred Walke. This was the unit to which the 442nd Regimental Combat Team would be attached about a year later. The 36th was to be followed across the beachhead by the 45th Infantry Division. The plan was for the 34th Infantry Division— which now incorporated the Nisei GIs of the 100th Infantry Battalion—to enter Italy through Naples as soon as it was captured. In the meantime, this division, along with the 3rd Infantry Division and the 1st Armored Division, constituted the Allied reserve force.

The Germans put up stiffer than expected resistance at Salerno, upsetting Clark's timetable and worrying Allied leaders. As the first troops were going ashore at Salerno, the reserve 34th Infantry Division embarked two of its three regiments from Oran, the 135th and 168th, to back up the 36th Division. The 133rd, to which the Nisei 100th Infantry Battalion was attached, was to remain in reserve and come in later, but the call came sooner than expected.

As the 133rd headed for Naples as planned before the battle, it became obvious that the port would not soon be in Allied hands, so they were diverted to Salerno. As it was now considered possible that Salerno would not be held, the 133rd was ordered to embark and prepare to fight its way ashore if the beachhead was lost. Working around the clock, the men waterproofed their vehicles, stored their noncombat gear, and got ready for action. The three ships carrying the 133rd managed to reach Salerno on September 22, D-day plus 13, only hours behind the two sister regiments.

The 100th Infantry Battalion arrived aboard the *Frederick Funston*, and began going ashore in the late morning in assault boats, although, thankfully, they were not greeted by enemy fire as the first waves going into Salerno had. The Nisei GIs were now in the combat zone. They and their equipment were part of 190,000 Allied troops, 30,000 vehicles, and 120,000 tons of supplies that came ashore through Salerno. By the following morning, all of the battalion's equipment had been unloaded, and the troops marched inland about five miles. As they reached the regimental bivouac area, Companies E and F of the 100th Infantry Battalion were assigned as the guard detail for the Fifth Army headquarters, where they would remain until mid-October.

The Germans had made Salerno costly for the Americans, but had failed to push the Allies into the sea. Only after September 15, when Field Marshal Albert Kesselring, commander of all German forces in Italy, made the decision to undertake a tactical withdrawal, were the Allies able to push inland. Meanwhile, the steep and rugged terrain presented as much of an obstacle to the Allied advance as did the tenacious German gunfire. The Germans had destroyed the few bridges crossing the deep ravines on the narrow mountain roads, so the Allies would soon resort to using mules to carry supplies.

The tough going would not get easier any time soon. Kesselring's strategy was not to stop the Allies, but to make them pay dearly for every inch of territory that they captured. If the Allies had any illusions about reaching Rome before the end of 1943, Kesselring had disabused them. He would delay their march to the Italian capital until the following summer, and the great bulk of the Italian peninsula would still lie farther to the north. Through a series of heavily fortified defensive lines, Kesselring would continue to make the Allied advance into Italy a difficult proposition for the next twenty months.

Though the Germans had withdrawn from the beachhead, they retained artillery positions on high ground that continued to cause serious damage. The 34th Infantry Division was ordered to form a task force to cut off the German line of reinforcements at Benevento, sixty miles north of Salerno. The centerpiece of the task force would be the 133rd Infantry Regiment. They moved out on September 28, soon making their first contact with the enemy at Montemarrano on the

Calore River. The heavily armed and armored troops of the German 26th Panzer Division gave the inexperienced Yanks a brutal baptism of fire, raining artillery fire on every switchback as the Yanks slowed in their climb up the steep mountain road. The advance was made even more difficult by persistent pouring rain.

It was on the following day that the Nisei GIs of the 100th Infantry Battalion first took enemy fire. Serving as the advance guard of the 133rd, they were tasked with capturing the high ground west of the town of Chiusano. Leading them was the squad led by Sergeant Joe Takata, the star outfielder from Waialua who had been such a mainstay of the Aloha baseball team when the Nisei were training at Camp McCoy a year earlier. Takata's men came under intense German 75 mm artillery fire, and he was wounded. Nevertheless, he urged the men to continue their advance.

Despite his injuries, he led them farther up the hill in a flanking movement to wipe out an enemy machine-gun nest. By the end of the day, they had taken their objective. For his actions that day, Joe Takata was awarded the Distinguished Service Cross. However, it was to be a posthumous award, for he died of his wounds before nightfall, the first Nisei soldier to be killed in action in World War II. His dreams of a postwar career in professional baseball would never be realized.

The Nisei men continued to fight their way toward the northwest, battling both the Germans and the rain, until they captured Montemiletto at the end of the day on October 1. The following afternoon, as the 133rd Infantry Regiment moved to positions near San Giorgio, orders came to capture Benevento and a bridgehead north of the Calore River. The 3rd Battalion of the 133rd was given the lead in this mission, with the 100th protecting their left flank south of Benevento.

At the end of the day, the 133rd occupied Benevento and had secured the bridgehead that was necessary for the Allied advance. By now, Allied troops had also finally captured Naples, a week behind schedule. From September 29 through October 5, when the 100th was briefly relieved for two weeks and placed in division reserve, their initial casualty figures were considered light. Three men had been killed in action, and thirty-one, including a pair of officers, had been wounded.

Before the Nisei GIs had gone into combat, they had many detractors among those in the division who thought that these "little Hawaiians"—who were small of stature and "different"—would not be able to hold up to the rigors of the battlefield. By October, they still had detractors, but there were very few—if any—among the men of the 133rd who had actually *seen them in action*. Far from being a hindrance, the fact that the Nisei soldiers were all from Hawaii was a bonus. Many of them had grown up with one another and had a camaraderie that gave them a rare unit cohesiveness. This would prove effective in making them one of the best battalions in the 34th Infantry Division.

The 133rd Infantry Regiment, with its Nisei battalion, was credited with having achieved the first major success of the 34th Infantry Division in World War II, and they were in the forefront of the next major Fifth Army advance. In order to hold Naples against counterattack, General Clark ordered the troops to advance to—and cross—the Volturno River, the next major natural barrier north of the city. Because the meandering river flows south before turning west toward the sea, the natural route north for the advancing Allies involved multiple crossings.

At the Volturno, the Allies faced the stiffest German defense since the Salerno beachhead. Meanwhile, the fast-moving river, with its steep banks, was also a formidable obstacle. The 34th Infantry Division made its crossing on the evening of October 12 under heavy fire. Division artillery returned fire as the Yanks struggled across and engineers made preparations to build a temporary treadway bridge. This was completed the next day, and American troops were able to get supplies to the bridgehead on the north side. By October 17, with the 168th Infantry Regiment in the van, the division fought its way north to Alvignano against heavy opposition from the German 3rd Panzer Grenadier Division.

Two days later, the 34th reached Dragoni, and once again the river needed crossing. The 133rd Infantry Regiment now took the lead in an attempt to capture an intact bridge. With backup from the 100th Battalion, the 1st Battalion crossed the river south of the bridge and captured it with an end run.

On October 20, the 133rd moved on Sant'Angelo, with the 1st and 100th Infantry Battalions capturing road junctions on the two flanks of the town. Two days later, the 100th and 3rd Battalions spearheaded a regimental assault in the direction of Alife. In the 100th Battalion sector, Companies A and C were in the vanguard when they came under intense machine-gun fire from several directions.

As the Nisei GIs hunkered down and hugged the dirt, they heard the rumble of German tanks. Private Masao Awakuni took out the lead tank with his bazooka at a range of twenty-five yards, and the remaining armored vehicles wisely chose to pull back and reverse their course rather than press on against the young Nisei, who that day earned a nickname as the "battalion tank buster"—as well as a Distinguished Service Cross.

The two 100th Battalion companies managed to secure Alife on October 24, and were relieved in their new position by Companies E and F. The Nisei men were next ordered to assault the high ground west of Castello d'Alife that the GIs nicknamed Castle Hill. By 9:00 the next morning, the men held a position a thousand yards from the top of the hill as other 133rd Infantry Regiment soldiers outflanked the hill and removed another in the mass of German strongpoints that lay before the Allies that autumn.

On October 29, the 100th Infantry Battalion bid farewell to Lieutenant Colonel Turner, the old Hawaii National Guard officer who had commanded the battalion since it shipped out from Hawaii more than a year before. His replacement, Major—later Lieutenant Colonel—James Gillespie assumed command as winter approached and as the 100th prepared for the next phase of the Italian campaign.

As the men of the 133rd Infantry Regiment secured the high ground around Sant'Angelo to protect the left flank of the 34th Infantry Division, they looked back to their first month in action. They had traveled 267 miles from Salerno, of which 122 miles were on foot. It was a major accomplishment for a first month, but there was a lot of work ahead. The Allies had covered barely a quarter of the distance from Salerno to Rome.

CHAPTER 8

Veterans Becoming Heroes

As October waned and the cold winds of winter began howling out of the Apennines, the once fresh-faced Nisei GIs of the 100th Infantry Battalion had seen their baptism of fire, and they were rapidly becoming battle-hardened veterans. Before the year was out, these veterans would become true heros, with many of them performing acts of bravery that would one day be recognized by America's decorations for valor in action.

The day-to-day life of the GIs grew more miserable as November brought the most inclement weather that they had yet seen in Italy. Rain fell constantly, bringing with it muddy conditions that made movement difficult. Clothes and footwear remained constantly damp, and trench foot—that painful potential precursor to gangrene— reached epidemic proportions. Winter overcoats and heavy underwear finally reached the frontline troops by the second week of November, and as the official history of the 34th Infantry Division reports, "A great effort was made to insure the supply of dry socks to the forward troops but this was not always possible."

Though pressed to the point of exhaustion, the Allies kept up the pressure on the Germans, who had dug in and reinforced a series of natural barriers that they called the Bernhardt Line. Despite these exceptional defensive positions, the German troops also suffered from shortages of dry socks—not to mention shortages of food.

During the last three days of October the Germans broke contact with the Allies, moving into defensive positions across the Volturno. This left the Allies in control of the left bank of the river. The 133rd Infantry Regiment, meanwhile, had consolidated its position overlooking the river on the right bank, with the 100th Battalion mopping up the last German holdouts there.

On the night of November 3, the 133rd Infantry Regiment negotiated a huge mine field in darkness as they crossed west of the Volturno. By daylight the next morning, they had made good progress, but just over a mile from the river, they ran into severe German defensive fire. The regiment dug in to try to hold their position on a ridgeline, but the following morning, the 1st Battalion was pushed back by a German counterattack. At first light on November 5, however, the regiment launched an attack in which the 1st Battalion retook their previous hill, and the 100th Battalion captured several adjacent hills against heavy German resistance. These included the one overlooking the town of Pozzilli.

As the Americans swept up the high ground, the German response was a counterattack to regain these lost positions. Their efforts were, however, thwarted by the determination of the American defenders, especially a trio of mortar platoon spotters from the 100th Battalion's Company D. Lieutenant Neill Ray and Corporals Bert Higashi and Katsushi Tanouye remained atop a hill, manning their observation post and precisely directing mortar fire each time the Germans attempted a counterattack. Despite continuous German artillery and mortar fire, the men kept up their work until the morning of November 6, when a single well-placed enemy shell ended their lives. By this time, though, the Germans had given up on their counterattack, and the American line held.

It was also on November 6 that the 100th Battalion lost its commander, although Lieutenant Colonel Gillespie succumbed not to enemy fire, but to his chronic problem with ulcers. Major Alex

McKenzie from the 133rd Infantry Regiment would take over, but only temporarily.

On November 15, as the Allied troops were suffering from the effects of both the rain and general exhaustion, Clark ordered Fifth Army to cease its offensive for two weeks of regrouping. For the troops on the front lines, there would be little rest from German shelling, although they wouldn't have to dig a new foxhole for several days!

The 133rd Infantry Regiment then went into VI Corps reserve and a period of training, while the 34th Infantry Division's other two regiments conducted reconnaissance missions. By this time, the Nisei men of the 100th Infantry Battalion had been in action for six weeks, during which time they had lost 3 officers and 75 enlisted men killed in action, and had more than 200 men seriously wounded. Though they were technically in reserve, the 100th continued to take enemy fire, with an artillery and mortar attack on November 27 causing 12 casualties.

After an uneasy two weeks of holding in place while trading fire with the Germans, the Fifth Army offensive resumed at dawn on November 29. The British X Corps, situated along the Garigliano River near the Tyrrhenian coast, attacked toward Monte Camino, while the American VI Corps attacked toward a series of mountains that included Monte Pantano—a bare stone edifice with an elevation of over 3,300 feet on which there would be no cover for the assaulting troops. Relieved of reserve status, the 133rd Infantry Regiment entered the VI Corps sector on the left flank of the 168th Infantry Regiment. Their objective was the menacing Monte Pantano and its German guns.

As the 100th Infantry Battalion moved out at 6:00 A.M. on November 29, their immediate objective en route to Monte Pantano was the village of Cerasuolo, while the 3rd Battalion targeted Cardito. German gunners on the high ground of Monte Pantano had an excellent overview of the battlefield that was obscured only by dense ground fog. This was not a hindrance to the German artillery, however, because their spotters had already lined up the coordinates of all the obvious approaches, and they knew where the Nisei GIs would be even without seeing them. Meanwhile, the lack of visibility made it very tough going for the Americans.

Casualties were extremely high from the artillery and, as the troops moved closer to the German positions, from machine-gun fire and infantry counterattacks. The Americans also came under fire from the Germans' feared six-barrel rocket projector known as the Nebel-werfer (smoke mortar) and to the Americans as the Screaming Mimi. Against all of this, the men of the 100th's companies A, B, and C fought their way up the sides of Monte Pantano and two adjacent hills and held on.

It was here and on this day that three Nisei soldiers of the 100th Infantry Battalion would earn the Distinguished Service Cross, America's second-highest decoration for valor. Each of these would later be upgraded to the Medal of Honor, America's highest decoration for heroism in military service.

As the men of Company B inched toward the approaches to Monte Pantano, Sergeant Allan Ohata, his squad leader, and three men were protecting their platoon's left flank when they were attacked by a force of approximately forty Germans armed with machine guns, machine pistols, rifles, and hand grenades. When a man near him was hit, the sergeant left his position and advanced fifteen yards through heavy machine-gun fire. Another man in Ohata's squad was Private Mikio Hasemoto, a Browning automatic rifle gunner. Pinned down by two approaching enemy machine gunners, Hasemoto burned through four clips returning fire before his Browning was damaged. Without faltering, he ran ten yards to the rear, grabbed another, and continued to fire until the second weapon jammed.

By this time, Hasemoto and Ohata had killed roughly twenty German troops, but again Private Hasemoto ran through a barrage of enemy machine-gun fire to pick up an M1 rifle. Continuing their fire, Hasemoto and Ohata killed another ten Germans. With only three enemy soldiers left, the Company B men charged, killing one German, wounding another, and capturing the last enemy soldier.

In total, Ohata and Hasemoto were credited with killing fifty-one enemy soldiers and capturing three. They continued to hold their position against repeated German attacks the next day. Private Hasemoto was killed in action on November 30, but Sergeant Ohata went on to earn his commission as an officer, retiring long after the war as a captain. He passed away in 1977 at the age of fifty-nine.

Meanwhile, Private Shizuya Hayashi of Company A, also under attack from the German onslaught on November 29, single-handedly counterattacked in the face of rifle and machine-gun fire. Firing his automatic rifle from his hip, he charged and overtook an enemy machine-gun position, killing seven Germans in the nest and two more as they fled. After his platoon advanced two hundred yards from this point, another German gun position opened fire on the men. Private Hayashi returned fire, killing nine more of the enemy, taking four prisoners, and forcing the remainder of their force to withdraw from the hill.

When the Distinguished Service Crosses awarded to the men for their heroism in the Cerasuolo fighting were upgraded to Medals of Honor by President Clinton in 2000, Shizuya Hayashi was still alive to receive his medal in person. In an interview with journalist Gregg Kakesako that appeared in the May 12, 2000, issue of the *Honolulu Star-Bulletin*, the eighty-two-year-old Hayashi said, "I still remember that day and the battle. We were cut off in a mine field. There were mines all around. I remember a sniper bullet passing by my neck. . . . A lot of boys got hit in that mine field. It was a rough time."

On November 30, when the dense morning ground fog finally cleared, the 133rd Infantry Regiment continued its advance toward Monte Pantano in the face of ruthless German counterattacks. The Germans were well concealed, and American casualties were extremely heavy. Indeed, two battalion commanders were lost in less than an hour. On the first day of December, American artillery launched a half-hour artillery barrage against German positions as the 168th Infantry Regiment joined the 133rd in a coordinated push. Despite withering fire from well-entrenched German positions, the

Yanks succeeded in seizing their objectives on the mountain. During this period, the 100th Infantry Battalion suffered 68 men killed in action and 211 wounded.

The men of the 100th Battalion were now veterans; they were becoming experienced in combat. However, most of the men, regardless of their experience, never really become *used* to the death and dying. In an interview that Ray Nosaka of Company B gave to the Go For Broke Educational Foundation, he described an incident in which there was a firefight, and several of the men, including Nosaka, took aim at a German motorcyclist. As he was hit, the moving BMW toppled and skidded across the ground to a stop. When the shooting subsided, the other Germans withdrew, leaving just the dead motorcyclist.

"I was curious," Nosaka recalled of his impressions as he approached the German. "I went across and saw his leg was stuck between the motorcycle fork. . . . He was backward and his eyes were closed, but his head [was] all shaved from the ground because the motorcycle dragged him. And he was dead. . . . When I looked at him, I said, gee, he must have parents. You cannot hate the guy. He must have brothers or sisters somehow. So I felt kind of pitiful. I felt bad that I was one of them that fired a rifle to kill the guy. . . . When you sit down and think about it . . . they're humans just like us. They have feelings, they have loved ones. . . . War is so strange. [We're] killing each other, but actually, they don't want to really kill you. But you have to defend yourself. . . . You either shoot, or they shoot you."

As December arrived and snow began to fall, the regiment maintained its foothold on Monte Pantano and consolidated its positions throughout the area. The Germans, too, dug in. The 100th Battalion held positions that were as close as a hundred yards from the German lines, and the two sides frequently traded mortar and artillery fire.

While each side probed the other with patrols, there were no major assaults launched in the vicinity by either side during early December. The reason was practical. Nobody wanted to move! The weather was so cold that the water in the canteens froze at night, and moving supplies of any kind in the steep and slippery terrain was extremely difficult. The U.S. Army had resorted to the use of mules as its princi-pal mode of logistical transport, but even they often had a hard time on the slopes.

Finally, on the night of December 8, the men of the 133rd In-fantry Regiment were relieved in the line by the 4th Moroccan Rifle Regiment of the Free French Army. Without the Germans observing their movements, the men of the 133rd Infantry Regiment came down from the mountain the following day, and moved toward the rear. During the previous week, the 100th Battalion had lost 2 officers and had suffered 4 men killed in action, while 5 officers and 135 men were wounded or injured. Six of the latter would die of their wounds. Companies E and F were so understrength that they had to be tem-porarily disbanded and their men consolidated into other companies.

By December 11, the men of the 133rd Infantry Regiment and the 100th Infantry Battalion were at a rest area near Alife, on the east-ern side of the Volturno, where they would remain through the end of 1943. The time was spent cleaning equipment, training, and integrat-ing replacements into the units. They also received a new battalion commander. Since Lieutenant Colonel Gillespie had been relieved a month earlier, Majors Alex McKenzie and William Blytt had been as-signed temporarily, but at Alife, Major Caspar Clough, formerly of the 1st Infantry Division, took over on a more permanent basis. While at Alife, many of the men also availed themselves of opportunities to travel to the military R&R facilities that had been established for American GIs in Naples. Men who had been written up for decora-tions were now formally awarded the medals they had so undeniably earned.

CHAPTER 9

From Cassino to the Gates of Rome

As the troops of the opposing armies on the front lines in Italy dug in for the coldest part of the winter of 1943–1944, the high commands on both sides of those lines pondered the future of the Italian campaign. The Germans had eleven divisions opposing the Allies between Naples and Rome, plus another dozen divisions in northern Italy. By contrast, the Allies had a total of fourteen divisions, with two more on the way.

For the Allied leaders looking forward to 1944, Italy was not the first thing on their mind. The pivotal event of the year in the European Theater would be Operation Overlord, the long-awaited invasion of northern France, which was scheduled to take place during or about the first week of June. It would be the largest single military operation of the war, and all of the resources under the command of the Supreme Headquarters Allied Expeditionary Force (SHAEF) in Europe would be focused on assuring the success of this mission. During the first half of 1944, all Allied operations were carried out with this in mind.

The Mediterranean Theater, and the Italian campaign, while important, would now become peripheral. Allied leaders in Italy would get what they needed in terms of men and materiel—but only so long as this resupply effort did not interfere with the stockpiling of resources for Overlord. In fact, the Mediterranean Theater would be asked to divert troops from the Italian front for an invasion of southern France that would be coordinated with Overlord, although this operation would not occur until August.

As 1944 began, the two principal Allied objectives in the Mediterranean Theater would be to continue whittling away at German fighting strength and to capture Rome. The capital of Italy had been the central focus of military campaigns for more than two thousand years, and now it was the turn of the Allies to target the Eternal City. Among the Allies, there was some disagreement between Field Marshal Alexander, who favored defeating the German armies as a primary objective, and General Clark, who thought that the symbolic victory of taking Rome should have the higher priority.

Opposing the Allies was Kesselring, the shrewd German supreme commander in Italy and commander of Germany's Army Group C. Within the Army Group C were the Tenth Army under General Heinrich von Vietinghoff, which directly faced the Fifth Army, and the Fourteenth Army under General Eberhard von Mackensen, which guarded the approaches to Rome farther north in the Apennines.

The Germans had the rugged Italian terrain on their side. To add to the natural barriers, Kesselring constructed the Gustav Line (a.k.a. the Winter Line), a system of fortifications to stymie the Allies. The Gustav was an extensive, coast-to-coast line that was more involved than the abbreviated Bernhardt Line into which the Germans had dug themselves at the beginning of November.

The mountain campaign of the fall and early winter of 1943 had been arduous and costly for the Allies, and they yearned for a decisive stroke to break what seemed to be devolving into a stalemate. To outflank the Germans, the Allies developed a plan called Operation Shingle, which would be an end run to the north of the Gustav Line. Timed to coordinate with a further push northward by the United States Fifth Army and the British Eighth Army, Operation Shingle was to involve an amphibious landing by VI Corps at Anzio, on the west coast of Italy north of the Gustav Line and south of Rome. The idea was that Shingle would force Kesselring to pull troops out of the Gustav Line to suppress the invasion. In a perfect world, this would weaken the line and permit a breakthrough by either the Fifth Army or the Eighth Army—or both. Furthermore, if Shingle succeeded, VI Corps would be in a position to race north quickly and capture Rome. The invasion at Anzio came on January 22, 1944, and at first it seemed like a huge success. However, as the Allies would soon discover, it was not a perfect world.

At the end of December 1943, as plans were afoot for Operation Shingle, the 100th Infantry Battalion and its parent regiment began the long march back to the front line near Presenzano. The bulk of the regiment arrived there at the II Corps assembly area late on December 30, and the 100th Infantry Battalion reached Presenzano amid a blizzard on New Year's Eve.

From January 5 though 15, prior to the Anzio landing, the Fifth Army resumed its advance across the breadth of the front, battling entrenched German forces in one mountain battle after another. The January weather in the Apennines made the rain and mud of November seem like an afternoon sprinkle on the beach at Waikiki. Heavy snow alternated with sleet, and the mountain roads were either impossibly icy or impassibly snowed in. Finally, on January 14, the Fifth Army broke through the Bernhardt Line and the Germans withdrew across another natural barrier, the Rapido River.

With the Fifth Army building up momentum again, General Mark Clark moved to assault the Gustav Line, planning his main thrust on January 22 to coincide with the landing at Anzio. Clark planned to cross the Rapido and Garigliano Rivers, and seize the high ground on both sides of the Liri Valley, which contained the main road and rail route through the Apennines to Rome. Clark intended to drive north through the Liri and link up with the Anzio beachhead.

This was easier said than done.

It would take months rather than days.

The first step was to establish a bridgehead across the Rapido at Sant'Angelo, near where it flows into the Garigliano, and where the

Liri too flows into the Garigliano River. A major effort involving the 36th Infantry Division was launched on January 20, but it was abandoned after two days as a bloody and extremely costly failure. Every man in the small American force that did manage to get across the river was either killed or captured. In all, the badly mauled 36th Infantry Division suffered nearly 2,000 casualties in those two days. Kesselring's forces were able to stave off and defeat the American assault, but the German commander was compelled to divert resources to this operation that would otherwise have been used on January 22 to push VI Corps into the sea at Anzio.

Though the intended Fifth Army push up the Liri Valley would not happen as planned, VI Corps did manage to secure and hold a large beachhead at Anzio. However, breaking out of this beachhead would, like breaking through the Gustav Line, take months rather than days.

Earmarked for II Corps Reserve, the 133rd Infantry Regiment had been sent into action with the 34th Infantry Division one battalion at a time during mid-January. The 100th Infantry Battalion was under the command and control of the 1st Special Service Force until January 17. During this time, the Nisei succeeded in capturing two heavily contested hills and the village of San Michele.

On the first night of the 36th Infantry Division's failed Rapido River operation, the 133rd had provided covering fire for the division advance, and then it was pulled out and sent north. On January 24 the regiment was tasked with crossing the Rapido at the base of a steep, 1,700-foot mountain called Monte Cassino.

High on Monte Cassino, the focal point of the 34th Infantry Division attack would be a fortress overlooking the Liri Valley. Actually, the fortress was the Benedictine abbey of Monte Cassino, a monastery dating back to the sixth century that housed an irreplaceable library of ancient books and a priceless art collection. Unfortunately for the cultural history of Italy, the Germans had turned it into a fortified position that served as the linchpin of the Gustav Line.

The reason that it was an important objective, and the reason that it would ultimately have to be destroyed, was that the German gunners and artillery spotters within the abbey literally controlled the entire valley below. Allied troops couldn't move without being subjected to artillery fire directed from the abbey.

At 11:30 P.M. on the night of January 24, the 133rd Infantry Regiment, as part of the 34th Infantry Division, launched the first attack toward Cassino, successfully crossing the Rapido River in the process. As the 36th Infantry Division licked its wounds from its abortive Rapido operation downstream at Sant'Angelo, the 34th Infantry Division succeeded. They had established a Rapido bridgehead, although it was about five miles upstream from the Liri Valley crossing that Clark had imagined for his unrealized ideal bridgehead.

In the 34th Infantry Division's Rapido operation, the 100th Infantry Battalion's Companies A, B, and C were tasked with establishing and holding the line of departure for the main assault across the river. On the morning of January 25, as Company B tried to move up to the river itself, the men were slammed with a ferocious artillery barrage. Only fourteen men actually reached the river, the others were killed, injured, or forced to withdraw. At the same time, Major Clough was also wounded, and the battalion was withdrawn to San Michele to regroup.

At San Michele on January 29, Major Lovell, the original battalion executive officer, temporarily took command of the 100th. The former McKinley High School coach, who had been with the Nisei men since Hawaii, had been wounded earlier in the year and had just returned from sick leave. He was ready to lead the battalion when it assaulted one of the foothills of Monte Cassino as part of a regimental advance toward the town of Cassino, located at the base of the mountain of the same name.

At daybreak on February 8, the 100th moved forward with tank support. During this attack, Nisei soldiers with bazookas succeeded in taking out a German tank and a self-propelled gun. For the next several days, the 100th led the way in suppressing enemy resistance within Cassino. Enemy resistance was fierce, and the unit took heavy casualties for four days until it was ordered to again withdraw into regimental reserve. Among those wounded was Lovell, who was injured on the first day. He was replaced briefly by Major Clough, until he, too, was wounded *again*.

By the time that Clough left the field the second time, Jim Lovell was able to resume command, and he remained commander for the next two months. Lovell led the 100th Battalion back into action in Cassino on February 18, but four days later they were withdrawn, along with the rest of the regiment.

During its weeks in action at Cassino, the 100th Infantry Battalion had lost 4 officers and 38 men killed in action, 4 missing or known to have been captured, and 15 officers and 130 men wounded or injured. It would eventually take four horribly bloody months before the Germans on the mountain were finally defeated. Assisted by large numbers of medium and heavy bombers, Allied troops made four attempts to eliminate the German garrison at the abbey. The first three, in the third weeks of January, February, and March, would all fail. Finally, on May 18, after a ferocious weeklong fight, the II Polish Corps under General Wladyslaw Anders would finally succeed in taking down the devastated citadel.

Between February 1 and the night of February 21–22, when they were relieved by the 6th New Zealand Brigade, the men of the 133rd Infantry Regiment were in the thick of the fighting to take the town of Cassino. Exhausted and badly depleted by the battles from the Volturno to Cassino, the regiments of the 34th Infantry Division were officially relieved by British Commonwealth units and sent back to Alife. The idea was to provide them with time to rest, reorganize, and integrate replacements, and then to send the division back into action at Anzio. As this was being done, the regiment's long-detached 2nd Battalion returned to the 133rd Infantry Regiment, but the 100th Infantry Battalion would remain attached to the regiment for the Anzio operation as a fourth battalion.

The 133rd shipped out from Naples aboard U.S. Navy landing ships the afternoon of March 24, arriving at the Anzio beachhead just before noon the next day. The situation that the unit found ashore at

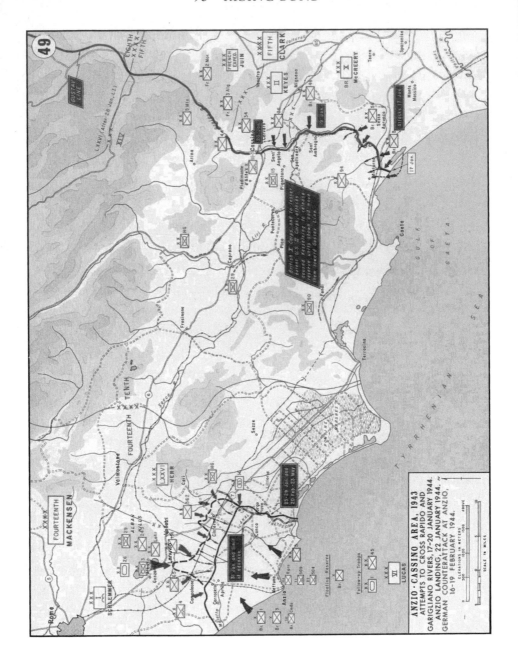

ANZIO-CASSINO AREA, 1943
ATTEMPTS TO CROSS RAPIDO AND
GARIGLIANO RIVERS, 17-20 JANUARY 1944.
ANZIO LANDING, 22 JANUARY 1944. ~
GERMAN COUNTERATTACK AT ANZIO,
16-19 FEBRUARY 1944.

Anzio was an enormous stalemate. The Allies occupied a vast patch of real estate into which they had flooded mountains of materiel and thousands of troops. However, the Germans still occupied the encircling high ground, from which they continued to shell the beachhead. German General Mackensen had given up on the idea of pushing the Allies into the sea, but the Allies had not yet achieved the critical mass of combat strength that would allow them to break out of their perimeter.

Through April, the regiments of the 34th Infantry Division would be consumed with continued training, and occasional reconnaissance patrols along the front to locate and identify German defensive positions, mine fields, and other obstacles. It was in April that Lieutenant Colonel Gordon Singles assumed command of the 100th Infantry Battalion, replacing Lovell. The thirty-eight-year-old, Pennsylvania-born Singles was a 1931 West Point graduate who came from a family with a long military tradition, but he had no combat experience. Perhaps sensing that he was a rookie commanding a veteran outfit, Singles was unpretentious and willing to listen to the ideas of others.

One of those from whom Singles was most likely to take advice was Captain Young Oak Kim, the adept and tenacious Korean-American who had commanded Company B during the 100th's early weeks in combat. At Cassino, Clough had promoted Kim to battalion intelligence officer, and Singles now made him the unit's operations officer.

Replacing Kim as commander of Company B was Lieutenant—later Captain—Sakae Takahashi, a graduate of the University of Hawaii who had grown up on the Makaweli Plantation on Kauai and who was an agriculture teacher at the junior high school in Aiea when the war started. Aiea is located just outside the perimeter of the Pearl Harbor Naval Base. Takahashi went on to be one of the best-regarded and highest-ranking Japanese American officers within the 100th Infantry Battalion.

In order to break out of the Anzio beachhead, the United States forces needed intelligence, and Captain Kim had an idea. It was a simple and straightforward idea, but it was a dangerous idea. He would lead a small group of men who would cross no-man's-land, penetrate the German lines, and bring back prisoners. It may have been a dangerous idea, but it was a dangerous idea with a precedent. Kim had done this previously on the night of November 4–5 when the battalion was in action near the Volturno River, and he came back with seven German prisoners.

At first, Kim offered to go alone, but he soon had men volunteering to join him. The first man was Honolulu native Irving Akahoshi, who had been drafted just twenty-two days before Pearl Harbor.

"Nobody wanted to send a damn fool to get himself killed," Akahoshi told an interviewer from the Go For Broke Educational Foundation. "It turned out that they found two damned fools."

By the time Kim and Akahoshi crawled forward on the dark night of May 16, they were accompanied by another four fools. Kim had long since earned the respect and admiration of the Japanese American GIs.

They inched forward through a drainage ditch and into a briar patch, continuously dreading unexploded mines or booby traps. They advanced through a wheat field until they heard the voices of two German guards. The GIs had gotten so close to the German lines that when one of the Germans raised his head, Kim was able to reach out and press the muzzle of his pistol into the man's forehead.

As they pulled out with the two prisoners, Akahoshi left an American hand grenade behind in the trench, so that when the enemy soldiers were discovered missing, the Germans would know that they'd been captured. He later explained that "I thought if I was captured, I wouldn't want my officer to think that I had betrayed my friends and be accused of having deserted."

For their foray into enemy territory that night, Kim and Akahoshi were each awarded a Distinguished Service Cross.

On May 23, as VI Corps finally achieved its critical mass of 90,000 troops, the Allies began the long-awaited breakout from the Anzio beachhead. Now under the command of Major General Lucian

Truscott, these men were ready to push due north through the Alban Hills and to knock on the gates of Rome, around which Mackensen had constructed a string of strongpoints that were known as the Caesar Line. This line was less well fortified than the Gustav Line and other such defensive positions, and it did not have the added feature of very difficult terrain. Nevertheless, it did have behind it the full weight of the German Fourteenth Army.

For the Anzio breakout, the 133rd Infantry Regiment and 100th Infantry Battalion were detached from the 34th Infantry Division to support the 1st Special Service Force, an elite commando group with which the 100th had served briefly at Cassino earlier in the year. One of the precursors to modern Special Forces, this 1,200-man unit had *by itself* controlled a quarter of the thirty-two-mile-long Allied perimeter at Anzio—while the rest was being held by *three divisions*. On the morning of May 23, the 133rd helped the 1st Special Service Force cut off the main road leading to the key junction at the town of Cisterna. The subsequent envelopment of this important crossroads assured the success of the Anzio breakout. As exemplified by the Distinguished Service Cross actions by Kim and Akahoshi, the 100th had played an important role in breaking the stalemate.

Restored to the 34th Infantry Division by May 25, the 133rd spearheaded the division advance northward toward the town of Lanuvio at the foot of the high ground of the Alban Hills. Two days later, the 133rd ran into heavy German opposition as it approached the rail line connecting Lanuvio with Velletri. With fortifications and mortar emplacements entrenched into the hillside above the rails, and with the village of Villa Crocetta fortified with infantry, tanks, and self-propelled guns, this marked the outer edge of the Caesar Line defenses. Here the Germans planned to stand and fight.

For the Nisei GIs of the 100th Infantry Battalion, their part in the assault on the Caesar Line would be to attack Lanuvio itself. During this battle on the second day of June, two men from the unit earned Distinguished Service Crosses that were upgraded to Medal of Honor status in 2000.

Technical Sergeant (later Lieutenant) Yeiki "Lefty" Kobashigawa's platoon encountered strong enemy resistance from a series of German machine guns. Spotting a machine-gun nest fifty yards from his position, the former southpaw pitcher from Hilo crawled forward with one of his men. He tossed a hand grenade and then charged the enemy with his submachine gun while a fellow soldier provided covering fire. He killed one German soldier and captured two prisoners.

Kobashigawa and his comrade were then fired on by another machine gun fifty yards farther ahead. They quickly moved forward to subdue the second machine-gun nest. After throwing grenades into the enemy position, Kobashigawa provided close supporting fire while the other GI charged, capturing four prisoners. On the alert for other machine-gun nests, Kobashigawa discovered four more, and adroitly led his squad in taking down two of them.

After the war, the unassuming left-hander went home to Oahu and raised two sons and a daughter at Waianae. He received the Distinguished Service Cross, but his family barely knew the details of his wartime valor. His son, Merle Kobashigawa, himself a veteran of fifteen years of service with the U.S. Army, learned of the full dimensions of his father's heroism only when his daughter saw her grandfather's name on display at the Smithsonian Institution while on a school trip to Washington, D.C.

In a 2005 interview with journalist Leila Fujimori of the *Honolulu Star-Bulletin*, Merle Kobashigawa recalled that when his father was invited to Washington, D.C., to receive the Medal of Honor, he told Secretary of the Army Louis Caldera, "It's so long ago, just send it in the mail."

The younger Kobashigawa told Ms. Fujimori that, to his father, the Medal of Honor award ceremony was "no big deal fifty-four years later, but for [the members of the family] it's a big deal."

Lefty Kobashigawa was talked into making the trip, and in June 2000 his medal was presented personally by President Bill Clinton at the White House. Kobashigawa passed away on March 31, 2005, at age eighty-seven, and was buried with full military honors at the National Cemetery of the Pacific on Oahu.

Even as Lefty Kobashigawa was depriving the Germans of their machine-gun positions, Private Shinyei Nakamine's platoon became pinned down by intense machine-gun cross fire not far from La Torreto. The German gunners were on a small knoll two hundred yards to the front. Deciding on his own that something had to be done, he crawled toward one of the hostile machine-gun nests. Reaching a point twenty-five yards from the enemy, he stood up and charged, firing his Thompson submachine gun as he ran. He killed three Germans and captured two.

Later that afternoon, Nakamine spotted an enemy soldier lurking on the right flank of his platoon's position. Crawling twenty-five yards from his position, he opened fire and killed the German. Looking around from this forward position, he could see a machine-gun nest approximately seventy-five yards away, so he crawled back to his platoon and led a Browning automatic rifle team toward the enemy. Under covering fire from the BAR, which was a hand-held light machine gun, Nakamine inched forward until he was about twenty-five yards from the machine-gun nest. He then tossed several hand grenades at the enemy soldiers, wounding one and capturing four. Spotting yet another machine-gun nest a hundred yards to his right flank, he led the automatic rifle team toward the hostile position, but as they approached, he was killed by a burst of machine-gun fire.

As with Sergeant Kobashigawa's actions that day, Private Nakamine's heroism was written up for a Distinguished Service Cross, which was upgraded to the Medal of Honor in 2000.

The 100th Infantry Battalion had won the Battle of Lanuvio, but at great cost. In just thirty-six hours, fifteen men had been killed in action, sixty-three were wounded, and one was listed as missing in action.

With the 100th Infantry Battalion in the vanguard, the Allied troops began pouring through the gap that they had opened in the Caesar Line. By noon on June 3, after the Nisei men made an exceptionally decisive assault on a roadblock on the main highway toward Rome, Mackensen's Fourteenth Army was in retreat. Allied fears of a renewed stalemate on the approaches to the Eternal City evaporated in the warm summer weather.

Kesselring was so furious with Mackensen's failure to stop the Allies that he sacked him and sent in General Joachim Lemelsen to replace him as Fourteenth Army commander. Lemelsen, too, was helpless to stop the flood of troops, tanks, and artillery as they surged northward.

On June 3, Kesselring declared Rome an open city, meaning that he would not fight to hold it. This status helped to spare its irreplaceable art and architectural treasures from the almost certain destruction that would have ensued in an artillery duel between Allied and Axis guns. The Germans began an orderly withdrawal from the city, completely abandoning the Caesar Line and moving to new defensive positions to the north. In a rare show of conciliation, Adolf Hitler himself had specifically ordered his troops *not* to destroy anything within Rome as they pulled out. This was in contrast to the situation in Naples eight months earlier, when he had demanded that the city's infrastructure be blasted beyond usability before it was abandoned to the Allies. Aside from several bridges and communications facilities around the outskirts, Rome was left intact.

Late on June 4, lead elements of the Allied units began entering Rome, having seized bridgeheads across the Tiber River to the southwest. Many bridgeheads that had lost their bridges to the retreating enemy were quickly retrofitted with temporary replacements by fast-working U.S. Army engineers.

By the morning of June 5, the 1st Special Service Force, as well as the 1st Armored Division, and the 3rd, 34th, 36th, 85th, and 88th Infantry Divisions were passing through the city. The first units entered the city in predawn darkness before most Romans realized that the Germans were gone and the Americans had arrived. By the middle of the day, though, the citizens were giving their liberators an enthusiastic welcome. Most troops, including the Nisei men, did not stay long.

They moved into the city and out without pausing to admire the sights.

Thanks to the 100th Infantry Battalion, the fall of Lanuvio provided the Americans with the key that unlocked the whole German defensive line. The Germans had prepared defenses in depth across a broad open valley to the east and between the hills and sea to the west, but the center had relied on the Lanuvio strongpoint. The Nisei GIs had effectively handed the Allied VI Corps a bus ticket to Rome and beyond.

The capture of the first of the three Axis capital cities on June 5 made headlines in the United States and around the world, but it was quickly overshadowed the following day by news of Operation Overlord, the enormous Allied invasion in Normandy. For the men of the 100th Infantry Battalion, Rome was quickly overshadowed as well. In their case, it was eclipsed by the work that was yet to be done up the coast toward the ancient city of Civitavecchia, forty-five miles from Rome.

By nightfall, the men of the 34th Infantry Division were well north of Rome and already trading fire with German forces retreating along the Tiber River. The 34th, together with the 1st Armored Division, had been tasked with pursuit of withdrawing German forces moving north and northwest from the Italian capital. While the 1st Armored Division encircled enemy forces around Viterbo, the 34th moved at top speed along the coastal highway, reaching Civitavecchia by the morning of June 7.

The 100th Infantry Battalion and the 133rd Infantry Regiment were now given the job of securing a line of hills near the town of Tarquinia, about seven miles north of Civitavecchia. Here they would fight their first major battle since Lanuvio. The enemy who met them were the elite troops of the 40th Jaeger Regiment, which had been brought in specifically to halt the Allied advance up Italy's west coast. Unfortunately, the new German regiment had not imagined that the Americans could have reached Tarquinia in forty-eight hours, and they were still in the process of digging their defensive positions when the Yanks struck from the high ground above them. Before sunset, the few surviving enemy who hadn't been killed or captured were in retreat up the coast.

The Battle of Tarquinia marked a fitting climax to the latest period of combat for the men of the 100th and 133rd. After being in continuous action since May 23, the 34th Infantry Division was formally relieved on the night of June 8–9 by the newly arrived 91st Infantry Division, whose 361st Infantry Regiment relieved the 133rd.

For the Nisei men of the 100th Infantry Battalion, this was the end of their direct association with the 133rd Infantry Regiment. They would now be assigned to a new regiment that had just arrived from the United States—the all-Nisei 442nd Regimental Combat Team.

CHAPTER 10

The 442nd on the Offensive

While the 100th Infantry Battalion was battling Hitler's legions in Italy, the men of the 442nd Regimental Combat Team had continued to train in the United States. For three weeks beginning on January 27, 1944, the regiment's infantry had been attached to the 69th Infantry Division for maneuvers in the DeSoto National Forest in Mississippi. At the same time, the 522nd Field Artillery Battalion was active on separate maneuvers in Louisiana.

Having passed muster with flying colors during the maneuvers, the 442nd was ordered to prepare its gear to ship out. Beginning on April 22, they began to make their way from Camp Shelby to the staging area at Camp Patrick Henry in Virginia. On the first of May, they boarded the troop transport at Hampton Roads under the watchful eye of Colonel Charles W. Pence, bound for the long-awaited opportunity to prove themselves, as the 100th Infantry Battalion already had. As with the Nisei men who had preceded them in August, they were destined for the Italian campaign.

"We were loaded onto Liberty Ships and started zigzagging across the Atlantic with a large convoy," Robert Ichikawa recalled. The zigzagging was a routine means of making the ships harder for German submarines to hit. "As we zigged, another big convoy joined us, and as we zagged again, there was yet another convoy. This happened four or five times, and pretty soon, there were hundreds of ships as far as you could see in all directions. This was in preparation for D-day in France, so most of the ships headed for England, while our group headed through the Straits of Gibraltar."

The 442nd landed at Naples and reached Civitavecchia by truck on June 10, three days after the Nisei men of the 100th Infantry Battalion. Here, the 442nd would be formally assigned to the 34th Infantry Division, still the parent division to the 100th. Meanwhile, the 100th Infantry Battalion was detached from the 133th Infantry Regiment, and reassigned to the 442nd, although it was not officially integrated into the Regimental Combat Team as an organic element until August.

According to Army organizational specifications, regiments contain three battalions, just as divisions are composed of three regiments. The 442nd had contained three infantry battalions while it was training in the United States, but it went overseas with two. The idea was that the 100th Infantry Battalion would become its de facto 1st Battalion.

Just as the 100th Infantry Battalion had served as a temporary and de facto 2nd Battalion within the 133rd Infantry Regiment, it would become the official and permanent 1st Battalion of the 442nd Regimental Combat Team. However, it would retain the 100th designation. The 442nd's original 1st Battalion had remained behind in the States, and would function as a training unit to prepare Japanese American replacements for the regimental combat team. A liberalization of the Selective Service laws at the beginning of 1944 had completely removed all Japanese Americans from under the 4-C Enemy Alien classification, and future Nisei draftees would almost all be earmarked as replacements for the 442nd.

During the second and third weeks of June, the 34th Infantry Division remained out of the line, integrating replacements and new outfits, such as the 442nd. In contrast to conditions the previous winter, the men now enjoyed warm and sunny weather on the hills overlooking the blue Tyrrhenian Sea. Finally, on June 24, the men of the

34th climbed aboard the trucks that would take them north through Grosseto to the front lines near Piombino on the Gulf of Follanica. From here, the 442nd turned inland toward Suvereto.

On June 26, the 442nd got its first combat assignment, to capture an important road junction that lay along the road that led north into the mountains from Suvereto to the small hill town of Sassetta. In between, high on a hill, was a patch of ground containing the tiny village—actually just a collection of buildings—that was known on the maps as Belvedere. This patch of high ground, held by an elite SS battalion, was the key to controlling the road junction.

As they went into action that morning, the green troops of the 442nd were anxious to prove themselves to the battle-hardened GIs of the 100th, and to their families back in the United States. News of the exploits and heroism of the Nisei GIs in action in Italy had reached the internment camps, and the new men were eager to establish their own reputations and to show the folks on the home front that they, too, were true Americans.

Meanwhile, the men of the 100th also wanted to show the recent arrivals how real veterans operated, but they would have to wait, because the 100th was in reserve that day, and the 2nd Battalion led the advance. They marched eastward flanking the objective to the right and moving slowly. The Germans spotted them and opened up with an artillery barrage that rained down with all the deadliness that the SS could deliver.

"We were pretty green," Lawson Sakai of the 2nd Battalion's Company E said, recalling the 442nd's first day in combat. "We didn't know that we were supposed to stay behind the hill, so we just ran over to the other side. We'd run into this low area, when all of a sudden mortar shells and artillery shells started falling. Machine-gun fire, too. I remember seeing these puffs of dust bouncing across the ground right at me, and there was a popping sound. Somebody was shooting a burp gun at me!"

There was no mistaking the sound of the German 9 mm MP40 submachine gun. It was referred to as a burp gun, because the noise it

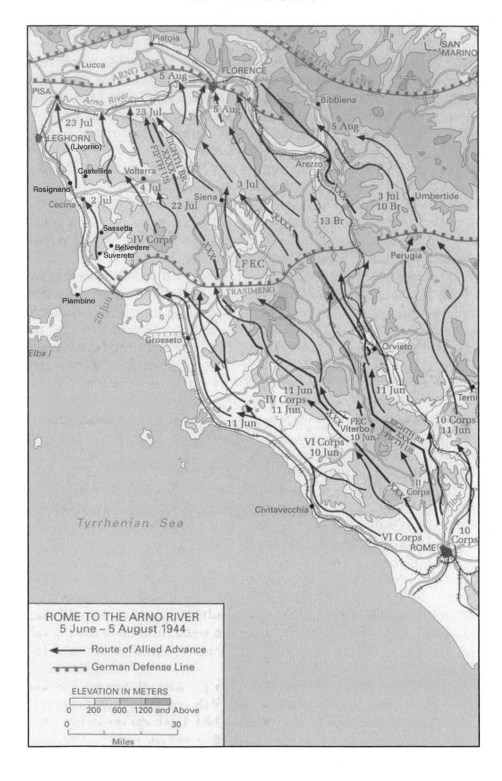

ROME TO THE ARNO RIVER
5 June – 5 August 1944

Route of Allied Advance

German Defense Line

ELEVATION IN METERS

0   200   600   1200 and Above

0   30

Miles

made sounded like a series of burps. It had such a high rate of fire that the continuous recoil made it hard for the user to keep the tip of the barrel from raising upward. If the German gunner had been able to keep the barrel level, Sakai's first day in battle would have been his last.

"Coming under fire the first time was kind of mesmerizing," he observed. "But then you started seeing the blood and men falling. No matter how you train, you can't be prepared for seeing people getting killed right in front of you. It was awful. We lost our company commander, and my platoon leader was killed."

The Company E commander killed on that first day of action was Captain Ralph Ensminger, the officer from Hawaii who had inspired such loyalty from his troops during their training at Camp Shelby.

Mas Tsuda, a BAR man with the 3rd Platoon of Company E, had just turned twenty on June 21, five days before the 442nd's baptism of fire. "The first prisoners we took were just a holding force," he recalled. "They didn't want us to shoot them up, so they just surrendered. It was easy compared to the action that we were going to see later on."

As the artillery fire around Suvereto reached its worst, Private First Class Kiyoshi Muranaga, a 442nd man from Arleta in California, found his company taking 88 mm rounds from a self-propelled gun that had a direct line of fire on his unit. Muranaga's mortar squad was ordered into action, but the terrain made it impossible for the men to set up their weapons, so the squad leader ordered the men to disperse and take cover.

The men continued to take heavy casualties, so Muranaga, who was the gunner in his squad, decided to try to take out the eighty-eight by himself. He set up his mortar position and opened fire on the enemy gun at a range of approximately four hundred yards.

It was a race with the clock. He had to fire a shot, then adjust his range and trajectory before firing again. All this time, however, the Germans continuously poured machine-gun fire in his direction. With his third round, Muranaga was able to correct his fire so that the shell landed directly in front of the enemy gun. Meanwhile, the enemy crew, aware of the source of the mortar fire, had turned their weapon directly on Muranaga's position. Before he could fire a fourth round, an 88 mm shell scored a direct hit on his position, killing him instantly. However, because of the accuracy of Muranaga's previous fire, the enemy troops decided not to risk further exposure to themselves, and they hastily abandoned their position.

For his heroism, Kiyoshi Muranaga was posthumously awarded a Distinguished Service Cross that was upgraded to Medal of Honor status in 2000.

Around noon, as the other battalions had worked themselves closer to the objective, the 100th was ordered to penetrate the space between the two encircling units and capture Belvedere.

Identifying a hill on the right that the Germans had apparently failed to fortify, Companies A and B quickly swarmed to its heights and secured it. This gave them a commanding view of the SS battalion command post at Belvedere. An hour earlier, the Germans held the highest ground on the battlefield. Now this situation was reversed. Moving quickly, Company A attacked Belvedere, while Company B circled around to capture a segment of the road to the south of Belvedere.

The amazing precision of the veteran 100th stunned the Germans. Suddenly they had Japanese American solders above them and behind them. The Nisei then proceeded to cut them up—isolating groups of defenders—and cut them down, overwhelming them and killing them. By late afternoon, the entire objective was in Nisei hands. Most of the SS unit had been killed or taken prisoner, and the Americans had also captured a great deal of German gear. They had killed 178 enemy troops, wounded 20, and captured 86. For its outstanding performance in neutralizing the SS command post at Belvedere, the 100th Infantry Battalion was awarded a Presidential Unit Citation. It was the first of three.

As Lawson Sakai summarized the 442nd's first battle in the company of the 100th, "the first day of action had been a real eye-opener.

We aged very rapidly, but gradually our training took over, and we knew what to do."

With momentum born of the success at Belvedere, the 442nd moved north on June 27 toward Sassetta. While the 3rd Battalion circled into high ground to the north of Sassetta and the 522nd Field Artillery Battalion brought down a barrage on the German positions, the 100th smashed its way into the town and captured it.

As the 133rd Infantry Regiment moved northward along the coastal road, the 442nd worked their way north on a parallel track about a dozen miles to the east in the inland mountains. The 168th Infantry Regiment, meanwhile, was operating on another parallel track even farther inland, and deeper in the rugged mountains.

By June 30, the Nisei troops had reached the Cecina River, about forty miles north of Suvereto. Intelligence reports indicated that the German units facing the advancing regiments of the 34th Infantry Division were scattered and moving north as small bands rather than cohesive units. The Americans had also learned that the Germans hoped to regroup and to make a stand somewhere north of the Cecina. Compared to the rivers that the men had been forced to cross earlier in the Italian campaign—such as the Volturno and the Rapido—the Cecina was merely a shallow stream.

The 442nd crossed this little creek with ease on July 1 and passed through the town of Cecina. They then headed north to seize and hold another key road junction about five miles way. With artillery support, the regiment was able to overwhelm the German defenders with relative ease. Things would not be quite so easy next time.

One of the roughest battles that would be faced by United States forces in the weeks following the capture of Rome came as the Nisei soldiers were working their way northward toward Pisa and the port city of Livorno.

Intelligence reports spoke of a probable major German defensive action somewhere north of the Cecina River. On July 2, they found the expected German bulwark about ten miles north of the river, on the road that reaches inland from Rosignano on the coastal highway to the hill town of Castellina Marittima. Kesselring had sent the 35th SS Panzer Grenadier Regiment to reinforce the 16th SS Reconnaissance Battalion.

As they reached this lateral road, the 442nd Regimental Combat Team and the 100th Infantry Battalion ran into a vicious barrage of mortar and machine-gun fire, backed with heavy artillery fire from the ridge above. Forward motion abruptly stopped as the men dug into defensive positions to return fire against the heavily fortified German strongpoints, many of which were in caves on the hillsides, especially a prominent edifice known as Hill 140. Interlocking fields of fire from numerous machine-gun nests made it very difficult for the Nisei GIs to find cover anywhere near enough to the German positions to fire on them effectively.

With the 100th in the lead, the soldiers made small gains against these obstacles over the next two days, and on July 4, the 3rd Battalion moved up to trade places with the battered 100th in the vanguard of the action, and the 2nd Battalion undertook to assault Hill 140.

At midnight, Robert Ichikawa's Company E platoon was ordered to take up positions on the north side of Hill 140. As they circled around and began to dig in, the men in the platoon did not realize that they were in the midst of a large group of sleeping Germans. The confusion ran both ways.

"We didn't realize what had happened until a German officer came up to one of our guys, and spoke to him in German as he was setting up his machine gun," Ichikawa recalled. "He didn't say anything, so the German officer took out his gun and shot him in the head. That's when all hell broke loose."

The Germans started shooting and the platoon returned fire. Frank Wada spotted two Germans carrying a machine gun and ammunition uphill, and he fired one round. Amazingly, the bullet passed through one of the enemy soldiers and hit the second one as well. Mineo Kodama tossed a hand grenade at another German machine-gun crew and blew them up.

As Ichikawa got up, the man next to him did as well. He spoke to the other man, but he didn't answer. It was so dark that the men could barely see one another. Suddenly, the man grabbed Ichikawa's rifle and started to try to pull it away from him. Ichikawa realized that it was a German, so yanked his gun back and pulled the trigger. Another German lunged toward him, and Ichikawa shot him as well. Two other Germans came to the aid of the first two, and Ichikawa shot four Germans before he moved on.

When the platoon got back to the staging area on the south side of the ridge, Captain Thomas Crowley, the company commander, asked how many Germans there were. Ichikawa told him that he had been too busy to count them.

On Independence Day, the bravery displayed by two recently arrived members of the 442nd Regimental Combat Team would warrant the award of Distinguished Service Crosses that were later upgraded to Medals of Honor. It was with great irony that one of these Medals of Honor for heroism on Independence Day would be awarded for the actions of a man who was recruited out of a relocation camp and whose family was still incarcerated there.

Born in Seattle, William Kenzo Nakamura had grown up in the Emerald City, but his family had been sent to the Minidoka Relocation Center near Hunt, Idaho, and it was here that he had entered service with the U.S. Army. His brother, who had been a star football player at Seattle's Garfield High School, also joined the 442nd Regimental Combat Team.

Half a world away from Minidoka, Private First Class Bill Nakamura's Company G platoon was pinned down by enemy machine-gun fire from a camouflaged bunker. He crawled twenty yards toward the hostile nest with fire from the enemy machine gun barely missing him. He reached a point fifteen yards from the machine-gun nest, and quickly raised himself to a kneeling position and chucked four hand grenades into the enemy position, killing or wounding at least three of the German soldiers. With this enemy weapon silenced, Nakamura crawled back to his platoon.

Later, when Company G was ordered to withdraw from the summit of the hill so that a mortar barrage could be brought down on this ridge, Nakamura remained in position to cover the withdrawal of his fellow GIs. However, while they were moving toward the safety of a wooded gully, Nakamura's platoon became pinned down by lethal machine-gun fire. He inched forward to a place from which he could get a bead on the enemy position and quickly opened fire to pin down the enemy machine gunners. His platoon was then able to withdraw to safety, but Nakamura was hit as he tried to follow, and he was killed in action.

As Bill Nakamura was fighting his last battle, another Company G man, Private First Class Frank Ono, was also in the thick of the action on Hill 140 that terrible Fourth of July. Less than a month past his twenty-first birthday, the young man from North Judson, Indiana, was part of a squad that was caught in a hail of formidable fire from well-entrenched German positions. Ono opened fire with his automatic rifle and succeeded in silencing one machine gun three hundred yards away. Advancing through incessant fire, he killed a sniper with another burst, and while his squad leader reorganized the rest of the platoon in the rear, Ono defended the critical position solo.

The Germans closed in on Ono, managing to shoot his gun out of his hands. Tossing hand grenades, Ono forced the enemy to abandon their attempted counterattack, defending the newly won ground until the rest of his platoon moved forward. Taking a wounded man's rifle, Ono again joined in the assault. After killing two more enemy soldiers, he boldly ran through withering automatic, small arms, and mortar fire to render first aid to his platoon leader and a seriously wounded rifleman.

Now in danger of being encircled, the platoon was ordered to withdraw. Volunteering to cover the platoon, Ono occupied a virtually unprotected position near the crest of the hill. From here, he engaged an enemy machine-gun emplacement on an adjoining ridge while at the same time exchanging fire with snipers armed with machine pistols. Ono made himself the constant target of concentrated enemy fire until the platoon reached the comparative safety of a draw.

He then descended the hill in stages, firing his rifle, until he rejoined the platoon.

Frank Ono was awarded the Distinguished Service Cross, survived World War II, and passed away in 1980, two decades before this award was upgraded to a Medal of Honor.

After the heroism of Nakamura, Ono, and all the men of the 2nd and 3rd Battalions on Independence Day, July 5 saw marked improvement in the tactical situation. During that afternoon, the 3rd Battalion overwhelmed several of the heavily entrenched German positions, and the 2nd Battalion worked its way into a preferable position to attack their wing of Hill 140. They went up the hill under cover of darkness, and as the sun rose, they had established a strong foothold there. In all, the 442nd Regimental Combat Team had inflicted about 250 German casualties in the space of about forty-eight hours.

Shortly after the Hill 140 battle, Ron Oba, a cook with Company F, found himself in an amusing situation that could have turned quite deadly. There is always the potential for trouble when you are delivering meals in the midst of a tank battle.

In an anecdote preserved in the archives of the Go For Broke Educational Foundation oral history project, Oba and a small detail of men were taking a hot meal to the men who were on the front line. One man carried the bread, another had a tray of meat, two were carrying five-gallon cans of water, and one had a large container of rice, always a staple side dish for a Japanese American meal. As the men crested the first hill, they came across an American M4 Sherman tank thunderously blasting away. Suddenly, 88 mm shells crashed down on the hill as a German Mark VI Tiger tank returned fire. Undaunted, Oba's catering crew carried on, carefully making their way through the exchange of gunfire.

The firefight let up, and Oba asked a Nisei lieutenant to direct him to Company F. The man pointed across the valley to the next hill. As the tank battle resumed, Oba led his men down off the ridge, following a faint trail going down into the valley.

"Come on," he said. "Follow me."

They went down the hill, through a vineyard, and up the other side, following the little pathway. They reached Company F, unloaded all the rations and headed back. As they came up the hill through the vineyard to where the tank crews were, Oba's contingent discovered themselves being applauded by the tankers.

"Hey, what's going on?" Oba asked the lieutenant.

"A Company H guy went through that mine field and he got blown," the lieutenant explained. "We couldn't even find his body. And you guys went both ways, that way and back."

"Why didn't you tell me there was a mine field?" Oba asked.

The lieutenant didn't answer.

As Oba related the story later, he surmised that the tankers were just "too busy fighting the enemy."

While the 2nd and 3rd Battalions were in their battle at Hill 140, the 100th Battalion had made an end run to the east, cutting off the road to Castellina Marittima and isolating the Germans. On July 7, the 100th turned their attention to wrenching control of the town of Castellina Marittima from the occupying Germans. As the battalion moved forward, men of Company C were pinned down by a German machine-gun position. Kaoru Moto, a twenty-seven-year-old private first class from Spreckelsville on Maui, carefully made his way to a point just a few feet from the machine-gun nest and promptly shot the gunner. When another German opened fire on him, Moto ducked out of sight, got behind him, and captured him.

Though he was weighed down with the responsibility of guarding a prisoner, Moto continued to focus on what he saw as his principal task at that moment, dealing with the enemy gunners who were peppering his unit with lead. He could see a building ahead that would make a good place for a German spotter to use to direct fire against the other GIs, so he decided to prevent them from using it by getting up there himself before they could. Taking his German prisoner with him, Moto got to within a few yards of the house.

As he and his unwitting charge were occupying this location, Kaoru Moto saw the Germans setting up a heavy machine gun nearby.

He was in an ideal position to open fire and he did, forcing them to run for cover. By this time, other men from 100th Battalion had reached Moto's position. Just as they thought the worst was over, Kaoru Moto was hit and seriously wounded by a bullet from the rifle of an enemy sniper.

The medics bundled Moto up to get him back to a first aid station. As they were making their way toward safety, Moto observed another German machine-gun nest. Not satisfied to leave it to someone else, Moto broke free of the medics and opened fire on the three men in the nest, wounding two of them. Refusing to leave a job partially done, the plucky Nisei then rushed the nest and took all three Germans into custody.

Also on July 7, as Kaoru Moto was proving himself to be one of the Third Reich's worst enemies, Technical Sergeant Ted Tanouye of the 442nd's Company K was leading his platoon in an attack to capture the crest of a hill in the ridgeline west of Castellina Marittima. It was hard going for the young soldier from Torrance, California, whose family had been shipped to the Rohwer Relocation Camp in Arkansas two years before. The enemy were vigilant and there was little cover. When he spotted a German machine-gun crew setting up their weapon to attack his men, Tanouye acted first, killing or wounding three Germans and putting two others on the run. Another group of Germans opened fire on him, but he returned fire and killed or wounded three more of the enemy soldiers.

As he continued to advance, Tanouye was severely wounded in his left arm. Nevertheless, he raked the German position with fire from his submachine gun and wounded several of the enemy. Running out of ammunition, he attacked yet another German position with a hand grenade, and crawled twenty yards to get additional submachine-gun clips from another GI. Next, he located yet another enemy machine gun firing down the slope of the hill, opened fire on it, and silenced it. Drawing a volley from a machine-pistol nest located above him, he returned fire and wounded three more of the Germans.

Before agreeing to let the medics give him first aid for his wounds, Tanouye insisted on organizing a defensive position on the back side of the hill that he had almost single-handedly captured. He survived the day and was taken to a field hospital, but he would die of wounds on September 6 after lingering for two months.

As the sun went down on July 7, the 2nd and 3rd Battalions had secured their objectives in the hills above the mountain road, and the 100th had captured Castellina Marittima. The battle, probably the toughest fight yet to be faced by a contingent of the 34th Infantry Division since Rome, was finally over.

And as the sun went down that day, the names of two more men, Moto and Tanouye, had been added to those of Nakamura and Ono on the roster of the Nisei men who would be written up for Distinguished Service Crosses that bloody week in July 1944. More than half a century later, all four would be added to an even more select roster, that of men who would be written up for the Medal of Honor.

It was in July 1944, in the wake of this extraordinary heroism by these men who were widely presumed to be unlikely as heroes, that *Time* magazine would write, almost in the form of a humble admission: "From a cautious experiment the Army has received an unexpectedly rich reward. A group of sinewy oriental soldiers only one generation removed from a nation that was fighting fanatically against the U.S. was fighting just as fanatically for it."

CHAPTER 11

Closing In on the Arno

During that first week of July, the American forces on Italy's west coast had seen the hardest fighting in a month. For the 442nd Regimental Combat Team, the days since June 26 had not been a gentle introduction to the harsh realities of combat in World War II. They had been tossed into a cauldron and they had endured. In fact, they had more than endured; they had triumphed. With three Medal of Honor actions in less than two weeks—on top of a fourth by Kaoru Moto of the 100th Infantry Battalion—the new 442nd had distinguished itself many times over. They had met and surpassed the call of duty. As Lawson Sakai had put it so eloquently, the men had aged very rapidly, and they now knew what to do.

The Allied armies had been in Italy for ten months now, and had several extremely difficult campaigns behind them. Mention of names such as Salerno, Cassino, and Anzio—not to mention the Gustav Line in general—brought a chill to anyone who had been there, for each represented an Allied victory that had taken longer and cost more in terms of men and materiel than Allied planners had expected. Yet there was more hard slogging and other extremely difficult campaigns ahead as the Allies continued their battle against the tenacious German troops, and in the jagged terrain that so favored their defensive positions.

Principally, there were four field armies fighting in Italy that summer, two on each side. The spine of the Apennines, running north to south through the Italian peninsula, formed a natural boundary between the two armies within the Allied 15th Army Group, as well as between the two German armies. Field Marshal Bernard Montgomery's mainly British Eighth Army was moving north on the east side of the mountains, while Mark Clark's mainly American Fifth Army—to which the 442nd and its parent, the 34th Infantry Division, were attached—moved north on the west side. Opposing the Allies was Germany's Army Group C, commanded by Kesselring. His Tenth Army faced the Allied Eighth, while his Fourteenth Army was situated on the western side of the divide facing the Allied Fifth.

In general, the immediate objective of the Fifth Army was the Arno River. Initial Allied plans had called for the 34th to be one of the divisions pushing north to, and across, the famous river. However, Allied planners decided instead to divert them toward the coast to capture Livorno and Pisa, the two major port cities south of the Arno.

Despite heavy resistance and an occasional setback, all the Fifth Army divisions were making slow but steady progress, pushing north toward the broad valley of the Arno, which flows east to west from Florence to the Ligurian Sea at Pisa. The Arno itself formed a barrier against the Allied advance, but it lay in generally flat terrain, so Kesselring planned to use the Arno as just a temporary defensive position. He would make the Allies pay dearly to cross it, but he had something even more costly waiting for them on the northern side of the valley. He put most of his considerable engineering and construction resources into fortifying the rugged Apennine Mountains roughly twenty miles farther north. Here Kesselring would create a major defensive line across the breadth of Italy. Known in Italian as *Linea Gotica*, the Gothic Line, this barrier lay in the mountains north of the Arno on the west side of Italy and north of the Foglia River on the east.

While the 442nd was fighting in and around Castellina Marittima during the first week of the month, a sister regiment within the 34th, the 363rd Infantry Regiment, had been overwhelmed and pushed back, albeit temporarily, by a 26th Panzer Grenadier Division counter-attack. Nevertheless, by July 8, the regiments of the 34th Infantry Division had slammed forward again through the German defenses and were pushing north toward the port at Livorno. The largest port city between Rome and Genoa, Livorno was referred to by its English name Leghorn on U.S. Army maps, and that name often appears in contemporary accounts of American combat actions in the area.

By the second week in July, the 442nd was past the ridges and into low-lying hills that were inland from the coastal cities. On July 10, the reserve 2nd Battalion relieved the 3rd in the line, and, together with the 100th Battalion, it was given the job of capturing the hill town of Pieve di San Luce, south and east of Livorno.

As they moved forward, the Nisei GIs began taking very heavy enemy fire from both Pieve di San Luce and Pastina, another hill town farther inland. The 100th Battalion was closer to the high ground, and was therefore tasked with taking down Pastina, while the 2nd Battalion took up positions below. Within the 2nd Battalion, Companies F and G were in the vanguard, with Company E in reserve.

On July 11, all three companies were located at the base of the hill, with their command post situated in a pinkish-colored house. The German artillery that constantly dogged the advancing Americans shifted its focus to the 2nd Battalion positions and field telephone communications were cut between the forward companies and the battalion headquarters. Robert Ichikawa was in the Company E platoon that was ordered to trace the telephone wires leading forward and to find and repair the breaks. Ichikawa and several other soldiers made their way up the sloping hill, following the phone line.

As the squad climbed toward the crest of the hill, the Nisei GIs came under fire from a German machine-gun nest higher on the slope of the ridge. The men in the advance squad took cover just as two 88 mm artillery shells slammed down, impacting near the pink house. Ichikawa's platoon sergeant was hit, with shrapnel entering his elbow and exiting his forearm. As the Germans pounded the GIs, there were mounting casualties. Seiji Kaneta—the man known to everyone as

"Brooklyn" because of his hometown and his heavy accent—was badly injured in his knee. A medic who came to his aid was mortally wounded.

Ichikawa, who had taken cover behind a haystack, urged the other men to crawl over to where he was. A badly injured GI named Seiji Isoda made it, but Brooklyn was unable to move. Ichikawa told Isoda to get rid of his pack and he would help him crawl to safety. Ichikawa dragged Isoda across the face of the hill, trying to keep the haystack between them and the German machine-gun nest.

"When we got near the top of the hill, the machine gunner spotted us again," Ichikawa recalls. "As he opened up on us, I grabbed Isoda, ran him across the top of the hill and threw him onto the other side. I shoved him into a hole and told him to stay there while I went to get a medic. I ran down the hill to a barn where the battalion medics had set up their headquarters, and told them about Isoda and Brooklyn. They got out a stretcher and a flag with a big red cross and ran up the hill. When they waved that flag, all the firing stopped. Even the Germans honored the red cross flag. While it was waving, everything stopped."

It wasn't until then that Ichikawa noticed that the wetness in his boot was his own blood, and that he had been wounded in the leg himself.

"When the medic patched me up, and I tried to stand, I couldn't." He laughed as he retold the story. "For some reason, after running all that distance, now I couldn't even stand up!"

After two days of heavy fighting and the precision artillery support of the 522nd Field Artillery Battalion, the 100th Battalion finally secured Pastina at about 11:00 P.M. on July 12. Bob Ichikawa was in and out of field hospitals for the next several months, but finally rejoined the 442nd Regimental Combat Team during the winter.

By the middle of July 1944, the U.S. Army was pushing hard against the last major German defensive positions on the south side of the Arno. For the advancing 442nd and the other units of the 34th Infantry Division, the major obstacles during the approach to the Arno in mid-July now were the poor quality of the roads, and the fact that German engineers had destroyed or damaged most of the bridges as they withdrew from positions south of the Arno. The major objectives included Livorno and towns that guarded the important road network in the hills inland from Livorno.

Despite their overall strategy of withdrawing into the Gothic Line, the German resistance remained fierce, especially whenever the GIs happened to run into an enemy strongpoint. Such was the case on July 15, as the 442nd Infantry Regiment was advancing toward another hill near Pieve di San Luce. The air was filled with lead and the muzzle sounds of high-powered rifles and heavy machine-gun fire. The men of Company G found themselves pinned down in a wheat field. Among them was Staff Sergeant Kazuo Otani, a twenty-six-year-old from Visalia, California, whose family was at the Gila River Relocation Camp in Arizona.

Sergeant Otani located one of the snipers who was trying to pick off members of his platoon, stood up, took aim, and killed him. This removed one danger, but still there were numerous German gun positions throughout the high ground. Otani discerned that the longer the platoon remained in the relatively open area, the greater their likelihood of being hit. Dashing across the field, he led most of his men to the cover of a cliff. When the platoon continued to draw heavy enemy fire, Otani hurried along the base of the ridge, deliberately exposing himself to the gunners. By diverting the attention of the Germans, he made it possible for the men closest to the cliff to get to cover.

Organizing the men at the bottom of the cliff to guard against the potential of an enemy counterattack, Otani again made his way across the exposed field to where a number of the men were still stranded. He moved toward the rear of the platoon, all the while making himself a lightning rod for German gunners. Taking cover in a shallow ditch, Otani directed other members of the platoon to provide covering fire so that the stranded men could get to safety.

When one of the men was hit, the young sergeant crawled to his side in the open terrain and began to provide first aid. It was at this point that Otani was mortally wounded by machine-gun fire. For these actions Sergeant Otani was posthumously awarded a Distin-guished Service Cross that would be upgraded to the Medal of Honor nearly fifty-six year later. Citations for medals often make mention of heroes who "completely disregard their own safety," but almost nowhere was this more true than with Kazuo Otani that day in the hills above the place called Pieve di San Luce.

On July 16, the morning after the heroic death of Otani, the 3rd Battalion of the 442nd Regimental Combat Team was to make a frontal assault on the town, while Otani's outfit, the 2nd Battalion, was tasked with encircling the Germans on the left flank. They traversed the ridgeline to the west of the crossroads town of Luciano, one of those important road junctions inland from Livorno. The objective here was to flank the town and cut the enemy rear. The Nisei GIs met stiff resistance, and the 522nd Field Artillery Battalion was called upon to lay down an artillery barrage. Backed by the Nisei gunners, the bat-talion was successful, and by the evening of July 17, the German resis-tance collapsed. The men of the 442nd had secured Luciano and its pivotal crossroads.

During the fighting south of the Arno, the accuracy of the 522nd Field Artillery Battalion earned high marks from the GIs in the in-fantry companies.

"One night my squad was on a reconnaissance mission near the Arno," recalled Don Seki of Company L, "We had crawled under-neath the barbed wire until we were in a dry canal a few yards from the German line of defense . . . We called in artillery fire. The 522nd was really sharp . . . boom, boom, boom . . . Right down the line."

On July 18, German opposition across the front finally began to crumble. The 100th Battalion of the 442nd, joined by elements of the 91st "Powder River" Infantry Division, entered Livorno, while the 3rd Battalion of the 442nd secured positions overlooking the Arno it-self. Over the next several days, the 2nd and 3rd Battalions of the 442nd would be tasked with staking out a defensive line along Highway 67, the road that parallels the Arno, leading inland from Pisa toward Florence.

From their new vantage point, the Nisei GIs could see the city of Pisa and its legendary Leaning Tower. Built in fits and starts in 1173–78 and 1272–84, and finally finished in 1372, the tower was a world-renowned architectural icon—and a high vantage point from which German artillery spotters could monitor the progress of the approaching American troops. While the Germans would frequently use the tall campanile, or bell tower, of an Italian city for such a purpose, there are conflicting reports as to whether the Germans actually used the Leaning Tower in 1944. There are also conflicting reports attesting to whether orders were issued to American troops to destroy the famous tower if it *was* being used by the enemy. It is improbable that orders to shell the tower were officially issued, because they would have been contrary to Clark's previously stated insistence that the GIs should spare the landmark.

Although a patrol from the 3rd Battalion of the 442nd did conduct a reconnaissance mission into a corner of Pisa overnight, on July 20–21, it was the 91st Infantry Division that would be given the high-profile job of occupying the famous city.

After several days of mopping up operations in the Arno Valley inland from Pisa, the 442nd was sent to the 34th Infantry Division rest area at Vada, on the coast south of Pisa. The bulk of the regiment arrived on July 24, followed by the 100th Infantry Battalion the next day.

Don Seki still has fond memories of the rest area at Vada. "Oh man, there were chickens there, and tomatoes hanging from the rafters," he recalls with a smile. "We made soup using the vegetables and the bouillon cubes [from the government-issue rations]. We went to the beach and borrowed an Italian skiff. We went out into the sea, took a grenade, pulled the pin, dropped the grenade and the concussion brought the fish up!"

Several organizational changes would occur to the Nisei units during the three weeks that the regiment was regrouping at Vada. The

Fifth Army was going through a great deal of shuffling of units in preparation for the campaign against the Gothic Line. On August 10, the unofficial status of the 100th Infantry Battalion (Separate) as the de facto 1st Battalion of the 442nd became official. However, no sooner had the 100th became an official part of 442nd than it was separated from the 442nd and sent into the line on the Arno east of Pisa.

The 442nd, meanwhile, was reassigned from the 34th Infantry Division to IV Corps, then transferred on August 17 to the 85th Infantry Division sector, which was farther inland, near Florence. For the first time since Nisei GIs had reached the Mediterranean Theater in September 1943, they were no longer affiliated with the 34th Infantry Division. The next day, the 442nd was reassigned briefly to the 88th Infantry Division of II Corps.

On August 19, a few days after the Nisei men left Vada and reentered combat near Pisa, Private Masato "Curly" Nakae of Company A became one of the men who earned a Distinguished Service Cross that was later upgraded to a Medal of Honor. That day, Company A was attacked by large number of German troops and Nakae's submachine gun was damaged by a shell fragment as he tried to return fire. He immediately grabbed an M1 rifle belonging to a wounded soldier and struck back. He fired a series of rifle grenades at the approaching enemy, but they continued to close in, so he lobbed a half dozen hand grenades into their midst, forcing them to scatter.

The Germans quickly reorganized for another attack, this time preceding their assault with a concentrated mortar barrage on the position occupied by the young Nisei GI who had just caused them so much grief. Curly Nakae was seriously wounded by a mortar shell, but he refused to give up. When the German infantry tried to assault his position again, he blasted away at them, inflicting heavy casualties and finally forcing them to retreat in disarray.

The twenty-seven-year-old native of Lihue on the island of Kauai recovered from his injuries and returned home, where he lived until his death on September 4, 1998. He was interred at the National

Memorial Cemetery of the Pacific nearly two years before his DSC was formally upgraded to Medal of Honor status.

On August 20, as the 100th remained committed in the Pisa area, the 2nd and 3rd Battalions of the 442nd moved into the line along the Arno near Scandicci, in hills overlooking Florence to the west. The city had been occupied by the Allies on August 12.

With Livorno, Pisa, Florence, and bridgeheads across the Arno now in Allied hands, the Allies could now concentrate on the Gothic Line. Their leaders realized that breaking through this formidable barrier was easier said than done. At nearly every step since the Italian campaign had begun, every battle had been harder that expected. The battles at Salerno, Cassino, and Anzio and all the fighting during the preceding winter on the Gustav Line had been more arduous than the Allies had foreseen. Now they faced the Gothic Line. It was, for the relatively short time expended in fortifying it, one of the most forbidding defenses yet faced by Allied troops in World War II, and it could be guaranteed to be an offensive challenge of enormous proportions.

On the other hand, the tactical rewards of getting through the Gothic Line would be considerable. When the Allies had gotten through the Gustav Line, they had faced yet more rugged, mountainous terrain that was well suited to the German defenders. However, across the Gothic Line lay the vast, flat Po Valley, which was tailormade for fast-moving, mobile offensive action. The valley offered few obstacles to the rapid advance of the many armies that had operated here through the centuries. If the Allies got through the Gothic Line, Kesselring would be out of naturally defensible terrain until he had his back to the Alps.

The Allied plan for breaching the Gothic Line, known as Operation Olive, called for the British Eighth Army to launch a major offensive east of the Apennines, while the Fifth Army crossed the Arno and worked its way north toward the Po.

Even as preparations for Olive were under way, the Allies launched another major offensive in the Mediterranean Theater—

Operation Anvil/Dragoon, the invasion of Southern France near Marseilles on August 15. This operation effectively opened a new front against the Germans, compelling them to divert the forces that they had committed to opposing the Allied armies that had swarmed into northern France after Operation Overlord in June.

However, Anvil/Dragoon *also* depleted the United States Fifth Army. The American 3rd, 36th, and 45th Infantry Divisions—which would certainly have been useful in operations against the Gothic Line—were pulled out of Italy to be reassigned to the Seventh Army, which would be the major U.S. Army force in the campaign in southern France.

On August 25, ten days after the invasion of southern France, the long-awaited attack on the Gothic Line finally began with a British Eighth Army thrust against the German Tenth Army. When the Fifth Army followed suit west of the Apennines crest on September 10, the 442nd was involved, although just briefly. The 100th Battalion was active in the VI Corps push north from Pisa in the coastal hills, while the 2nd and 3rd Battalions crossed the Arno near Florence in the II Corps sector of the front.

Shortly after the initial actions, though, the Nisei men were ordered out of the line in order to join the exodus of American units that were being pulled out of Italy to be relocated to southern France for reassignment to the Seventh Army. The men were trucked south to the port at Piombino, which they had last seen three months earlier, and coasted south to Naples. Here, on September 26, they boarded the transport ships that would take them to France and the campaign that would earn them enduring fame within the annals of the great regiments of the U.S. Army.

As the 442nd Regimental Combat Team departed Naples for Marseilles, the unit was at its peak strength of 224 officers and 4,034 enlisted men, including both combat troops and support personnel. Combat losses had been made up by a flow of replacements that had been drafted from the relocation camps across the Western United States.

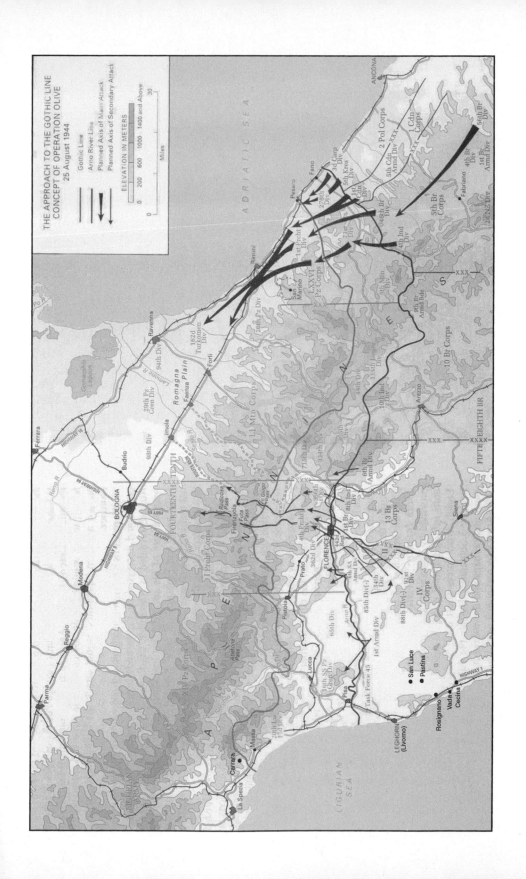

THE APPROACH TO THE GOTHIC LINE
CONCEPT OF OPERATION OLIVE
25 August 1944

Gothic Line
Arno River Line
Planned Axis of Main Attack
Planned Axis of Secondary Attack

ELEVATION IN METERS

0   200   600   1000   1400 and Above

Miles
0   10   20   30

CHAPTER 12

On the Other
Side of the World

W hile the accomplishments of the Nisei GIs of the
442nd Regimental Combat Team in the war
against the Third Reich were well known and in-
deed well publicized during World War II, the activities of those who
served in the Military Intelligence Service (MIS) against Japan were
just the opposite. Because of the sensitive nature of intelligence operations, few details of the MIS activities were known during the war,
and the full breadth of the Nisei contribution to the Pacific Theater
actions would not be known until after large numbers of long-secret
World War II intelligence documents began to be declassified in the
1970s.

The work done by the MIS men in the Pacific was much different than that the infantrymen did in Europe, but it carried challenges
that were unique to the conditions. In the Pacific, the Nisei men knew
that if they were captured they could very well be executed. Imperial
Japan considered the ethnically Japanese soldiers, even the American-
born Nisei, to be Japanese citizens. Therefore, wearing a United States
uniform automatically made them traitors. For the Japanese authorities, it was considered impossible for such people to have allegiance to
the United States.

The work that the linguists did was absolutely indispensable.

Without them, countless important documents and communication intercepts would have remained incomprehensible to Allied intelligence officers. Well trained in the heigo military language at the Military Intelligence Service Language School in Camp Savage, the Japanese American linguists were able to translate unencrypted military messages with ease. Except for high-level strategic communications, the leadership of the Imperial Japanese armed forces made little effort to encrypt or obfuscate their radio transmissions. When the Nisei linguists got into the field, they discovered that much of what they were overhearing was like listening to an ordinary telephone conversation. The enemy arrogantly assumed that the Allies employed no one who was conversant in the Japanese language. Thanks to the secrecy that surrounded the work being done at Camp Savage, they would retain this misconception until the end of the war.

For operations in the vast reaches of the Pacific, Allied military commanders had divided the theater into three administrative areas, and MIS units were assigned to each. These three were the South Pacific (referred to by the acronym SOPAC), containing the island chains such as the Solomons; the Southwest Pacific, including the Philippines and New Guinea; and the Central Pacific, which contained island chains such as the Marianas and Japan itself (except Hokkaido). The U.S. Navy considered operations involving Alaska to be in the North Pacific Area. The Joint Chiefs of Staff later simplified the geography of the Pacific by placing the Southwest Pacific Area (SWPA) under U.S. Army jurisdiction, with General Douglas MacArthur as supreme commander, with all the rest combined under U.S. Navy jurisdiction. This region, containing the North Pacific, Central Pacific, and South Pacific, would be known as the Pacific Ocean Areas (POA). Here Admiral Chester Nimitz would be the supreme commander. The SWPA contained much more land area so it was natural to assign an army commander, while the POA was mainly ocean, so the U.S. Navy took the lead. In the myriad of islands in the POA, surface actions would be conducted primarily by the U.S. Marine Corps, although the U.S. Army would also be involved in major POA actions, including the Marianas campaign. A majority of the Nisei linguists, though certainly not all, served with the MacArthur's SWPA Command.

Though unencrypted communication was understood by the MIS men right away, by the spring of 1943 the linguists were even starting to achieve major breakthroughs in deciphering the Imperial Japanese codes. In his Center of Military History study of military intelligence in World War II, John Finnegan gave a great deal of credit for the Allied successes in the Pacific to the Nisei linguists, saying, "Events of the spring of 1943 would reshape the entire structure of Military Intelligence. In April Army cryptanalysts scored their first success against Japanese military codes."

In April 1943, five months before the Nisei 100th Infantry Battalion first entered combat in Europe, Harold Fudenna, a Nisei Military Intelligence Service officer operating with the Signal Corps at Port Moresby, interpreted one of the most important intercepted radio messages of the Pacific War. This encrypted Imperial Japanese Navy communiqué revealed the itinerary of an inspection tour by Admiral Isoroku Yamamoto, the architect of the attack on Pearl Harbor and the commander of the Imperial Japanese Navy Combined Fleet. As a result of the intercept, Yamamoto's airplane was shot down on Bougainville on April 18. Untangling the cryptogram was a painstaking task in itself, but Fudenna's skills were especially vital to the undertaking because without his ability to read and understand both the Japanese language and military terminology, the coded message was not even *approachable*, much less decipherable. For his work, and for the momentous content of the message that he revealed, Fudenna was awarded the Bronze Star.

The work of the Military Intelligence Service even gave the United States a bargaining chip in its relations with its British allies. One of Britain's most vital wartime secrets was the fact that they had managed to break the extremely secret German Enigma code, which was considered to be impervious to decoding. Accomplished in the summer of 1940, cracking Enigma was one of the major espionage triumphs of the war. It was also so secret that the British maintained it

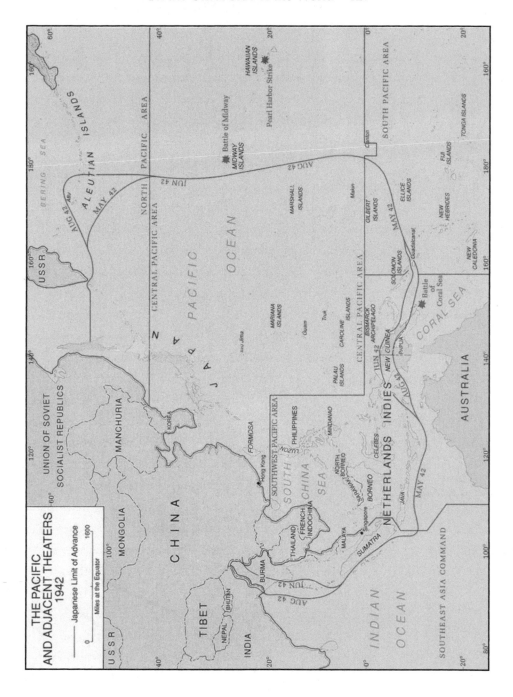

THE PACIFIC
AND ADJACENT THEATERS
1942

——— Japanese Limit of Advance

0   1600

Miles at the Equator

as a state secret until 1974. They were even hesitant to make this information available to their American allies during World War II. However, after the Yanks shared the details of their having broken the Japanese codes, all this changed. Only one month after Harold Fudenna's dramatic decryption of the Japanese naval code, the British invited a party of officers from the MIS and the Signal Security Agency to visit the British government code and cipher center at Bletchley Park, near London, and learn all the details.

This pivotal moment in American intelligence is best described by Finnegan, who wrote: "For the first time, American Military Intelligence became aware of the dimensions of the British success against high-level German communications. British efforts in breaking the German Enigma and other ciphers used on command links had laid bare many of the most important secrets of the Nazi high command. The intelligence derived from this source, known as Ultra, was disseminated by the British under rigidly controlled conditions. Although such intelligence had been provided to Eisenhower during the invasion of North Africa, U.S. Army Intelligence had not been fully aware of its origins. Now the British agreed to share this intelligence with the U.S. Army on an unrestricted basis, in exchange for reciprocal access to American communications intelligence on the Japanese."

Though much of their work was done safely behind the lines, the Nisei MIS linguists often went into the hot zone with combat troops—as during the invasion of New Georgia in July 1943 and the Marianas a year later—to act as translators and interrogators.

Though they were U.S. Army ground forces personnel, their activities were not restricted to operating with ground forces. The Nisei linguists also flew on bombing and reconnaissance missions with the U.S. Army Air Forces, and they served aboard U.S. Navy ships at sea. As the Americans expanded their counteroffensive across both the SWPA and Pacific Ocean Area, Nisei linguists were assigned to both the U.S. Army and Marine Corps at the regimental, division, and corps level. In the actions on Bougainville in October 1943, information provided to the Marine Corps by the MIS is credited with a substantial reduction in American casualties. Though the men served with, and provided valuable services to both the U.S. Navy and Marine Corps, the attachments to non-army units were on a temporary duty basis, and the men remained in army uniforms.

As many as three dozen MIS linguists were also sent to India and assigned to work with the South East Asia Command, headed by British Admiral Louis Mountbatten. Primarily, they translated documents in New Delhi, but occasionally they were sent to Old Delhi to interrogate Japanese prisoners of war.

Ken Akune, from Turlock, California, who joined the MIS while interned at the Amache Relocation Camp in Colorado, was among those linguists who were sent to the China-Burma-India Theater, where he was given the task of interrogating prisoners to get basic miliary information.

"We were also looking for material that we could use for propaganda broadcasts," he said. "We wanted to get them talking about the morale situation, and their poor living conditions, so we could use that against the Japanese army. The enemy troops were so isolated that they knew nothing about what was going on in the outside world, so if we could show them that we knew what conditions were really like where they were, then they would believe what was going on in the war beyond Burma. Most of those guys couldn't believe that Japan was losing the war."

In general, the enemy troops reacted to the Military Intelligence Service men with a mixture of shame at being captured and puzzlement at facing a Japanese across an interrogation table. MIS linguist George Takabayashi recalled in an interview with the Go For Broke Educational Foundation oral history project that it was "sort of perplexing if anything for the enemy to see somebody with the same facial features, physical features. Brown eyes, black eyes, black hair. But I will never forget the first POW that I interrogated. The first thing he said was, 'Please do not let my family in Japan know that I am a prisoner of war.' And you can understand why this was uttered by this particular individual. . . . Although in the heart of every mother who sent her son or husband or father to war, inside I'm quite sure, mothers whether they are Japanese, black, Caucasian, want to see their dear ones come back alive. But in Japan this was not so. The training that they received was to be ashamed to be captured, so we had to get them out of this particular mode of thinking, that because they are POWs, they should be ashamed of themselves. No, they did their job. Unfortunately they got captured."

The MIS interrogators found that the Japanese prisoners were unprepared for interrogation. American GIs had been told to divulge only their name, rank, and serial number if captured, but the Japanese solders never had been trained for what to do *if* captured because they had been told not to allow this to happen. Much of the credit for developing practical interrogation techniques goes to Harry Fukuhara. A SWPA MIS linguist, he determined that a lot of the captured troops were so poorly trained that a skillful interrogator could trick them into revealing just about anything. The Seattle-born Fukuhara had been taken to Japan by his widowed mother at the age of thirteen, but he returned five years later. Recently graduated from Glendale Junior College in California, he was interned in 1942, but he volunteered for the MIS and was assigned to the Allied Translator and Interpreter Service after completing his MISLS course at Camp Savage. Having received a battlefield commission as a second lieutenant in 1945, Fukuhara served in Japan during the occupation and continued as an Army intelligence analyst through the Korean and Vietnam Wars before retiring as a colonel in 1970.

As Maui-born Milton Murayama, who served with the MIS detachment assigned to the British command in India, explained, "There was no cat-and-mouse, we just asked the questions and they told us everything they knew. They had no connection with the [other Imperial Japanese] troops they left behind."

The fact that only the U.S. Army officially accepted Japanese American personnel led to peculiar situations throughout the Pacific, especially at the naval base at Pearl Harbor. Though Japanese Americans were a sizable part of the population of surrounding Hawaii, and

Japanese American Hawaiians were serving bravely in Europe with the 100th Infantry Battalion and the 442nd Regimental Combat Team, Japanese Americans continued to be barred from setting foot inside the gate at Pearl Harbor without being escorted by a Caucasian officer. This became an issue when the army and navy created their Joint Intelligence Center for the Pacific Ocean Area (JICPOA), which was headquartered on the grounds of Pearl Harbor. This location led to a peculiar dilemma. The JICPOA had an obvious and pressing need for trained Japanese-speaking linguists—but these most important of personnel couldn't go there!

To address this dilemma, did the U.S. Army insist that the U.S. Navy modify its arbitrary rules? No, the people from both services at JICPOA simply bypassed the problem by setting up the JICPOA Annex Group in an abandoned furniture store on Kapiolani Boulevard in Honolulu, about ten miles east of the Pearl Harbor gate.

Despite this foible, the JICPOA itself represented a milestone in interservice cooperation. Prior to World War II, the U.S. Army's Military Intelligence Division (MID) and the Office of Naval Intelligence barely communicated, much less cooperated on complex operations. The staggering intelligence failures in December 1941, especially at Pearl Harbor, were a rude wake-up call to such a system. In the aftermath, both General George Marshall, the army chief of staff, and Admiral Ernest King, the chief of naval operations, became boosters of *joint* intelligence. By 1943, with the United States on the offensive in the Pacific, where cooperation was vital, the need for joint intelligence was absolute. To address this, the JICPOA was formally established on September 7, 1943. It was charged with the collection and evaluation of strategic and tactical intelligence, as well as its distribution to all American forces, so that everyone was literally on the same page.

The first group of Nisei soldiers to staff the JICPOA Annex included a group of seventeen volunteers from Hawaii who had graduated from the Military Intelligence Service Language School at Camp Savage in June 1943. After completing their basic training at Camp Blanding, Florida, they shipped out to their first assignment at an "undisclosed overseas location." Imagine their surprise when they discovered that it was in downtown Honolulu!

Nisei linguists from the MISLS also served stateside at the Pacific Military Intelligence Research Section (PACMIRS) that was set up in August 1944. Located at Camp Ritchie, Maryland, outside Washington, D.C., the organization was tasked with reviewing captured documents for information that might aid the Joint Chiefs of Staff in long-range planning for strategic operations against Imperial Japan.

One of the key intelligence coups achieved at PACMIRS by a Nisei MIS linguist was the Imperial Army Ordnance Inventory. It was part of an estimated fifty tons of enemy documents that were captured on Saipan in 1944. Shipped to Camp Ritchie sorted into boxes marked "No Military Value," the inventory was discovered and translated by Master Sergeant Kazui Yamane, a Hawaiian-born graduate of Waseda University in Japan. The document contained a detailed survey of weapons and ammunition that had been cached at dispersed locations *within Japan*. Its discovery permitted the U.S. Army Air Forces to target these locations, and the information would be extremely valuable in the postwar disarmament of Japan.

By August 1944, as the battalions of the 442nd Regimental Combat Team were being pulled out of the line in Italy for redeployment to France, the Military Intelligence Service Language School had outgrown its original rural home at Camp Savage and was relocated to Fort Snelling in Minneapolis. At this same time, the United States was gearing up for major operations against Japanese-held territory in the South and Southwest Pacific during 1944. The MIS men at JICPOA and those attached to operational units would play an indispensable role.

On the opposing side, the Imperial Japanese Navy was developing its "Z Plan," a strategy for its Combined Fleet that involved the defense of the same territory that the Allies were preparing to recapture, while massing its naval power for a decisive battle with the United States. Since the Battle of Midway, the Imperial Japanese Navy had lost the initiative, and the idea was to reverse the tide of the war during 1944. The Z Plan was the brainchild of Admiral Mineichi Koga, who had succeeded Admiral Yamamoto as commander in chief of the Japanese Combined Fleet.

Like his predecessor, Koga was not a lucky airplane passenger. On March 31, 1944, he and his chief of staff, Rear Admiral Shigeru Fukudome, set out in separate aircraft from Palau in the Caroline Islands to Davao, on Mindanao island in the Philippines. Both airplanes went down in bad weather and Koga was killed. Fukudome survived, was captured by Filipino partisans, but was released in a prisoner swap. However, he had lost his briefcase.

The briefcase, which contained the Z Plan documents, was recovered by the partisans and sent to the Allied Translator and Interpreter Section in Australia. Here Nisei linguists Sergeant Yoshikazu Yamada and Sergeant George Yamashiro translated the top-secret Combined Fleet Order Number 73, signed by Koga, that set out Japanese navy plans. The translation of this and other documents gave the U.S. Navy a tremendous advantage and aided the major American campaigns, and victories, in the Pacific for the remainder of 1944.

These translated documents were in the hands of American commanders in time for Operation Forager, the largest amphibious operation yet conducted in the Pacific. The goal was the capture of the Mariana Islands, specifically Saipan, Guam, and Tinian. The landings took place on June 15, July 21, and July 24, respectively. For these operations, teams of Japanese American MIS linguists were attached to combat units, including the 27th Infantry Division and the 2nd and 4th Marine Divisions. Two of the men, Ben Honda and George Matsui, earned Silver Stars during the campaign.

By the middle of August the Marianas were essentially secured from the Imperial Japanese forces, and the Nisei linguists were given the difficult task of risking being shot while going into caves to try to coax Japanese civilians and a few holdout troops into giving up.

The next major campaign in the Pacific was to be the reconquest of the Philippines. When he left the Commonwealth, where he had spent much of his life, General MacArthur had promised "I shall return." On October 20, 1944, it was time to make good on that promise. Four U.S. Army divisions went ashore at Leyte, a major island located at the center of the archipelago that makes up the Philippines. With these troops came about one hundred Nisei linguists from the MIS.

Meanwhile, offshore, the U.S. Navy was fighting the Battle of Leyte Gulf, one of the largest naval battles in world history. Here the Imperial Japanese Navy hoped to win the "decisive battle" that Admiral Koga had envisioned in the Z Plan. However, thanks to the Nisei linguists, the United States naval commanders had read the Z Plan. The overwhelming American victory essentially marked the irrevocable defeat of the Japanese navy, in the last major naval battle of World War II.

Ken Akune's brother, Lieutenant Harry Masami Akune, was one of the MIS men who distinguished himself in the fight to recover the Philippines from the Japanese. Attached to the 33rd Infantry Division in New Guinea, Harry took part in the airborne landings on the island of Corregidor in Manila Bay. In May 1942, the island—known as "the Rock"—was the last stand of American and Filipino troops in the Philippines. In February 1945, retaking it from the invaders was part of MacArthur's strategy to recapture western Luzon and the area around Manila, the Philippine capital. Having it in American hands was important, because enemy artillery located there could harass and sink American ships that tried to use Manila's harbor.

Landing troops on Corregidor was problematic because its steep cliffs constituted formidable natural defenses, and before the war, the United States had built heavy fortifications here that the Imperial Japanese forces now controlled. With the Rock so well defended against naval action, MacArthur decided against an amphibious operation, Instead, he would send his troops in from above. The American assault on the Rock was spearheaded by the U.S. Army's 503rd Parachute Infantry Regiment, the first airborne regiment to fight in the Pacific as an independent unit. Though he had not previously made a parachute jump, Harry Akune was asked personally by Colonel George Jones, the 503rd's commander, to join his "Rock Force" as their MIS interpreter.

When he agreed to volunteer, Akune didn't realize that he would make his first parachute jump without his helmet and weapon. They were misplaced on the morning of the assault and he went without. As he described in an interview with the Go For Broke Educational Foundation, one of his biggest concerns on February 16, 1945, was avoiding landing in the waters surrounding the Rock.

"We had two small areas to land in," he explained. "My landing area was . . . closer to the cliff . . . and the rest of it is ocean. So I thought, oh no, I don't want to go back. I don't want to go in the ocean. So I grab[bed] the rear end of the riser . . . so I wouldn't drift forward . . . As I descended, the shoreline became wider, so I said, 'I'm not going to go into the ocean.' By that time I looked down and there was a bomb shattered tree. 'Oh no, I'm going to get impaled . . . I can just feel the pain of getting impaled.' I got excited and let the rear riser go and pulled on the front one as hard as I could. Well, I'm not supposed to do that I understand, because as soon as I did that, the parachute started oscillating and turning. Now I was coming in backward. . . . A few seconds later I saw the shattered tree go by. I said, 'Oh boy, I'm safe now, I got it made.' Then my feet suddenly touched lightly. It was a really light landing. Everybody else on that parachute run really got banged up."

The paratroopers quickly joined up into combat squads to defend themselves from the sizable number of Imperial Japanese Army troops who promptly counterattacked. Harry Akune picked up a rifle and fought alongside the infantrymen. The situation was graphically evident in the notations in the official U.S. Army "Rock Force" war diary: "Sniper and machine-gun fire pouring all about us from the east . . . heavy fire from enemy heavy machine gun. . . . Can't locate medical bundles . . . dispensary swamped . . . heavy casualties."

By the end of the day, the soldiers had formed a defensive perimeter, and Akune started studying captured documents. From these he was able to ascertain that the Americans were opposed by a force of about 5,000, including Imperial Japanese Marines, not just the 850 service troops that had been expected. He also determined that the enemy commander had been killed. All of this information was to be vital in organizing a defense. The former was bad news for the outnumbered GIs, but knowing that the Japanese commander was dead was good news because it ruled out a coordinated mass counterattack by the full enemy force.

As he worked his way through the captured paperwork, Harry Akune also was able to determine the locations of some sources of fresh water, which saved the Americans a great deal of aggravation, and possible loss of life.

He debriefed what few prisoners were taken, including a small number of Japanese sailors. From them, he was able to learn the location of about a hundred Q-boats, small motorboats loaded with explosives that could be used to attack American ships.

Two weeks after the initial landing, Corregidor was securely in American hands. Harry Akune went on to serve in the Allied Prisoner of War Recovery Team, and he ended the war with numerous decorations, including the Paratrooper Badge and the Bronze Star. In 1996, he would be named to the Military Intelligence Corps Hall of Fame.

CHAPTER 13

They Also Served

As noted above, despite the best efforts of those who pointed to the exemplary performance of the Nisei GIs in the 100th Infantry Battalion and the 442nd Regimental Combat Team, the U.S. Navy, the Marine Corps, and the U.S. Army Air Forces refused to officially accept Nisei men as sailors, marines, or airmen. Whereas Nisei linguists of the Military Intelligence Service were not deemed adequately trustworthy to set foot in the JICPOA headquarters at Pearl Harbor unescorted, they *were* good enough to sail aboard navy ships and listen to enemy radio transmissions. The Nisei men weren't acceptable as marines, but were good enough to wade ashore under fire *with* the marines.

Despite the best efforts of the U.S. Navy, Marine Corps, and the USAAF brass to exclude them, there *were* some sons of Japanese immigrants who slipped through the cracks. Notable among them was Technical Sergeant Ben Kuroki, a Nebraska farm boy who not only managed to enlist in the USAAF, but to fly fifty-eight combat missions. An urban legend that has been told, usually with a chuckle, around the tables at Nisei veteran events is that the USAAF must have thought that Kuroki was a Polish name!

Ben was born in Gothenburg, Nebraska, one of ten children of Issei immigrant parents. Shosuke Kuroki and his wife Naka had a farm in Lincoln County, near the small town of Hershey, that to this day boasts a population of barely five hundred. They grew potatoes and sugar beets, and the kids helped out.

In the wake of Pearl Harbor, Ben and his brothers drove into nearby North Platte to sign up for the service. They stood in line with young Caucasians who looked just like the friends and class-mates they had known all their lives. The recruiters were happy to see each one of these young fellows until the Kuroki boys reached the head of the line. For the first time, they knew what it was like to be told they were not good enough because they were different. Having been refused in North Platte, they drove east to Grand Island. The re-cruiters there had not yet figured out that Japanese Americans need not apply. Maybe, as the urban legend goes, the recruiter thought that Ben Kuroki was Polish.

Ben signed up for the USAAF, and went overseas with the 93rd Bombardment Group as a top turret gunner in a Consolidated B-24 Liberator, the most widely produced American heavy bomber to serve in World War II. The 93rd was deployed to England, where it was as-signed to the Eighth Air Force and flew its first combat missions over German-occupied France in October 1942. Two months later, a siz-able detachment was sent to the Mediterranean Theater for two months of operations against enemy targets in North Africa and Italy.

In June 1943, the 93rd Bomb Group sent another detachment to North Africa, this time to prepare for Operation Tidal Wave, an attack on the petroleum refinery complex at Ploesti, Romania, then the largest cluster of such facilities in German-occupied Europe. Damag-ing this refining capacity was seen as an important blow against the German war effort. Ben Kuroki was a gunner in one of 177 B-24s that reached Ploesti in the historic low-level mission on August 1. His Liberator was one that survived the withering German antiaircraft fire that cost the lives of so many 93rd Bomb Group crewmen that day.

After Ploesti, the 93rd Bomb Group's Mediterranean detach-ment flew missions in support of the Allied landings in Italy in Sep-tember before returning to the group's main base at Hardwick in

England, from which it would operate until Germany was defeated in May 1945.

Early in the war, the USAAF required its aircrewmen to complete twenty-five combat missions, after which they were entitled to stand down and go home. Then the service upped that requirement to thirty missions. Ben Kuroki completed his twenty-fifth mission, and finally his thirtieth.

By the time the U.S. Army announced the creation of the 442nd Regimental Combat Team in February 1944, Ben Kuroki was back in the states on a furlough, having already fought the Germans thirty times. He had been awarded two Distinguished Flying Crosses, as well as the coveted Air Medal with four Oak Leaf Clusters—*and* he had volunteered for more.

It was on February 4 that Ben Kuroki, the decorated war hero, was invited to speak to the business leaders and power brokers at the prestigious Commonwealth Club in San Francisco—in a city and state where Japanese Americans had not been allowed to walk the streets for nearly two years. He spoke of his experiences overseas, and the experiences of a Nisei GI walking the streets of California. On the street outside, he had received suspicious stares, but inside the Commonwealth Club, he received a standing ovation. Monroe Deutsch, the vice president of the University of California, later said that Kuroki's appearance that day set a positive tone that carried over in the reacceptance of Japanese Americans into California society after World War II.

When Ben Kuroki signed up to fly missions against Imperial Japan, this was unheard-of for a Japanese American airman. However, many things that Ben Kuroki had done were without precedent. Initially, the thought of sending a Japanese American man on missions over Japan raised some eyebrows. What if he was shot down and captured? The USAAF was inclined to deny his request. Of course, under USAAF rules, he shouldn't have *already* flown thirty missions over Hitler's Reich, so why not break another rule? Kuroki persisted, and his persisting went all the way to Secretary of War Henry Stimson, who reviewed his record and finally signed off on the Nisei airman's request.

In 1944, the USAAF's new superbomber, the Boeing B-29 Superfortress, was ready for combat, and General Henry "Hap" Arnold, the USAAF's commanding general, decided to concentrate them in a strategic air offensive against Japan. By that time all of Hitler's Third Reich was within range of existing B-17 and B-24 heavy bombers, but these aircraft did not have the range to strike Japan's industrial heartland from any bases then occupied by Allied forces. Japan was even out of range for B-29s, except from hard-to-supply forward bases in China, but this situation changed in the summer of 1944 with the capture of Guam and the Mariana Islands. On the islands of Guam, Saipan, and Tinian, USAAF at last had the bases that it needed for the task at hand. With the B-29s now becoming available from four new factories in the United States, they also had the planes. In Ben Kuroki, they had the man—the type of enthusiastic and patriotic airman who was an inspiration to others.

Kuroki went on to fly twenty-eight Superfortress missions with the XXI Bomber Command of the USAAF Twentieth Air Force out of the big bomber base on the island of Tinian, and he would have flown more had he not run afoul of racial hatred that was very out of character for the fellow airmen he had come to know.

Through his more than three years in the service, the likable farm boy from Nebraska was well regarded wherever he had gone. He had gotten along well with his fellow crewmen, who nicknamed him "Most Honored Son." On Tinian, where there were still some Japanese holdouts hiding in the hills, his Caucasian buddies escorted him everywhere so that a guard wouldn't mistake him for an Imperial Japanese soldier in a pilfered American uniform.

Suddenly, Kuroki's good relations with his fellow airmen changed abruptly. One night in July 1945, in the barracks on Tinian, a drunken ground crewman pulled a knife, called Ben Kuroki "a damned Jap," and lunged. He cut a gash across Ben Kuroki's head. Ben went down and the man lunged again, this time for the kill. However, by now, Master Sergeant Russell Olsen, a B-29 flight engineer, was in the way. He ordered the would-be assailant to surrender his weapon, and this was done.

Ben Kuroki was bundled off to the base hospital, where twenty-four stitches closed the wound. By the time he had recuperated, World War II was over and Kuroki's combat career had ended with fifty-eight missions. He went home to enroll at the University of Nebraska in Lincoln, where he earned a journalism degree. He worked in the newspaper business across the United States, finally retiring as an editor at the *Star Free Press* in Ventura, California, in 1984.

In August 2005, thanks to the efforts of Senators John McCain and Ben Nelson, as well as University of Nebraska Regent Charles Wilson, members of the 93rd Bomb Group Association, and fellow Nebraskan Carroll "Cal" Stewart of Lincoln, who served with Kuroki in the war, Ben Kuroki was awarded the Distinguished Service Medal.

"I'm just the luckiest man on the planet," Kuroki said on the night that he received the award. "To have these Nebraska friends go to bat for me, I cherish that as much as I do receiving the medal."

Speaking of his being awarded the medal, he continued: "I feel that it gives credence to the word 'democracy,' and it's Americanism at its very best. I feel that more so than any personal glory it gives to me."

Russell Olsen was in the audience at the Cornhusker Hotel in Lincoln that night, and Kuroki thanked him again for saving his life.

Of course, there were also a handful of Nisei men in the other services when the war began. One such man was Douglas Wada, who was a naval intelligence officer stationed at Pearl Harbor at the time of the attack, and who interrogated the first Japanese prisoner of war, the crewman of the midget submarine captured on Oahu reef on December 8, 1941. A University of Hawaii graduate, he had played baseball with Joe Takata of the 100th Infantry Battalion before the war, and he went on to a long career in the U.S. Navy that lasted until his retirement in 1975.

Meanwhile, just as it is important to mention Nisei men who served with military units other than the 442nd Regimental Combat

Team and the 100th Infantry Battalion, it is equally important to mention that not all the Nisei to serve their country in uniform during World War II were *men*. Nor was language training at Fort Snelling an all-male fraternity. Beginning in 1943, the U.S. Army trained more than fifty Nisei members of the Women's Army Corps (WAC) at Fort Snelling to work as translators. Those daughters of Japanese immigrants were assigned to a number of locations, including the Pacific Military Intelligence Research Section (PACMIRS) at Camp Ritchie, Maryland. After the war, many were sent to Tokyo to work as translators during the military occupation.

In addition to the WACs, a large number of Nisei women had volunteered for the U.S. Cadet Nurse Corps, formed in June 1943. Lieutenant Colonel Mary Walker of the U.S. Army Nurse Corps supervised the program in army hospitals and coordinated with other agencies. Though the women wore military-style uniforms, the organization was managed by the U.S. Public Health Service under the surgeon general. The idea was to guarantee that the United States had enough nurses to meet the wartime needs of both military and civilian hospitals.

A Japanese-American draftee during "hold and squeeze" rifle training at a U.S. Army induction center in Hawaii, circa 1941. *(Courtesy of the U.S. Army Signal Corps via the National Archives)*

During their training at Camp Shelby, Mississippi, in 1943, these Nisei GIs of the 442nd Regimental Combat Team prepare to cross a stream. *(Courtesy of the U.S. Army Signal Corps via the National Archives)*

A pair of Nisei GIs from the 100th Infantry Battalion repair the engine of a truck during their training at Camp Shelby. *(Courtesy of the U.S. Army Signal Corps via the National Archives)*

Troops of the 100th Infantry Battalion move up toward the front in the vicinity of Valletri, near Lanuvio, in Italy on May 28, 1944. *(Courtesy of the U.S. Army Signal Corps via the National Archives)*

Secretary of War Henry L. Stimson greets 442nd Regimental Combat Team officers north of Cecina in Italy on July 6, 1944. General Mark Clark, the commander of the U.S. Fifth Army is in the back seat of the Jeep. *(Courtesy of the U.S. Army Signal Corps via the National Archives)*

Gunners of the 442nd Regimental Combat Team's 522nd Field Artillery Battalion fire their 105 mm Howitzer at enemy positions during the Battle of Livorno on July 12, 1944. *(Courtesy of the U.S. Army Signal Corps via the National Archives)*

The 522nd Field Artillery Battalion's fire control center near Livorno on July 12, 1944. *(Courtesy of the U.S. Army Signal Corps via the National Archives)*

A platoon of Nisei GIs moves forward during the 442nd Regimental Combat Team advance near Livorno on the west coast of Italy on July 15, 1944. *(Courtesy of the U.S. Army Signal Corps via the National Archives)*

This Nisei sniper with the 100th Infantry Battalion saw sixteen straight days of fighting during the July 1944 Battle of Livorno. *(Courtesy of the U.S. Army Signal Corps via the National Archives)*

This 100th Infantry Battalion mortar crew is blasting the high ground near Montenero, Italy, to silence the German snipers firing at the Nisei GIs from the hills on August 7, 1944. *(Courtesy of the U.S. Army Signal Corps via the National Archives)*

Cited in War Department General Orders on September 12, 1945, the 100th Battalion of the 442nd Regimental Team received a Presidential Unit Citation at a ceremony in Livorno, Italy. *(Courtesy of the U.S. Army Signal Corps via the National Archives)*

Brigadier General Frank Merrill flanked by two of his Nisei translators, Tech Sergeant Herbert Miyasaki of Pauuilo, Hawaii, and Tech Sergeant Akiji Yoshimura of Colusa, California. (*Courtesy of the U.S. Army Signal Corps via the National Archives*)

A Nisei bugler plays taps after a rifle squad has fired a salute at a July 30, 1944 memorial service for seventy-two members of the 2nd Battalion of the 442nd Regimental Combat Team who were killed during the first month of combat in Italy. (*Courtesy of the U.S. Army Signal Corps via the National Archives*)

On December 8, 1941, Tech Sergeant Thomas Tsubota of Honolulu helped capture the first enemy in the Pacific war when his unit apprehended the crewman aboard a Japanese midget submarine on a Hawaiian reef. Tsubota went on to serve with Merrill's Marauders. *(Courtesy of the War Relocation Authority; photo by Charles Mace)*

Sergeant Henry "Horizontal Hank" Gosho served for sixteen months with Merrill's Marauders in Burma and India. Frequently exposing himself to enemy fire while directing American guns, he earned his nickname because "he hit the ground so much he wore it out." *(Courtesy of the War Relocation Authority; photo by Hikaru Iwasaki)*

Somewhere in the Vosges Mountains in France on October 12, 1944, a Nisei soldier stands guard at the 100th Infantry Battalion bivouac while his unit prepares to go to the front. *(Courtesy of the U.S. Army Signal Corps via the National Archives)*

Private First Class Sadao Munemori was the only Nisei soldier to be awarded the Medal of Honor prior to 2000. It was awarded posthumously in 1946 for his actions on April 5, 1945 near Seravezza in Italy. *(Photo courtesy National Archives)*

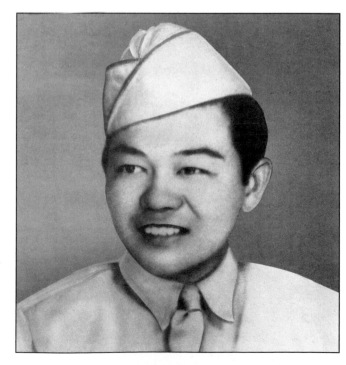

Nisei GIs of the 442nd Regimental Combat Team take cover during a German artillery barrage in or near the hilltop village of Seravezza on April 4, 1945. *(Courtesy of the U.S. Army Signal Corps via the National Archives)*

These vets of the Italian campaign recuperating at Dibble Hospital in Palo Alto, California, in July 1945 include Nisei GIs and their Caucasian buddies. In the front are PFC Walter Heirakuji; PFC Bud Schultz, who fought alongside the Nisei; Corporal Minoru Yoshida; PFC Andy Anderson; and Private Masao Hayashida. In the back row are Corporal Steve Shimizu; PFC Kiyotaka Uchiyama; Sergeant Jack Kawamoto; and PFC Roy Tsutsui. *(Courtesy of the War Relocation Authority; photo by Hikaru Iwasaki)*

Two weeks after the formal end of World War II in Europe, members of the 100th Infantry Battalion load confiscated German materiel onto a trailer at the Fifth Army concentration area in Brescia, Italy. *(Courtesy of the U.S. Army Signal Corps via the National Archives)*

Aboard the S.S. *Shawnee* in Los Angeles Harbor on November 30, 1945 a Nisei sergeant converses with a girlfriend. *(Courtesy of the War Relocation Authority; photo by Charles Mace)*

Nisei GIs and young ladies from New York City enjoy a party at the Nyack, New York, U.S.O. in March 1945. Seen here are U.S.O. hostess Mrs. J. Knapp, Private Katsumi Sakotomi, Flora Tanji, Julie Tanji, and Private Tomizo Saiki. Both GIs were from Hawaii. The Tanji cousins were originally from California, but were sent to the Granada Relocation Center in 1942. By 1945, both were working in New York. *(Courtesy of the War Relocation Authority; photo by Tōge Fujihira)*

On the rainy afternoon of July 15, 1946, President Harry Truman presented the 442nd Regimental Combat Team with their seventh Presidential Unit Citation at the White House in Washington, D.C.. (*Courtesy of the National Archives*)

A Nisei veteran of the 442nd Regimental Combat Team is welcomed by a hula dancer. (*Courtesy of the U.S. Army Signal Corps via the National Archives*)

Lieutenant Colonel Alfred Pursall, the commanding officer of the 442nd Regimental Combat Team's 3rd Battalion, is seen here conferring with Masao Yamada, the former regimental chaplain of the 442nd. (*Courtesy of the U.S. Army Signal Corps via the National Archives*)

Anxious to get their feet on the red dirt of the Islands once again, Nisei GIs of the 442nd Regimental Combat Team stream down the gangplank of the U.S.S. *Waterbury Victory*. (*Courtesy of the U.S. Army Signal Corps via the National Archives*)

The "Go for Broke" slogan of the 442nd Regimental Combat Team decorated the bridge of the transport U.S.S. *Waterbury Victory* as it pulled into Honolulu on August 9, 1946. *(Courtesy of the U.S. Army Signal Corps via the National Archives)*

The 442nd Regimental Combat Team Color Guard marches in the Honolulu Veterans Day Parade at Kapiolani Park on August 15, 1946. *(Courtesy of the U.S. Army Signal Corps via the National Archives)*

Army Secretary Louis Caldera inducts Nisei soldiers into the Pentagon's Hall of Heroes on June 22, 2000. Ken Inouye, left, represented his father, Hawaii Senator Daniel Inouye, at the Pentagon Hall of Heroes induction ceremony. Secretary Caldera, center, applauds as Army Chief of Staff General Eric Shinseki presents a certification of induction. *(American Forces Press Service photo by Rudi Williams)*

On June 21, 2000, the Medal of Honor was bestowed on *(left to right)* Private Shizuya Hayashi, Private George T. Sakato, Technical Sergeant Yeiki "Lefty" Kobashigawa and Technical Sergeant Yukio Okutsu. *(American Forces Press Service photo by Rudi Williams)*

CHAPTER 14

Frank Merrill's Samurai

While the majority of the Military Intelligence Service personnel served in General Douglas MacArthur's Southwest Pacific Area, or with the JICPOA and ATIS, one of the most colorful cadres of Nisei GIs was the group assigned to the 5307th Composite Unit (Provisional), an organization that is considered to be a grandfather outfit to the modern Special Forces.

The idea of the 5307th was for a temporary United States commando unit to operate deep behind Japanese lines in the mountainous jungles of Burma. The goal was the disruption of enemy communications from within and paving the way for the recapture by Chinese forces of the Burma Road, the only major supply route into China that was passable by motor vehicles. As they penetrated into Burma, the Americans would be opposed by the Imperial Japanese Eighteenth Army, a vastly superior force, and the enemy unit responsible for the defeat of both Malaya and Singapore.

The concept for the 5307th was loosely based on the British Chindits commando organization that was commanded by Brigadier General Charles Orde Wingate. The Chindits already performed a similar function within the greater China-Burma-India (CBI) Theater, but the U.S. Army wished to have a unit of its own under American command. When General Joseph Stilwell, the American theater commander of the CBI, selected Brigadier General Frank Merrill to lead the 5307th, the nickname "Merrill's Marauders" was born.

The volunteers for the Marauders came from experienced combat unit that had already seen combat in campaigns such as Guadalcanal and New Guinea. The first of the volunteers reached India in October 1943, where they began to train as a unit and to develop tactics. Among the latter would be the widespread use of aircraft for delivering supplies to remote operating locations. Considered standard operating procedure for special forces today, this was still an innovative technique in 1943.

Since the Marauders would be operating deep behind enemy lines, the need for people with Japanese language skills was obvious, and fourteen MIS linguists volunteered to become Marauders. They did so knowing that they would be operating in perhaps the most dangerous possible environment. As noted previously, Japanese American GIs were considered fair game for torture and execution as traitors by Imperial Japanese troops. Because they were ethnically Japanese, they ran the parallel risk of being shot by Americans in cases of mistaken identity. Still they went.

Known unofficially as the "Marauder Samurai," the fourteen Nisei in the 5307th Composite Unit included seven Hawaiians and seven mainlanders. Among the Hawaiians was Technical Sergeant Thomas Tsubota of Honolulu, who already had the distinction of having been among the first GIs of any ethnicity to see combat in World War II when he helped capture the one-man submarine Ha-19 on December 8, 1941. Three other men from Oahu were Roy Nakada and Robert Honda, both recent graduates of the University of Hawaii, and Edward Mitsukado, a court recorder in Honolulu. From the Big Island of Hawaii came Herbert Miyasaki of Pauuilo and two men from Hilo, Howard Furumoto and Russell Kono. When the war started, Furumoto was a veterinary student at Kansas State University, while Kono, whose father was a veteran of the U.S. Army in World War I, was studying law at the University of Hawaii.

Most of the mainlanders in the Marauders were from California,

with Calvin Kobata from Sacramento and Akiji Yoshimura from Colusa, and three from Los Angeles: Ben Sugata, Jimmie Yamaguchi, and
Roy Hiroshi Matsumoto. While many Nisei men who joined the Military Intelligence Service had attended school in Japan and had relatives living there, Matsumoto's entire family had moved back to
Hiroshima before the war. His father, Wakaji Masamoto, a professional
photographer, was descended from Wakamatsu Matsumoto, who had
been one of the first Japanese Americans to operate a large farm in
southern California. Roy's mother, Tei Kimura, was a picture bride
and the daughter of Shinjiro Kimura, who taught the art of kendo in
the court of Lord Asano in Hiroshima. Roy had spent three years in
Hiroshima with the Kimura family. He was the only member of his
family in the United States when the war started.

Henry Hiroharu Gosho was born and raised in Seattle, where his
parents operated a drugstore. When the relocation order came, Henry
and his pregnant wife were hustled off to the Minidoka relocation
camp in Idaho, where their daughter, Carol Jeanne, was born in 1943.
Despite having dependents, Gosho was eager to volunteer for the U.S.
Army and eager to prove his loyalty to the United States.

Grant Jiro Hirabayashi, originally from Kent, Washington, south
of Seattle, had attended high school in Japan from age twelve, before
returning to the United States to graduate from Kent High School.
He joined the U.S. Army in December 1941—three weeks past his
eighteenth birthday—on the Thursday before the United States entered World War II. In October 1942—even as his family was uprooted and evacuated to the Heart Mountain relocation camp in
Wyoming—Grant volunteered for the Military Intelligence Service
Language School, where he soon proved to be one of its star linguists.
Unfortunately, he discovered that he was allergic to one of the ingre-
dients in army K rations. Despite this, he insisted on volunteering for
Merrill's regiment.

Highest ranking among the Nisei Marauders was Lieutenant
(later Captain) William Laffin, whose mother was Japanese. Ironically,
on December 7, 1941, he was actually *in* Japan on a business trip for

the Ford Motor Company. He managed get back to the United States in 1942 in an exchange of civilians. He volunteered for the Military Intelligence Service, graduated from Camp Savage in 1943, and became the intelligence officer for the Marauders.

In February 1944, the three battalions of the 5307th deployed into Burma, hiking approximately eight hundred miles from India. The Marauders outflanked the enemy at Maingkwan, and fought their first major battle at Walawbum between March 4 and 6. They managed to cut off enemy lines of communications here, and to penetrate deep into the Japanese-held area. Climbing through the high mountains south of the Hukawng Valley and east of the Burma Road, battling the enemy in small-unit actions as they went, the Marauders fought their second major battle at Shaduzup.

From here, the Americans outflanked the Imperial Japanese Army again, marching seventy miles though virtually impassable terrain in just three days. They cut the enemy supply route at Inkangatawng on March 23, but the hugely outnumbered Americans were forced to withdraw under heavy enemy pressure. Pursued by the enemy, the 2nd Battalion of the Marauders went into defensive positions at Nhpum Ga—known to the Americans as "Maggot Hill"—where they held off the Japanese in a ferocious battle lasting from March 28 through the first week of April. Finally, the other units of the 5307th, supported by Chinese troops, relieved the 2nd Battalion and routed the enemy.

During early May, the Marauders crossed the Kumon Range into the valley of the Irrawaddy River, where they engaged the Japanese in numerous skirmishes before fighting their climactic battle, a siege of Myitkyina that lasted until August 3.

In an article that appeared in the May 17, 1944, issue of *The New York Times*, the war correspondent Tillman Durdin wrote of the 5307th: "No other American force except the First Marine Division, which took and held Guadalcanal for four months, has had as much uninterrupted jungle fighting service as Merrill's Raiders. . . . No other American force anywhere has marched as far, fought as continuously or has had to display such endurance, as General Merrill's swift-moving, hard-hitting foot soldiers."

The Nisei linguists who fought with the Marauders distinguished themselves repeatedly. Attached to the 2nd Battalion, Sergeant Roy Matsumoto earned the Legion of Merit for his performance at Maggot Hill. While the battalion was surrounded there, he went out each night, creeping close enough to the Japanese lines that he could hear conversations among the enemy officers. One night, he was able to ascertain the time and place of a major attack, and the Marauders successfully set a trap. In the ensuing confusion, Matsumoto stood up and shouted in Japanese, ordering the enemy reserve troops to attack a separate section of the line where yet another ambush had been prepared.

In the 3rd Battalion, Staff Sergeant Henry Gosho had signed up as a linguist, but, as often as not in Burma, he fought as a rifleman. Gosho, whose wife and newborn daughter were still inmates at Minidoka, often volunteered for the dangerous task of directing machine-gun fire for his platoon's gunners. As such, he was frequently exposed to enemy fire. Indeed, he was pinned down on the ground so often by enemy fire that his comrades started calling him "Horizontal Hank."

Grant Hirabayashi, the Nisei linguist who was allergic to K rations, was attached to the 1st Battalion and began the hike into Burma while still recovering from a broken arm that he suffered while in training in India. His food allergy forced him to live off the land, scrounging food wherever he could, and eating what little in the rations that didn't make him sick. Nevertheless, he bravely continued to do his work under conditions that were difficult for everyone, and doubly difficult for him. This work often found him crawling behind enemy lines to eavesdrop on conversations. He fully expected to be executed if caught.

After the Maggot Hill fight, Hirabayashi was evacuated by air, suffering from amoebic dysentery, high fever, and severe weakness. Nursed back to health, he volunteered to return to the Marauders. He arrived in time for the Myitkyina campaign, where he earned a Bronze Star with Oak Leaf Cluster for his actions.

Captain Laffin, the intelligence officer for the 5307th, was the only Japanese American Marauder to be killed in action. On May 17, 1944, as the unit was marching toward Myitkyina, he was in an L-1 observation aircraft observing Japanese defensive positions when enemy fighter planes attacked. The small, defenseless aircraft had no chance.

The provisional 5307th was disbanded after Myitkyina, having accomplished its task of penetrating the enemy rear and disrupting Japanese lines of communications. The Marauders were amazingly successful, defeating enemy forces that often greatly outnumbered them. They had captured several important objectives, including the important communications center at Myitkyina. They paid a high price, however, with a third of the Marauders killed in action, and another third severely wounded. Merrill himself suffered two heart attacks.

When the unit was officially terminated, Grant Hirabayashi, Calvin Kobata, Roy Matsumoto, Ben Sugata, Akiji Yoshimura, Howard Furumoto, and Roy Nakada all went on to the Sino Translation and Interrogation Center (SINTIC) in China. Robert Honda and Edward Mitsukado joined the Office of Strategic Services (OSS) and remained in action in Southeast Asia.

Wounded in action in Burma, Horizontal Hank Gosho also suffered from malaria, typhus, and a long list of other illnesses. He went on to lose one kidney, and was given a medical discharge. After recuperating, he was reunited with his wife and daughter, who had by then been released from Minidoka. As a civilian, Gosho went to work for the U.S. State Department, and at the Public Affairs Office of the American Embassy in Tokyo during the postwar reconstruction of Japan.

Later in 1944, Roy Matsumoto joined the 475th Infantry Regiment of the Mars Task Force, the successor organization to the Marauders, and served with Chinese Nationalist Army commando units behind Japanese lines, where he continued to work as a linguist and interrogator. After the war, he served for a year with the U.S. Army's China Command headquarters in Shanghai, where his duties involved escorting captured war criminals from China to occupied Japan. He was later transferred to U.S. Army headquarters in Tokyo. While in Japan, he was reunited with his family, who had survived the August 1945 nuclear strike on Hiroshima. He retired from the army in 1963. Along with Grant Hirabayashi and Henry Gosho, Roy Matsumoto was subsequently inducted into the U.S. Army's Ranger Hall of Fame at Fort Benning, Georgia.

General Frank Merrill had nothing but praise for the men who comprised the Marauder Samurai. "As for the Nisei group," Merrill observed, "I couldn't have gotten along without them. Probably few realized that these boys did everything that an infantryman normally does plus the extra work of translating, interrogating, etc. Also they were in a most unenviable position as to identity as almost everyone from the Japanese to the Chinese shot first and identified later."

CHAPTER 15

In the Darkness
of the Vosges

In August 1944, as the Nisei Military Intelligence Service linguists were in action from Myitkyina to the Marianas, the men of the 442nd Regimental Combat Team were preparing for redeployment from Italy to France.

The chief element of Allied strategy in Europe during the summer of 1944 was bringing the war to the doorstep of the Germans in northern Europe. Aside from the southern half of the long Italian peninsula, the Germans had held most of continental Europe in their grasp for four long years. The first step in reversing the fortune of the Germans on the Western Front was the Operation Overlord landing in Normandy on June 6, 1944. On August 15, this was followed by the Operation Anvil/Dragoon invasion of southern France. The United States Seventh Army, commanded by General Alexander "Sandy" Patch, spearheaded this Allied thrust that swiftly swept the Germans back, liberating both Marseilles and Toulon in less than two weeks.

The 442nd Regimental Combat Team had remained in Italy during the invasion of southern France in August, but the Nisei unit had contributed its antitank company for the operation. After twelve days of tactical glider training near Rome, the company was attached to the 1st Airborne Task Force for Anvil/Dragoon. They went in on August 15 carrying jeeps and antitank guns, and landed near Le Muy to help support the American paratroopers of the 517th Parachute Infantry Regiment, who had landed before them.

Staff Sergeant Frank Seto was a jeep driver in one of the gliders. "We cracked up in the mountains," he recalled. "I hurt my leg, and both glider pilots broke both of theirs. Our radio operator was knocked a little cuckoo."

Born in San Diego, Seto was raised in a Catholic Boys Home in the Boyle Heights neighborhood of Los Angeles. He never knew his mother, and his father put him in the home because he was a fisherman and was never home. He didn't find out until 1983 that he was part Hispanic. He had been 4-F before he was 4-C, having been rejected for the service before the war because he had suffered a broken eardrum while fighting as a professional boxer. When ordered to report for internment, Seto had gone into Santa Anita, and he was later sent to Glasgow, Montana, to pick sugar beets. He volunteered for the 442nd and was inducted at Camp Jerome, Arkansas.

"The carriage on the American 57 mm antitank guns was too high to fit in the gliders, so we had to borrow six-pounders from the British," Seto explained. "We were supposed to set up covering the beach where they expected the Germans to be retreating, but they never did come through, so we were lucky. On the third day we did knock out two light tanks in the valley, but that was all the Germans we saw. Our officer decided we should practice, so everybody started shooting at the tanks. Later, after they were full of holes, everybody claimed that he was the one who knocked out the tanks in the first place!"

On August 18, Seto and the antitank company, still attached to the 517th, participated in the American drive that pushed the Germans eastward toward Col du Brouis and Sospel on the Franco-Italian border. The company would not rejoin the 442nd until the last week of October.

Meanwhile, the remainder of the 442nd had been pulled out of operations against the Gothic Line, and had arrived in France on the last day of September. After three days en route by ship from Naples, the 442nd went ashore at the French port of Marseilles. By this time, the Germans were long gone, and the men left the ships at the pier and went ashore unopposed. Still under the command of Colonel Charles Pence, who had led them on their first combat action on June 26, the 442nd was clearly a battle-hardened outfit. Two of the 442nd's battalions—and more than two-thirds of its personnel—had been in action for just three months, but these months had to have seemed like an eternity. They had seen some very hard fighting by now, and the Nisei GIs of the 2nd and 3rd Battalions, like their brothers in the 100th, could certainly be called veteran soldiers.

Only six weeks had passed since the Allies had made their invasion of southern France on August 15, but tremendous progress they had made. This was in stark contrast with the slow slogging through Italy over the preceding year. As the 442nd was preparing for redeployment, the Seventh Army had quickly overcome German resistance as they pressed north. In the vanguard of the advance, the 36th Infantry Division, one of three assigned to Seventh Army for the invasion, reached Montelimar eight days after the invasion, having traveled the 250 miles. Here the division met and defeated the German 11th Panzer Division and 198th Infantry Division. With this victory, the Rhone Valley lay open.

The 442nd's new home would be as a regiment of the 36th Infantry Division, commanded since July 1944 by Major General John Dahlquist. Known as the "Lone Star Division" or "Panther Division," the 36th was originally formed of National Guard units, mainly from Texas, but also from Oklahoma. Known informally as the T-Patch, the 36th insignia incorporated an olive drab "T for Texas" and a blue flint arrowhead representing the Indian Territory heritage of Oklahoma.

In Italy, the "Texans" of the 36th Infantry Division had operated alongside the 34th Infantry Division, to which the 442nd and the 100th Infantry Battalion had been attached. Coincidentally, the 36th was the parent division to the 131st Field Artillery Regiment with which Sergeant Frank "Foo" Fujita had been probably the first Japanese American combat soldier to go overseas in World War II.

After having participated in the breakout from Anzio at the end of May, the T-Patch men had been pulled out to take the lead in the Southern France operations, and lead the way it had. As September came to a close—and as the 442nd was coming ashore at Marseilles—the 36th Infantry Division command post was at Eloye, near Épinal, almost four hundred miles north of Marseilles and nearly at the same latitude as Paris.

Here in the foothills of the rugged Vosges Mountains, the terrain was becoming steeper and more difficult even as the weather grew cold and rainy. When the 36th had gone ashore along the Riviera in August, the weather was good and the lay of the land conducive to a swift advance. Now the topography was getting to be as difficult as it had been in Italy, but with the added frustration that the steep hillsides were heavily wooded. The tangle of underbrush made it a literal jungle except for a few narrow, often unpaved, roads.

Because of the density of the forest, it was hard for the American units to stay within sight of one another, and doubly difficult to remain in communication. This would soon be a problem. As the days grew shorter and dark clouds covered the sky, the deep, dark woods of the Vosges turned daytime into perpetual twilight, and night into abysmal blackness. As was the case in Italy, the Germans would use the terrain to their defensive advantage in the coming battle.

It was into the darkness of the Vosges that the Nisei men of the 442nd rode in their two-and-a-half-ton trucks—universally known as "deuce-and-a-halfs." They reached the 36th Infantry Division front on October 14, in time for the beginning of the assault on the town of Bruyères, which was to begin the following morning. An important road junction, Bruyères was the nexus of five roads that were essential to the control of a section of the Vosges where most of the topography was impassable for vehicles except on the roads.

As the 442nd was positioned at the leading edge of the 36th Infantry Division advance, there was a sense of urgency in the air. The Allies were anxious to take the war home to Germany itself, and for the Texas Division, the German border was only about fifty miles away. Naturally, there was a rivalry among Seventh Army divisions on the front over which one would be the first. Dahlquist was anxious that it should be the 36th.

Dahlquist's urgency was fused with overconfidence. Compared to operations in Italy and the Normandy front during the summer, the Allied advance across southern France had been almost like the proverbial pat of butter in a hot skillet. German resistance had been relatively light, and that made many American officers assume that such good luck would continue. As Lawson Sakai of Company E remembers, "When we got to Bruyères, General Dahlquist was telling everybody that there were no Germans up ahead. He was pushing his units fast and far."

If that was the impression under which Dahlquist was operating, nothing could have been farther from the truth. The German forces that had allowed themselves to be pushed four hundred miles in six weeks would now be less inclined to give ground with their fatherland so close.

Another factor that Dahlquist appeared to ignore was that all of the American divisions who were racing one another for the German borders were also racing against another competitor—the impending winter. Americans and Germans alike knew that heavy snow would make already difficult terrain impassable.

Nevertheless, Dahlquist was indeed pushing fast and far, and the next step on what was then seen by the general as his fast track to Berlin was Bruyères. In this operation, the 442nd Regimental Combat Team was tasked with capturing four hills overlooking the town. The 100th Battalion, commanded by Lieutenant Colonel Gordon Singles, would go west to take the tallest of the four, which the army planners called Hill A. The 2nd Battalion, under Lieutenant Colonel James Hanley, was to capture Hill B on the north side of town, while Hill C would be assaulted by the 100th after the first two had been captured. The 3rd Battalion would then enter Bruyères itself, and the 2nd and 3rd would then target Hill D, known locally as Mont Avison.

Rain was falling and the temperatures were hovering around

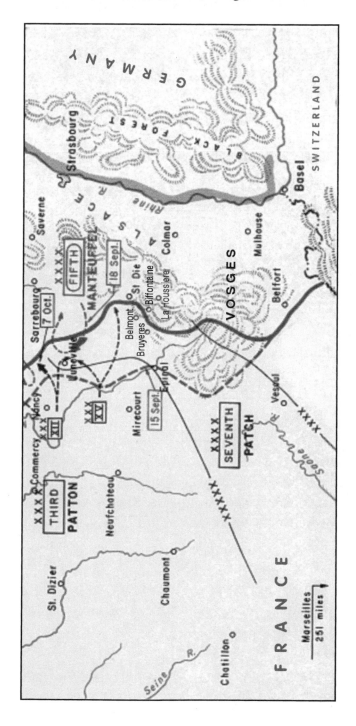

freezing as the Nisei GIs moved out. The German defenders were ready, and they proceeded to suck the Americans into what would be a vicious four-day artillery and small-arms battle in the thick jungle of the Vosges Forest.

By the morning of October 17, the 100th had worked its way to the base of Hill A under artillery support from the 522nd Field Artillery Battalion, but was meeting very concentrated enemy resistance. The 2nd Battalion, meanwhile, had reached Hill B, but its Companies E and F were fighting off a major German counterattack.

As Lawson Sakai recalled, "They were heavily wooded mountains, but when the artillery was finished, there wasn't a tree standing."

"It was raining, it was cold, and the foxholes would fill up with water," Sakai continued. "The guys had trench foot because they couldn't take their boots off for a week at a time. It was late October and there was no sunlight. It was so foggy and so dark. We could hear the Germans talking, and they could hear us, but we couldn't see each other."

Mas Tsuda, a BAR man with the 3rd Platoon of Company E who had come ashore with the 442nd at Civitavecchia in June, was among the many who described the days after Bruyères as "cold and miserable," and as the worst period of action that the regiment would experience. However, there were brief and incongruous moments of calm. He recalls one improbable moment that came when his unit was attacked by German machine-gun nests while crossing a field. The platoon's medical contingent was headed by a litter bearer named Taira, because all of the medics had been put out of action.

"He waved the red cross flag, and stopped the war." Tsuda said. "The Germans stopped shooting at us, and we were able to go out and collect our wounded. Then Taira waved his flag, saluted the Germans and the war started again!"

The BAR, such as Mas Tsuda wielded at Bruyères and as Shinyei Nakamine used in the Lanuvio action that earned him a Medal of Honor in July, was one of the key infantry weapons used by American soldiers in World War II. It was especially potent in close unit actions such as the Yanks faced in the Vosges. The GIs usually referred to it by the initials BAR rather than by its intuitive acronym "bar." Originally developed during World War I, but not widely used until World War II, the BAR was a durable and versatile gun whose twenty-round magazine made it a very potent weapon compared to the M1 infantry rifle with its eight-round clip. "We never aimed," Mas Tsuda explained. "We'd just spray the area." The twenty .30 caliber rounds chewed up anything that got in the way.

However, the BAR was a heavy piece of equipment, weighing about eighteen and a half pounds when empty, compared to nine and a half pounds for an M1 rifle. Tsuda and others have recalled that the gunners would usually unscrew the flash suppressor and the bipod that made the tip of the barrel very awkward to carry and to handle. Some soldiers even cut the stock off to shorten it and make it a bit lighter.

Late on the morning of October 18, the 100th made a final push against Hill A with Company B taking the lead, supported by tanks against a fusillade of hostile fire. As they approached the crest of the hill, German resistance finally collapsed, and enemy troops surrendered in large numbers. By 2:47 P.M., Captain Sakae Takahashi, the Company B commanding officer, was able to report that his men had secured the hill.

About that same time, the 2nd Battalion had effectively outmaneuvered the German defenders at its objective. They combined a determined frontal attack with a simultaneous flanking maneuver to the side and behind the enemy position. With attacks materializing from what seemed to be all sides, the Germans threw up their hands and resistance foundered. At 4:25 P.M., the 2nd Battalion reported that Hill B had been secured, and other 442nd troops, mainly the 3rd Battalion, began moving into Bruyères itself. On October 19, elements of the 2nd and 3rd captured the steep Mont Avison.

It was in the course of the fighting over the next several days that Private Barney Hajiro of Company I emerged as one of the stellar heros of the 442nd Regimental Combat Team. On October 19, he was serving as a sentry when he observed that some troops were under

sniper fire as they were moving toward the German lines. He intervened to help them by laying down covering fire with his BAR. In the
process, he killed or at least wounded two enemy riflemen.

Three days later, Hajiro and another man hid themselves about
fifty yards to the right front of their platoon, and ambushed a heavily
armed, eighteen-man German patrol. They killed two, wounded another, and took the rest as prisoners. For these, and for later actions in
the Vosges on October 29, Barney Hajiro would be awarded a Distinguished Service Cross.

On October 20 during action in the hills surrounding Bruyères,
Staff Sergeant Robert Kuroda of Company H demonstrated the heroism that also earned him a Distinguished Service Cross. Leading his
squad in a move to clear out snipers and machine-gun nests, Kuroda
encountered heavy fire from Germans on a densely wooded slope.
Unable to pinpoint the hostile machine gun, he made his way through
heavy fire to the crest of a ridge. Once he had located the machine
gun, he crawled to within ten yards of the nest and killed three enemy
gunners with hand grenades.

Sergeant Kuroda then fired clip after clip of rifle ammunition,
killing or wounding at least three of the enemy. As he went through
the last of his ammo, he saw that an American officer had been hit by
a burst of fire from a German machine gun located on a nearby hill.
He ran to the man's aid, but found that he was already dead. Picking
up the man's submachine gun, Kuroda advanced through continuous
fire toward a second machine-gun nest and destroyed it.

As he turned to fire upon additional enemy soldiers, he was killed
by a sniper. It was remembered in his Distinguished Service Cross citation that Sergeant Kuroda's courageous actions inspired his fellow
troops and ultimately helped to finally clear the woods and mountains
around Bruyères of the enemy.

The 100th Infantry Battalion fought a seesaw battle on Hill C,
beginning their assault at around midnight on October 19. They
reached the top by noon the following day, just as Dahlquist ordered
Pence to withdraw most of the battalion, leaving just one company to

hold the hill. His eye was still on continuing the 36th Infantry Division advance toward Germany.

Singles, the 100th's commander, and Captain Young Oak Kim, the unit's S-3, or operations officer, both protested because there was still a sizable German force on the opposite side of the hill. Pence noted their points of view, but ordered them to follow the general's order. Singles and Kim were concerned that a lone company could not hold the summit in the face of a determined German attempt to recapture the hill. They were right. The Germans counterattacked using tanks and retook the hill by early evening on October 20

As they bedded down for the night, the men of the 100th Battalion had assumed that they would resume operations against Hill C the following day. However, Dahlquist had other ideas. He personally ordered them to move east overnight toward the small hamlet of Biffontaine, about six miles due east of Bruyères. This order has always been controversial because it deployed the 100th at a moment's notice—without adequate rest and preparation—to an isolated and overextended position.

The order to actually capture Biffontaine did not come until the morning of October 22, by which time the battalion was meeting German resistance along the road and running short of supplies. They had left so quickly on the early morning of the previous day that they had shorted themselves on rations when they packed. When they reached the outskirts of Biffontaine, the Nisei were able to scrounge some cabbages and root vegetables from a farmer's field. The capture of Biffontaine was anticlimactic, as there were only a handful of service troops left in the town and the Nisei scooped them up with little difficulty. In addition to these prisoners, the 100th captured a substantial German supply stockpile.

Though the battalion was now in control of Biffontaine, they were still some distance from the rest of the 36th Infantry Division and precariously isolated. Smarting from the recent loss of Bruyères, the Germans moved into the high ground separating Belmont from Biffontaine, and prepared to counterattack against Biffontaine. Despite the best efforts of the men of Companies E and F, the men of the 2nd and 3rd Battalions in Belmont were unable to link up with the 100th because the enemy now held the intervening ridge.

While the men of the 100th Infantry Battalion had fought their way in to capture Biffontaine, the other men of the 442nd were also on the move toward the east and deeper into the Vosges Mountains. As he had ordered Pence to move on Belmont-sur-Buttant with the 100th, Dahlquist had ordered the colonel to send another task force northeast from Bruyères. This task force would consist of Companies F and L, commanded by Major Emmet O'Connor, the executive officer of the 3rd Battalion. Under rainy skies, they moved out early on the morning of October 21 in the direction of the isolated village of Belmont-sur-Buttant, about five miles northeast of Bruyères and about three miles from Biffontaine.

With Company L in the lead, the O'Connor Task Force succeeded in routing a German patrol in a firefight in the dense forest near Belmont, while capturing several prisoners. In turn, they captured several buildings that were occupied by the enemy, and which provided a good view of the German lines of communication. From this observation post, Nisei spotters were able to call in precision artillery strikes on German reinforcements moving forward toward the fighting.

Thanks to the work of the task force, the 442nd was able to capture the whole ridge above Belmont, while capturing fifty-six Germans, and killing eighty. This action provided both security for the hard-won crossroads at Bruyères, and a jumping-off point for Allied operations in the direction of the Meurthe River.

The men of the 442nd would later relish telling stories of how surprised the German prisoners always were to see Japanese soldiers in American uniforms. "Our guys would try to fool 'em," Lawson Sakai laughed. "The ones who could speak English would ask whether we weren't supposed to be on *their* side, but we'd tell them that we had been, but we switched. We're on *this* side now!"

By now, the overextended 100th Infantry Battalion was about to experience the downside of being so far away from the rest of the 442nd. By the afternoon of October 22, the Germans had essentially surrounded Biffontaine, and they launched their assault aimed at retaking the town. The men of the 100th, who had dug into defensive positions, returned fire. As they ran short of ammunition for their own weapons, they switched to captured German Mausers and "potato-masher" hand grenades that they had scrounged from the supplies they found in the town. German demands that they surrender were met with rude taunts, and the firefight continued.

Early on the afternoon of October 23, Colonel Pence was at the regimental headquarters when he heard from Singles, the 100th Battalion commander, who was in Biffontaine. Singles explained that the battalion was holding the town, but was unable to clear the enemy out of their higher positions on the ridge.

In the meantime, the 100th had made an attempt to move eleven wounded men, including Lieutenant Sam Sakamoto, the Company A commander, back to the American lines near Bruyères, but they had been captured. A separate group of ten wounded men, including Captain Takahashi, the Company B commander, had also attempted to reach the rear, but they had turned back to Biffontaine.

On October 24, Pence ordered the 442nd's 3rd Battalion, spearheaded by Company K, to make a push to drive the Germans off the ridge, and this was done. At the same time, units of the 36th Infantry Division's 141st and 143rd Infantry Regiments reached Biffontaine to relieve the 100th Battalion's positions. By the end of the day, after nearly a week of vicious close-in combat, all three battalions of the 442nd had been reunited at Belmont-sur-Buttant.

"It was one banzai attack after another. Bayonets had to be attached, and it was face to face, head to head," said Company E's Lawson Sakai, describing the bitter fighting in the Vosges. "We were in close contact for four or five days. We'd make counterattacks. They'd make counterattacks. We were moving, but slowly. It took us five days to cross two hills. There was no other way to go. I saw a friend of mine, Tsune Takemoto from Hilo, the platoon sergeant for the 3rd

Platoon, lead one charge after another. He was yelling and shooting, and I was sure he was going to get killed. He didn't, but he was finally wounded so badly that they had to take him out."

It was one night near Biffontaine that Don Seki of Company L lost his arm. "The Germans were very clever," he recalled many years later. "One machine gun was shooting tracer bullets six feet off the ground. Another one, without tracers, was shooting down below. That's the one that got me. It tore off my arm."

As units of the 36th Infantry Division were consolidating their positions around Belmont, preparations were being made to continue the fast—some would say reckless—forward momentum. However, there was trouble brewing up ahead in the dark woods.

CHAPTER 16

The Story of the Lost Battalion

During the long, hard months in Italy, there had already been myriad moments of gallantry under fire by the members of the 442nd Regimental Combat Team and the 100th Infantry Battalion, including the first Presidential Unit Citation action, and fifteen acts of heroism that would one day warrant the awarding of Medals of Honor. Yet the signature moment of sacrifice and courage by which the Nisei GIs are best remembered came in the cold darkness of the Vosges Mountains as October faded into November in 1944.

The three battalions of the 442nd had hit the ground running when they reached the front at the middle of October, and they had been in almost continuous fighting ever since. On October 24, after battling their way from Bruyères to Belmont-sur-Buttant by way of Biffontaine, the regiment paused to catch its breath. The regimental commander, Colonel Charles Pence, told them that they would have a very well-earned two-day break.

Even as they did, a fellow regiment within the 36th Infantry Division was pressing forward into the Vosges jungle to keep the pressure on the defenders of the Third Reich. This regiment, the 141st, is recalled as having been one of the finest in the 36th Infantry Division, and their 1st Battalion could be counted among the best of the best.

On August 15, when the Allied forces swarmed ashore near Marseilles, the 1st Battalion of the 141st was in the vanguard, coming ashore at the heavily defended Blue Beach. On the high ground above the beaches, German defenders poured an endless barrage of hot lead and high explosive ordnance on the Yanks landing below. For their heroism and for their brutal efficiency in taking out these enemy gunners, the 1st Battalion had earned their own Presidential Unit Citation.

On October 24, elements of the 1st Battalion, mainly Companies A and C, were preparing to move out, probing enemy positions to the northeast, through the woods known as Domaniale de Champ. Ultimately, the goal was to outflank the German forces in the Laveline-Corcieux Valley. They had been moving quickly and steadily against the Germans, unaware that they were moving through the thick woods into a trap. As they had attempted to do with the 100th Infantry Battalion at Biffontaine, enemy troops infiltrated their rear and attacked. With Germans behind, as well as ahead, the 1st Infantry Battalion of the 141st Infantry Regiment found themselves surrounded. Communications with their regimental headquarters were severed, and the unit became the Lost Battalion.

The Germans surrounding the Lost Battalion fired from all sides, exacting heavy casualties. When the 141st Infantry Regiment figured out where the Lost Battalion was, the unit's 2nd and 3rd Battalions were ordered to break through the three miles and rescue their colleagues. The initial attacks failed, with the other battalions taking heavy casualties themselves from German heavy mortar and machine-gun fire.

At 2:30 on the afternoon of Wednesday, October 25, General Dahlquist, the division commanding officer, showed up on the doorstep of the 442nd Regimental Combat Team command post. With him was none other than General Alexander "Sandy" Patch, the three-star commander of the entire Seventh Army. The forty-eight-hour respite that the Nisei men had been promised on Tuesday was canceled. The regiment was to move into line on the flank of the main body of the 141st. Dahlquist then went to call on Singles at the command post of the 100th Infantry Battalion. Singles was to prepare his men for possible action to save the stranded men of the 1st Battalion. Singles recalled his own recent experience of having his 100th Battalion surrounded inside Biffontaine. He understood what it was like, although, luckily, his unit had not borne the brunt of a concentrated attempt by the Germans to annihilate them.

Unfortunately, this is exactly what the men of the Lost Battalion were facing. Things were going from bad to worse for the surrounded Yanks. The Germans had poured more troops into the encirclement, and they were probing the American defensive perimeter with tanks. They were looking for a decisive victory against the 36th Infantry Division, and it seemed to be within their grasp.

In the early hours of October 27, the long-awaited orders came for two battalions of the 442nd to go to the aid of the Lost Battalion. The 3rd Battalion, commanded by Lieutenant Colonel Alfred Pursall, moved out at 4:00 A.M., followed by the 100th an hour later. Members of the 442nd remember that, even after daybreak, the woods of Domaniale de Champ were as dark as night. It was raining heavily, and the roads and trails through the pines were rivulets of sticky mud.

The 442nd's 2nd Battalion was earmarked as the regimental reserve for the operation. They attempted to move their armor forward, but one of their two tanks was stopped by a random land mine, and the constricted pathway into the dense Domaniale de Champ proved impassable for the other. Despite these difficulties, the worst fear that morning was that the Nisei GIs, like the unfortunate Lost Battalion, might be encircled by the enemy.

About four hours after they jumped off, the 3rd Battalion was detected by the enemy, and they were treated to a furious artillery barrage. The 100th also came under fire, but the 3rd took the brunt of the German fury that terrible morning. As the Germans prepared to counterattack against the 3rd early on the afternoon of October 27, Lieutenant Colonel Pursall got a message from Dahlquist, who nervously asked why he hadn't reached the Lost Battalion yet. It had been hoped that this could have been accomplished by midmorning, and Dahlquist was wringing his hands. To Pursall, just keeping his battalion alive under the circumstances was an accomplishment.

An estimated seven hundred German troops had unleashed a tank and infantry attack against Company K, the 3rd Battalion spearhead. They were met by determined fire from the Nisei soldiers, and the enemy finally broke off their assault, despite the fact that they outnumbered the Japanese Americans by more than four to one.

Through the remainder of that wet Friday and into the night, the 3rd Battalion's position was a nervous stalemate. The two sides were close to one another in the jungle of underbrush beneath the thick pine canopy, with neither side exactly sure of the location and strength of the other. That evening, Dahlquist ordered Pence to order Pursall to move out at 6:30 on Saturday morning.

At dawn on October 28—or rather at the time dawn might have occurred had the battlefield not been covered by a leaden overcast—the 3rd Battalion was under way as ordered. Companies 1 and K led the way, moving slowly because of the almost total lack of visibility. Pursall kept Company L in reserve until late morning, when enemy fire grew especially intense.

The 3rd Battalion commander also contacted Pence at the regimental command post to request artillery support. However, as they both knew, the use of the big howitzers was problematic in the heavy Domaniale de Champ woods. Artillery spotting was nearly impossible because the terrain was obscured by fog and tall trees. Meanwhile, it was also difficult for tanks to move on steep and slippery hillsides that were covered by a tangle of underbrush and fallen trees.

Down inside this jungle, the Nisei men were taking heavy casualties, and the medics were working overtime. One young medic who was to be singled out for his especially conspicuous bravery during the next several days was twenty-four-year-old Technician Fifth Grade James Okubo. Born in Anacortes, Washington, he grew up in nearby

Bellingham, where his parents, Kenzo and Fuyu Okubo, ran the Sunrise Cafe on Holly Street. James was one of six siblings, but the family grew to a dozen when Fuyu Okubo's sister passed away and three nephews and a niece came to live with them.

A football star at Bellingham High School, James later attended Western Washington University, also in Bellingham. Here he was a member of the skiing club, and just another American college student—until Pearl Harbor. Like other Japanese Americans living in Washington, the Okubos were interned early in 1942. They were sent first to the Tule Lake Relocation Camp in northern California, but later moved to Heart Mountain in Wyoming. In 1944, they were released when they agreed to resettle in Detroit, Michigan, two thousand miles from their home near Puget Sound.

Amazingly, five young men from the Okubo household enlisted to serve in the U.S. Army. James's two brothers Hiram and Sumi joined, as did his cousins Isamu and Saburo Kunimatsu. All but Saburo were members of the 442nd Regimental Combat Team.

As the Nisei men of the 442nd were pinned down and taking heavy enemy fire on October 28, James Okubo distinguished himself by crawling 150 yards, about three-quarters of the way from his position to the German lines, to aid wounded soldiers. As he was carrying men to safety, he was the target of a great deal of enemy fire, and he had two hand grenades thrown at him. Over the course of the next two days, he treated twenty-five injured soldiers. For these and for actions in early November, Okubo would be awarded a Silver Star, America's third highest medal for gallantry under fire. It would later be upgraded to the Medal of Honor—the highest award.

On October 29, as the Nisei continued their slow, but deliberate progress toward the Lost Battalion, the encircled Yanks were growing desperate. Even as they fought to slow the Nisei men, the Germans were tightening the noose around the 1st Battalion of the 141st. They noted that, although a few American aircraft had been able to drop in some food and ammunition, the Lost Battalion's drinking water and medical supplies were all but exhausted. The battalion's killed in action personnel were wrapped in shelter halves and placed behind the battalion first aid station in an ever-lengthening row.

Avoiding a mine field, Lieutenant Colonel Pursall and the men of the 3rd Battalion moved to outflank the German left, while the 100th encircled them to the right. At about 9:30 A.M., Singles received a visit from General Dahlquist and his young aide at the 100th Battalion command post. This routine visit was to be anything but for Dahlquist. As he sat down with Singles to discuss the tactical situation, he asked to see a map. Because Lieutenant James Boodry, the 100th Battalion's map man, had been killed in action on Saturday, Singles did not have a map within reach. Dahlquist's aide stood up to retrieve his map. Suddenly, a burst of German automatic-weapons fire ripped into his chest, and he collapsed onto the general.

The blood-spattered general was stunned. He had seen men killed in action before, but this was different. The dead lieutenant was Wells Lewis, the Harvard-educated son of Sinclair Lewis, the celebrity author of works such as *Main Street, Babbit,* and *Elmer Gantry,* who had been, fourteen years earlier, the first American to be awarded the Nobel Prize for literature.

Dahlquist, who seemed to be in a state of shock, simply wandered off without finishing his meeting with Singles. Lewis had been assigned to him as a special charge, more than as an aide, and Dahlquist had lost him. Sinclair Lewis, who later received a handwritten note from Dahlquist, would never be the same. He had just divorced his second wife, and his career was in a decline from which it would not recover.

For Singles and Pursall, and for the men under their command, there was still work to be done, and having to deal with a dazed Dahlquist made their lives that much more difficult. From the 100th Battalion command post, Dahlquist ambled off to contact Pursall. The 3rd Battalion's initial attack on the morning of October 29 had bogged down in the face of oppressive German fire, but Dahlquist demanded that Pursall resume the assault. To do so would mean pushing up a heavily defended ridge that would come to be known as Suicide Hill.

At about 2:30 in the afternoon, Companies I and K were ordered to fix bayonets and charge. This they did, exchanging automatic-weapons fire with the Germans at nearly point-blank range. Pursall himself led a contingent of the men, firing his Colt .45 automatic pistol. He reminded some of the men of a character from a Western movie. Lieutenant Edward Davis, leading Company K, took a round which shattered his leg, and he went down, but his men were not deterred.

When Company K was pinned down by a German machine-gun nest, Sergeant Fujio Miyamoto of the company's 2nd Platoon was hit badly in the right arm, but he switched his rifle to his left and kept firing. He worked his way up to the emplacement, killed two gunners, and, during the ensuing two-hour firefight, held the position and killed five Germans who unsuccessfully attempted to dislodge him. For this, Miyamoto would be awarded the Distinguished Service Cross.

A number of other Nisei men would be also cited for bravery during the fighting on October 29. Among them were two Company E men, George "Joe" Sakato, the young man from Colton, California, who had tried twice to join the U.S. Army Air Forces, and a young Texan named Saburo Tanamachi. The fourth of a dozen siblings, Tanamachi was born in Long Beach, California, but grew up in Beaumont, Texas, and was later a football star at Brownsville High School. He would earn a Silver Star that day, and Sakato would bring home a Distinguished Service Cross. Sakato's citation would record that as the platoon came under heavy fire, "he personally led a counterattack which overwhelmed two German defensive positions."

As Lawson Sakai recalls, it was Saburo Tanamachi's death that inspired Sakato's heroism that day. As Tanamachi was shot, Sakato watched him collapse into his foxhole. Joe crawled out of his own foxhole and picked him up. As Tanamachi tried to say something, his body went limp and Sakato knew he was dead.

"Sakato held him until he died," Sakai recalls. "As the Third Platoon guys told us just afterward, Joe charged up the hill toward the machine guns, until he was wounded so badly that he couldn't go any more. Meanwhile, other guys started charging too. That's what happens. They see one guy charging, then you have five or six guys going, and others join with them."

Another man to receive the Distinguished Service Cross for his actions on Suicide Hill was Private Barney Hajiro, whose heroism had been so evident during the fight for Bruyères the previous week. Hajiro initiated an attack up the slope of Suicide Hill, running about a hundred yards under enemy fire. He then advanced ahead of his fellow Company I men for around thirty feet, drawing fire as he went. At this point, he located two camouflaged machine-gun nests, both of which he annihilated single-handedly. To top it off, he next pinpointed two more German snipers and killed *them*.

The charge up the hill was one of the finest moments in the regiment's combat history. As the official War Department report observed, they were "killing or seriously wounding the enemy gun crews, but [with] themselves sprawling dead over the enemy positions they had just neutralized."

Both Sakato and Hajiro would live to see their Distinguished Service Crosses upgraded to the Medal of Honor more than half a century later.

Despite the punishment dealt to the men of the 3rd Battalion, the specter of the Japanese Americans staging their bayonet charge seemed to have thoroughly intimidated the Germans, who abandoned the hill. Companies I and K sustained heavy casualties, but they took the hill. They were also able to beat back two stubborn counterattacks.

At 3:45 that afternoon, Pursall put in a radio call to the 442nd Regimental Combat Team headquarters to explain the battalion's precarious situation. "We have no officers left in Company K. We are up on the hill but may get kicked off," Pursall reported in a radio message that was transcribed in the official log of the regiment. "There is a roadblock, and we are having a lot of casualties."

The 3rd Battalion commander went on to report that, according to a German prisoner, enemy defensive positions between the hill and the location of the Lost Battalion were substantial. General Dahlquist, who was then at the 442nd command post, interrupted to promise that a patrol from the 141st Infantry Regiment was somewhere near the hill. Pursall told the general that he couldn't see them anywhere, and repeated that his command had lost a lot of men taking the hill. When he asked the general for more infantry support to bolster his battered battalion, Dahlquist replied that all he could send would be some engineer personnel. The general was not endearing himself to the heroic men of the 442nd.

That night the temperature plummeted, and there was ice in the foxholes of the men of the 442nd and of the Lost Battalion. For the men of the Lost Battalion, things were reaching the breaking point. A passage in the booklet *The Story of the 36th Infantry Division,* a collection of excerpts from *T-Patch,* the division newspaper, is particularly poignant in its description of communications between division command and the Lost Battalion: " 'Send us food, ammunition, medical supplies, and radio batteries,' came the weak voice. Caught in an advance, 1st Battalion, 141st, was surrounded. For five days [doughboys] nursed scanty stocks they had carried until P-47s dropped provisions and supplies. There was little water; both Germans and Yanks fought for the nearest water hole. Some supplies were shot by base ejection shells. For six days and nights the 'Lost Battalion' threw back successive attacks, conserving ammunition, killing Germans, five or more for every one of its own casualties. The men fought on, not knowing when relief would come."

The "when" would be October 30. At 9:00 that morning, with both rain and occasional German artillery fire pouring down, the 3rd Battalion and the 100th Battalion moved out in a coordinated pincer assault against the German ring of steel. The seven companies involved in the push had been battered to the nub. They averaged just 81 men, when the official authorized strength of a rifle company was about 190 men. Company I had the fewest, just 71 men and 2 officers.

Two of its officers had been transferred to Company K, which had lost all of its own officers on the slopes of Suicide Hill.

For a second day in a row the exhausted Nisei GIs faced enemy opposition of staggering dimensions. On top of this, they found themselves fighting yard by yard through a mine field. Nevertheless, they hammered at the outer ring of the German encirclement all morning, while the inside ring of Germans continued to pummel the Lost Battalion.

By midday, with the hail of bullets filling the woods from every direction, Sergeant Bill Hull of the Lost Battalion's Company C heard something moving in the underbrush. He carefully pointed his rifle and waited. Abruptly the foliage parted and he looked up to see an unfamiliar face, a Japanese American face.

Private First Class Matt Sakumoto, a twenty-year-old from Waialua on the Island of Oahu, glanced at the dirty, bearded man and said calmly, "Say, do you need any cigarettes?"

Sakumoto was the point man in a small group of men under the command of Sergeant Takashi "Tak" Senzaki who represented the entirety of I company's first two platoons. There were only eight men left in those two platoons, but they had accomplished their mission: They had reached the Lost Battalion.

The German position atop Suicide Hill turned out to have been the anchor for their line of encirclement around the Lost Battalion. When that was taken by the GIs, the German line began to unravel.

Soon the men from Company K also began reaching the Lost Battalion, and they undertook the process of moving them back across the hill and down to American lines. The Nisei soldiers had rescued the 211 survivors of the 275 men who had been encircled as part of the Lost Battalion, but it cost them 140 of their own killed in action, and many times that number wounded. They had paid a terrible price, but they had done their job. It was the combat action for which the regiment is still best remembered to this day. Nearly every man in the 442nd who fought in the heroic mission was awarded the Purple Heart and the Bronze Star, and many received a Silver Star. As described above, Barney Hajiro, Fujio Miyamoto, and George Sakato would be awarded Distinguished Service Crosses. It was also during the Lost Battalion rescue mission that future United States Senator Daniel Inouye distinguished himself as a platoon leader, earning himself a battlefield commission to second lieutenant.

When he received word that the Lost Battalion had been rescued by the men of the 442nd, General Dahlquist coolly ordered these sons of Japanese immigrants to remain in the woods of the Domaniale de Champ, and be prepared to move out and to capture the *next* hill.

CHAPTER 17

La Houssière
and Beyond

After having rescued the Lost Battalion, the 442nd Regimental Combat Team remained in the line, their only rest being in foxholes that were best described as pools of icy rainwater. The 3rd Battalion was under orders to remain in place and hold the positions that they had captured on October 29, despite the fact that the entire battalion now numbered only about 200 exhausted men—the official strength of a *company*. Company I had just 44 men left. Company K had 76, but they still had no replacements for the 100 percent loss of officers. When 3rd Battalion commander Pursall explained this to General Dahlquist, the division commander, the general reiterated that the battalion was to remain in place and hold their position.

The rest of the 442nd Regimental Combat Team was not faring well either. The four companies in the 100th Battalion (Companies A through D) now averaged only 60 men and 5 officers, while the four companies of the 2nd Battalion (Companies E through H) averaged 79 men and fewer than 5 officers. Meanwhile, the loss of officers reached all the way to the top. Pence, the 442nd's commander, had been injured on October 28 when a shell exploded near his jeep, and he had been replaced by Lieutenant Colonel Virgil Miller, the regimental executive officer.

Lieutenant Ben Rogers, the commander of the regiment's anti-tank company, was also a victim of the fighting. Since there were few enemy tanks in the Vosges, the men of the company were operating as litter bearers or going on patrol with Company H as riflemen. It was while several of the men were holed up in a house during a patrol that Rogers lost his life.

"There was a French family living in a basement and the smoke from their cooking fire was coming up through the chimney," Staff Sergeant Frank Seto of the antitank company recalls. "Lieutenant Rogers told me to go tell them to put out the fire. I crawled out the back window [and] just then a German shell hit behind the house. Then another shell landed in front, and I knew they were bracketing the place. The next one hit right smack on that house, and it killed Lieutenant Rogers and wounded the radio operator. Years later, when I visited the cemetery at Epinal, the lieutenant was listed, but not his company. I told the caretaker that Ben Rogers was with the antitank company. Two years later, when I went back, I noticed that they had gotten it listed correctly."

As the Nisei men continued to battle the Germans in the deep, dark woods of the Domaniale de Champ, James Okubo, the Company K medic from Bellingham, Washington, continued to distinguish himself in the series of heroic actions that dated back to October 28. On November 4, an M4 Sherman tank that was supporting the Company K advance was hit. As it was quickly engulfed in flames, Okubo dashed seventy-five yards amid streams of enemy machine-gun fire to pull a man from the burning tank. Still taking fire, Okubo remained with the injured man until he was stabilized, thus saving his life.

James Okubo was recommended for the Medal of Honor, but the Silver Star was authorized instead because he was a medic, which technically prevented his receiving the higher decoration. In a 1999 interview that appeared in the *Honolulu Star-Bulletin*, Ed Ichiyama, a 442nd Regimental Combat Team comrade who was later instrumental in compiling the documentation for Okubo's upgrade to Medal of Honor status, told journalist Gregg Kakesako that "mortar and artillery shells don't discriminate, and it doesn't matter if you are a medic and a noncombatant."

His Silver Star was awarded in 1945 by the Fifth Army commander, General Truscott, at a ceremony conducted while the 442nd was in Italy. After his discharge from the service, Okubo joined his family in the Detroit area, where he attended Wayne State University on the GI Bill. He later married a fellow student, Nori Miyaya, whose family had relocated from Buena Park, California, and he went on to graduate from the University of Detroit dental school. Dr. Okubo set up a private dental practice, and also served on the faculty of his alma mater. He was killed in a car crash on January 29, 1967, and was buried in Woodlawn Cemetery in Bellingham, although his wife remained in Michigan. His name continues to be mentioned with reverence at Company K reunions.

It was also on November 4, as James Okubo was saving the life of the wounded tanker, that the division commander finally authorized the men of the 442nd to rotate out of the line long enough to take showers.

On October 30, in the bloody aftermath of the Lost Battalion rescue mission, Reverend Masao Yamada, a chaplain with the 442nd, had succumbed to emotion and dashed off a letter to his old friend, Colonel Sherwood Dixon, now on the staff of the War Department in Washington. At Camp Shelby, Dixon, then a lieutenant colonel, had commanded the 3rd Battalion of the 442nd during its training, and he was generally well liked by the Nisei GIs. Dixon came from a family with a long military tradition that hailed from Dixon, Illinois, today best known as the boyhood home of Ronald Reagan.

"Dixon was a very good tactician. We never lost on maneuvers," Don Seki of Company L remembers. "He wanted to go overseas with us, but he was too old. He could barely keep up with us on a march." Instead, he had been given a desk job in Washington.

Reverend Yamada wrote to Dixon explaining that General Dahlquist had "commanded the 442nd to push. It is quite a strain to go forward, regardless of machine gun nests and their well-prepared de-

fense. . . . The cost has been high. I admire the courage and the discipline of our loyal men. . . . I am spiritually low for once. My heart
weeps for our men, especially for those who gave all. Never had combat
affected me so deeply as has this emergency mission. I am probably getting soft but the price is too costly for our men. I feel this way more because the burden is laid on the combat team when the rest of the 141st
[Infantry Regiment] is not forced to take the same responsibility."

The answer, penned on November 22, might have provided some
solace, as Dixon tried to put things in context. Sounding as much like
a chaplain as the chaplain himself, Dixon explained, "The best troops
are called upon to do the hardest fighting. Whenever a general finds
himself up against a tough proposition he sends for the best troops he
has. In a critical situation he can't take chances with anything less than
the best. So when you are called upon again and again it is really a
kind of backhanded compliment. A man who is being shot at daily has
a hard time recognizing it as a compliment when, dead tired, bruised
and battered, he is called upon to make one more effort to risk his life
another time, but it is a compliment."

Both memos are preserved for posterity in the files of the 442nd
at the National Archives in College Park, Maryland.

While the infantry battalions of the 442nd were involved in their
heroic campaign to rescue the Lost Battalion, their unsung brothers in
the 442nd's component 232nd Engineer Combat Company were also
distinguishing themselves. When General Dahlquist made the decision
for the 36th Infantry Division to move east from Bruyères through the
Domaniale de Champ woods in late October, and into the Laveline-
Corcieux Valley, the Nisei engineers had been handed the job of turning a mountain footpath into a supply road capable of supporting
truck traffic.

The 300-plus men who served in the 232nd were under the
command of Captain Pershing Nakada, a second-generation U.S.
Army man who had earned his mechanical engineering degree from
the University of Nebraska before the war. He was named for General
John J. Pershing, who had commanded the American Expeditionary

Force during World War I, and under whom Nakada's father had served as an orderly. The key engineering officers on Nakada's staff during World War II included Lieutenant Peter Iwatsu, a New Yorker who had graduated from the Massachusetts Institute of Technology, Lieutenant George Nagai, an engineering grad from Texas A&M, and four men with civil engineering degrees from the University of Hawaii: Lieutenant Francis Fujita, Lieutenant Gilbert Kobatake, Lieutenant Walter Matsumoto, and Lieutenant Yoshiharu Tsuji.

If the terrain was difficult for infantry to walk on, and virtually impossible for tanks to move across, one can easily imagine how difficult it must have been to build a road. The steep hillsides crossed by the narrow, winding trail rose as high as a thousand feet above the valley floor, making the road a major engineering challenge. On top of this, the engineers had to contend with many of the same obstacles as the infantry, including artillery barrages and enemy snipers—not to mention having to locate and remove land mines that the Germans had sown into the trail.

Occasionally, the Germans would infiltrate troops behind the American lines to ambush the engineers. The men would then have to trade picks and shovels for M1 rifles and submachine guns and become infantry soldiers. More often than not, many of the men would continue working on the road even as armed engineers were trading shots with the Germans. Indeed, the engineers captured twenty-seven German prisoners as they worked.

The men of the 232nd employed a variety of construction techniques. The driving rain and rivers of mud precluded building a simple dirt road in many places, so the men had to cut, split, and place logs to create a corduroy roadbed. Elsewhere, they were able to fill the road with gravel, and occasionally they used flat stones to cobble the road in the manner of the Romans who had built the first paved roads through the same region many centuries before.

Having built the road, the 232nd Engineer Combat Company were tasked with maintaining it as the tanks and heavy vehicles tore constantly at its surface. Working continuously from October 23 to

November 11, the engineers got their road up and running and *kept it open* to a continuous two-way flow, with troops and supplies moving up and wounded being brought back from the front. They sustained fifty-seven men dead or wounded, and endured unremitting rain and snow to keep their road operable. Thanks to the Nisei engineers, the U.S. Army had a line of communication through the heart of the deep forests of the Vosges Mountains from Bruyères all the way to the Meurthe River.

During the first week of November, even as the engineers were immersed in the backbreaking task of maintaining the supply road, the men of the 232nd were reassigned to support the combat battalions of the 442nd, which was in critical need of replacements. Beginning on the morning of November 6, the 1st Platoon of the 232nd officially relieved Company A of the 100th Battalion in a defensive sector near Biffontaine. The platoon conducted active patrols in cooperation with the 100th's Company C, filling in until Company F could take over.

Throughout this time, the combat troops of the 442nd remained in action, pushing ever deeper into the German defensive positions in the Vosges. Of particular note was the fighting in the steep and heavily wooded ridges near La Houssière, about five miles southeast of Biffontaine. It was here, on November 7, that Private First Class Joe Nishimoto earned a Distinguished Service Cross that was later upgraded to a Medal of Honor.

His action came at the climax of a three-day stalemate during which the GIs had been attempting to dislodge the Germans from a strongly defended ridge. Nishimoto, as acting squad leader, crawled forward through a heavily mined and booby-trapped area to destroy a machine-gun nest with a well-placed hand grenade. Circling to the rear of another machine-gun position, he opened fire with his submachine gun at point-blank range, killing one German gunner and wounding another. He then chased the surviving Germans off the ridge.

That night, for the first time since the Nisei men had reached the Vosges, the rain turned to snow. As if there was any doubt after weeks of freezing rain, winter had at last come to the Vosges Mountains.

According to the regimental log, it was on November 8 that the 36th Infantry Division headquarters asked the 442nd's intelligence officer whether the regiment was "pushing" south from La Houssière. The regimental officer snidely replied: "I might call it patrolling, not pushing, when one company has four men and another seventeen men."

The next day, the 442nd Regimental Combat Team received word that it was *finally* to be pulled out of the line for a rest. By then, the men had been in almost ceaseless combat for nearly a month. The regimental operations officer asked the division: "Will you check with the colonel and find out when we will come back [into the line]? It makes a difference with us for if it's only one or two days we'd rather stay [and rest] where we are."

"I checked and the general [Dahlquist] says he wants you to move out for you need some rest," came the reply. "He thinks you will be out longer than you think."

This was true. The 442nd was leaving the front lines in France for good. By evening, nearly all elements of the 442nd had been pulled back to the rest areas.

On November 12, the men assembled for one final inspection by General Dahlquist. As the band played the national anthem, Dahlquist snarled at Lieutenant Colonel Miller, the regimental commander, that he was disappointed by the turnout for the inspection. He saw fewer than a third of the number of men that should constitute a regimental combat team, and he reminded Miller that he had ordered the *entire* unit to turn out.

Miller replied that this *was* the entire unit. The 442nd had arrived in the Vosges in mid-October with 2,943 combat soldiers. They had lost 161 killed in action and 43 missing. Of the more than 2,000 who had been wounded, 882 had been pulled out of action with serious injuries, and at least that many were in various army hospitals throughout France with lesser wounds.

"We were really beat up," Lawson Sakai explained later. "There was no chance to get replacements because the 442nd needed to have

Americans of Japanese ancestry, and they were still in training at Camp Shelby. We had no replacements except the walking wounded. If you were ambulatory, you had gone back to the unit."

It was in the Vosges that the 100th Battalion earned the second of its three Presidential Unit Citations, being, in the words of the official document, "cited for outstanding accomplishment in combat during the period 15 to 30 October 1944, near Bruyères, Biffontaine, and in the Forêt Domaniale de Champ, France. During a series of actions that played a telling part in the 442nd Regimental Team's operation which spearheaded a divisional attack on the Seventh Army front, this unit displayed extraordinary courage, endurance, and soldierly skill."

The 2nd Battalion of the 442nd would later also be given a Presidential Unit Citation that mentioned "outstanding performance of duty in action," on October 19, 1944, near Bruyères, and for its role in the Lost Battalion rescue on October 28 and 29, as well as for later actions in Italy in April 1945.

The 3rd Battalion was given a Presidential Unit Citation, which extolled the "intrepidity and fearless courage" of the Nisei GIs as they took down Suicide Hill and rescued the Lost Battalion.

"The mission was more difficult than it first appeared," the citation described with a touch of understatement. "For four days the battalion fought the stubborn enemy who was determined to stop all attempts to rescue the besieged battalion. . . . Despite effective enemy fire the determined men pressed the assault and closed in with the enemy nearing the enemy machine-gun and machine-pistol positions, some of the men charged the gun emplacements with Thompson submachine guns or BARs, killing or seriously wounding the enemy gun crew, but themselves sprawling dead over the enemy positions they had just neutralized. Completely unnerved by the vicious bayonet charge, the enemy fled in confusion after making a desperate stand. Though seriously depleted in manpower, the battalion hurled back two determined enemy counterattacks, and after reducing a heavily mined roadblock finally established contact with the besieged battalion."

Companies F and L, the O'Connor Task Force, also received a

Presidential Unit Citation for its actions near Belmont, which noted "the fearless determination, daring, and intrepidity displayed by the officers and enlisted men."

A Presidential Unit Citation issued to the 111th Engineer Combat Battalion, with 232nd Engineer Combat Company attached, would round out a total of four such citations awarded to the Nisei GIs for their actions in the Vosges. (A subsequent fifth citation would mention actions both in the Vosges and in Italy in 1945.) As for individuals, there were countless heroes during those awful weeks, and among them Barney Hajiro, Joe Nishimoto, James Okubo, and George Sakato would one day be awarded Medals of Honor.

General Alexander Patch, the Seventh Army commander, certainly had the men of the 442nd in mind when he wrote in commendation of the 36th Infantry Division: "In the Vosges foothills, you dislodged a desperate and skillful foe from positions which gave him every natural advantage. You fought for weeks . . . to pave the way for a breakthrough. Despite unfavorable weather, terrain and savage resistance, you pushed on with tenacious courage."

In the preceding three months, Patch's Seventh Army had experienced what was, in the context of wartime, the best of times and the worst of times. The month following their invasion of southern France on August 15, 1944, the Seventh Army had advanced quickly and had suffered few casualties—relative to the fighting elsewhere, such as in northern France during the Overlord landings and the recent breakout from Normandy, and in Italy where the fighting had been especially brutal for the past year. With this in mind, the GIs called this month after the August 15 invasion the "Champagne Campaign."

By the time the men of the 442nd Regimental Combat Team arrived in France in mid-October, however, the figurative champagne had stopped flowing, as the easy days were abruptly superseded by some of the hardest fighting of the war.

The Nisei GIs may have missed the original Champagne Campaign, but they had their own three months later. When they finally were pulled out of the darkness of the Vosges and redeployed to the sunny south of France, the men found themselves on the Cote d'Azur, where the beautiful people of prewar—and postwar—French society came to bask in the warm water beneath the warm sun. It was the closest thing to the climate of Hawaii or southern California that the Japanese American solders had seen in Europe. The contrast between this locale and the harsh environment of winter in the Vosges couldn't have been more extreme.

Most of the various elements of the 442nd reached Nice during the third week of November 1944, traveling by truck from Bruyères, by way of Dijon and Valence. The 442nd was assigned to the Department of Alpes-Maritimes—a 4,300–square kilometer administrative district roughly equivalent to a United States county—located in the southeastern corner of France. The Nisei GIs occupied a line extending inland from the Mediterranean Sea at Menton to the mountain village of Sospel, about a dozen miles inland. The first major French city west of the Italian border, Menton is about thirty miles east of Nice and about nine miles east of the tiny principality of Monaco. Though Menton was a Cote d'Azur resort town, its location on the border between Allied-occupied France and German-occupied Italy made it potentially dangerous. There was no large-scale combat in the Menton-Sospel area during the winter of 1944–45, but both sides continuously patrolled the border, occasionally exchanging shots and mortar fire.

The job of the 442nd for the four months that they were posted to the Alpes-Maritimes was to defend the border against incursions by the occasional German reconnaissance patrol and to prevent a possible, albeit unlikely, major German invasion.

As the nickname suggests, their Champagne Campaign was largely a period of rest and relaxation for the Nisei GIs. Leave to visit the pleasures and nightlife of Nice was frequent, and the men were generally well received by the French population in the area along the border. The friendly Japanese Americans were a far cry from the arrogant and often bullying German occupation troops. The men of the 442nd even helped to put together Christmas parties, complete with plenty of

American chocolate for the kids. For the men of the 232nd Engineer Combat Company, the months in southern France included both laying mines and deactivating mines and booby traps rigged by German engineers. The 232nd also strung more than ten thousand yards of barbed wire and built trestle bridges at both Sospel and Menton.

During the 442nd's months in the south of France, the 232nd is perhaps best remembered by the regiment for its resourcefulness in having created an imaginative shower unit for the men. The hot-water tank was salvaged from a brewery, and the water was heated by parts from a German mobile electric power plant. They used a jeep motor to power a German-made dynamo that was capable of producing 380 volts of electricity. Other parts included a control valve from a French welding torch, an electric blower from the ventilating system of a old French fort, a fuel-pump motor from an Italian self-propelled gun, and showerheads and hoses from an abandoned resort hotel. This mobile unit was a tremendous boost to the morale of men who had so recently gone for weeks without a bath—not to mention a hot shower!

On December 19, the engineers, with the help of some of the other 442nd men, even retrieved a German one-man submarine that had become beached on a sandbar in the Mediterranean near Menton. It was reminiscent of the incident three years earlier when Sergeant Thomas Tsubota and other members of the Hawaii National Guard captured the one-man Japanese submarine Ha-19 when it had ran aground at Waimanalo on the east coast of Oahu on December 8, 1941.

"A couple of us waded out to it," Staff Sergeant Frank Seto recalled with a chuckle as he described capturing the sub near Menton. "The German who was inside was asking us to push him to get him off the sandbar so he could get away, but we didn't. I guess he thought we were on his side. Finally he came out, and all of us were trying to get souvenirs off the submarine. I got part of a compass, but the officers made us put everything back because the engineers had to study it."

The submarine was later placed on long-term display near the royal palace in nearby Monaco.

The dangers of this deceptively sunny front were underscored by an incident on November 30, shortly after the 442nd arrived. On that day a German tank made a hit-and-run raid against the Company K bivouac at Sospel. Without being detected, the tank dashed across the border, shot up a group of men who were probably less vigilant than they should have been, and quickly withdrew. Both Corporal Larry Miura and Sergeant Kenji Sugawara were killed in this episode.

The people of Sospel later erected a memorial in the courtyard of the school. The marble tablet recalling the young "Militaires Hawaiiens" (Hawaiian soldiers) still remains. Two additional "Hawaiian" soldiers from Company G, Private First Class Herbert Kondo and Lieutenant Minoru Kurata, were killed while on patrol on January 16, and an average of twenty men were wounded in action each month from December through February during a campaign that was much easier than the hell that the men had endured in October and early November.

As they patrolled the border and continued to take casualties, the 442nd Regimental Combat Team was being slowly rebuilt from the terrible losses suffered in the Vosges. Of the nearly 2,000 sons of Japanese immigrants wounded in France, only 265 returned to the unit, but there was a new generation of 1,214 replacement troops. As had been the case with the original makeup of the 442nd, many of the new arrivals were from the relocation camps, eager to be part of the outfit. In the months since the unit had first gone into combat, the Nisei soldiers had achieved the status of folk heroes back home. Local and national media carried stories that praised their heroism and determination. Even behind the insulting barbed wire of the camps, families were proud to point to *their* boys in the 442nd.

CHAPTER 18

The Spring Offensive

T he 442nd Regimental Combat Team had suffered greatly during the campaign in the Vosges in October and November 1944. They had withstood a staggering casualty rate but kept on fighting until Bruyères and Biffontaine were securely in American hands—and until the Lost Battalion was lost no more.

By mid-March 1945, the four months of rest and rebuilding came to an end, and the 442nd was mobilized to return to large-scale combat operations. Except for the 522nd Field Artillery Battalion, which was detached on March 9 and reassigned to the 63rd Infantry Division for the attack across the Siegfried Line into Germany, the 442nd Regimental Combat Team was earmarked to return to an old and familiar front, the Gothic Line in Italy. The regiment had made an excellent reputation for itself in Italy during 1944, and the Fifth Army wanted it back.

On March 20, 1945, about a week after the artillerymen were reassigned, the remainder of the 442nd shipped out aboard a Landing Ship, Tank (LST), bound for Livorno, a city in whose liberation the unit had participated eight months before. The 442nd was now commanded by Colonel Virgil Miller, who had taken over when Pence was injured in the Vosges, while Lieutenant Colonel James Conley had taken over command of the 100th Infantry Battalion from Singles.

The 3rd Infantry Battalion continued under the command of Pursall, who had led them during their rescue of the Lost Battalion.

Much to the chagrin of the Allied leadership, the front had changed little since the 442nd had left Italy for France in September 1944. Even as the Nisei men were pulling out to redeploy, the 15th Army Group was launching Operation Olive, a maximum effort by two Allied field armies to break through the Gothic Line. It ultimately ground to a disappointing and anticlimactic halt as the winter fell across the Apennines.

As they had the previous winter, when their advance stalled at the German Gustav Line south of Rome, the Allies halted their offensive operations, dug in, and waited for spring. Winter in the Apennines was no time and place for offensive operations, especially when facing so formidable a barrier as the Gothic Line.

It is axiomatic that high ground is a force multiplier for defenders, and there were few places in Europe where this axiom was better illustrated in World War II than in the Gothic Line. Between La Spezia on the west coast and Pesaro on the east, virtually the entire 120-mile breadth of Italy is mountainous, and it was across this line that the Germans had spent the autumn and winter building the Gothic Line.

Organization Todt, the German military engineering unit responsible for fortifications, drilled bunkers out of solid rock, using 15,000 Italian laborers to construct gun positions and other fortifications along the ridgelines from coast to coast. This included sites for 2,376 machine-gun nests, each one about a hundred yards from the next, to provide interlocking fire. The terrain that was covered by these gun positions was mostly open hillside with only the occasional patch of brush to provide cover for infantrymen attempting the perilous task of trying to climb the slopes. Such a defensive line in this terrain was as close to being impregnable as it could be. The fact that fortifications were cut from solid rock and that they were in such rugged terrain prevented them from being attacked effectively with either artillery or aircraft.

It was against this formidable barrier that the Allies would launch their spring offensive. General Mark Clark, a man who had been outspoken in his admiration of the Nisei soldiers when he commanded the United States Fifth Army, had now assumed overall theater command in Italy. He had moved up from Fifth Army command, replacing Field Marshal Alexander. Meanwhile, General Truscott, formerly the United States IV Corps commander, had moved up to command the Fifth Army.

For the spring offensive west of the Apennines, Clark and Truscott planned to use the United States II Corps to launch a major thrust north of Florence toward Bologna. While the Americans flanked Bologna from the west, the British Eighth Army would do so on the east. Reaching and enveloping Bologna would put Allied forces into the broad Po Valley, where the Allies would face no natural barriers of consequence until they reached the Alps.

As II Corps attacked, the other United States corps, VI Corps, would attempt to pierce the Gothic Line at its western anchor, along the coast between Pisa and the big Italian naval base city of La Spezia, which was fifty-five miles northwest of Pisa. The front was now about thirty miles northwest of Pisa.

The 442nd was assigned directly to the Fifth Army command structure, but for operations the unit was attached to the 92nd Infantry Division, which was in turn one of the elements of VI Corps. Commanded by Major General Edward Almond, the 92nd had arrived in Italy at the end of August 1944, and was the only mostly African American division to serve with the U.S. Army in World War II. Its insignia, a black buffalo on an olive drab patch, made reference to the service of African-American units such as 9th and 10th Cavalry Regiments in the Indian Wars. In the nineteenth century, the Indians had referred to the African American troopers as "Buffalo Soldiers," and the nickname was adopted by the troops themselves.

On March 25, the Nisei men returned to Pisa, which they had helped to capture nine months earlier. Here, with the western spur of the Apennines visible in the distance from the top of Pisa's famous leaning tower, they were briefed on their role in breaking through the Gothic Line.

Essentially, for the six weeks that remained in World War II, the 442nd would be moving in a northwesterly direction through steep and rugged terrain on a line parallel to the coast and about ten miles inland. Most of their engagements for the rest of the war would be fought in or near small- to medium-sized hill towns along this corridor. Other units, especially the 473rd Infantry Regiment of the 92nd Infantry Division, would be tasked with pushing north along the coastal road on the 442nd's left flank.

As the 442nd moved forward initially, it did so with its 2nd Battalion in the center, the 3rd Battalion on the right flank, and the 100th Battalion on the left, adjacent to the 473rd Infantry Regiment.

The 442nd's initial objective would be on a steep line of hills in the Apuan Alps, known in Italian as *Alpi Apuane*. This spur of the Apennines overlooks the coastal cities of Massa and Carrara, which are located about forty miles and forty-four miles, respectively, north of Pisa.

Because the coastal roads pass through Massa and its environs, these towns were literally the gateway to La Spezia and northern Italy for the IV Corps offensive. Having Massa in American hands would ensure the smooth movement of Allied forces along the coast, and control of the mountain roads radiating from Carrara was a prerequisite for controlling the coastal roads.

Situated slightly more inland than Massa, Carrara is a city that has been famed for centuries because its marble quarries fueled Italian art and architecture from Roman times to the Renaissance and beyond. As with Pisa, Carrara's name is known around the world. It has been famous since ancient days, before the rise of Imperial Rome, for the white or blue-gray marble of exquisite quality that is taken from the quarries in the mountains above and around the city. Carrara marble was used to build the Pantheon and Trajan's Column in Rome, and during the Renaissance sculptures such as the works of Michelangelo were carved from this prized stone. The fascination with Carrara marble continued into the twentieth century, although during the distractions of the 1940s, there was a great deal less sculpting going on than in other times.

For the American GIs, Carrara's marble would present an altogether different challenge. As they moved into the mountains around Carrara, the Americans quickly discerned the downside of operating in this area. When they attempted to dig foxholes most places, they discovered that a foot or so below the surface soil, the ground was solid marble!

The line of hills near Carrara that the 442nd would have to capture included, from west to east, Monte Cerreto, Monte Folgorito, Monte Carchio, Monte Belvedere, and Monte Altissimo. However, to call these "hills" is to belie their true nature. They were steep, most with sixty-degree slopes, and they were tall. Many topped 3,000 feet, rising from valley floors that were not far above sea level. There were also a series of smaller hills, which the Americans code-named Georgia, Florida, and Ohio 1, 2, and 3. Belvedere was considered to be especially important because it was the key observation and artillery spotting point covering the roads leading into and through Carrara and Massa.

Assaulting the enemy positions in these hills presented an immense challenge, but Colonel Miller, along with Conley and Pursall, developed what they decided was the only plan that had a ghost of a chance of working—a surprise attack at night. To assault the Gothic Line in such steep terrain without the element of surprise would have been suicidal; therefore, they would have to go at night. In this terrain, the difficulties of operating at night are obvious, but the officers were sure that the Nisei GIs were up to the challenge. The idea was to begin with a two-battalion pincer movement. Then the 2nd Infantry Battalion would assault Monte Belvedere when the initial objectives had been secured by the other battalions.

Beginning on the evening of Tuesday, April 3, the troops were on the move. They had been trucked to the village of Pietrasanta, in the hills about eight miles southeast of Massa, which was far as the deuce-

and-a-half trucks could travel without alerting the Germans to the sound of the troop movement. From here, the men shouldered their packs to continue the march on foot. Lugging heavy cases of ammunition on top of their other equipment, the Nisei men moved quietly into the foothills, guided by Italian resistance operatives who knew the lay of the land.

That night, the 3rd Infantry Battalion took up a position to the southeast of Monte Folgorito, while the 100th Infantry Battalion circled to the west of 4,300-foot Monte Cerreto. The 3rd Battalion passed southeast of Monte Folgorito, reaching the village of Azzano by morning.

Early on Wednesday, the 100th Infantry Battalion relieved the American troops that had been holding ground southwest of Folgorito, and the Nisei GIs concealed themselves from the German observers high up on the slopes. They rested through the day, and after dark, they moved out again, rounding the flank of Monte Cerreto and moving toward the hilltop village of Seravezza.

Stealthily, Company I and Company L of the 3rd Infantry Battalion, together with the Company M machine gunners, made their way up the steep pass east of Seravezza that separated Monte Folgorito and Monte Carchio. By dawn on Thursday, they had reached the top of the ridge line and had outflanked the German defensive positions. The enemy was now between the positions occupied by the two Nisei battalions.

As the GIs made their way up Monte Folgorito, Company L's 3rd Platoon was in the lead. Shig Kizuka, the Nisei GI from Watsonville who had told his parents that he was drafted—rather than volunteering—into the 442nd, recalled that "it was so dark, we were hanging on to each other so that we wouldn't get separated. We were told that if anyone falls or gets lost, we should just keep moving. We taped our dogtags together so that they wouldn't rattle and make noise."

The 3rd Platoon finally reached their objective at first light after eight hours of stumbling through the darkness. Shig Kizuka was in the lead with two other men. "I saw a bunker on the left," he recalled. "And I said to myself, 'This is it.'"

The Germans had not expected Americans to be able to scale the steep, overgrown slopes of Monte Folgorito in the darkness, so they were taken by surprise. "If they'd been awake, that would have been a different story," Kizuka chuckled. In thirty-two minutes, Company L had done what the Fifth Army had failed to do in five months, they had punched an irreparable hole in the Gothic Line.

At 5:00 A.M. on April 5, the 3rd Battalion companies attacked westward toward the base of Monte Folgorito, but the Germans managed to launch a counterattack. The Nisei GIs rallied, with Company L defeating the German assault as Company I pushed the enemy back toward Monte Carchio.

Throughout the day, the Nisei GIs continued to battle their way up Monte Folgorito and the adjacent hills. Private First Class Hiro Asai was with the 2nd Platoon of Company E during the assault on Folgorito. It would have been a difficult climb under any circumstances, but the German mortar fire made it that much worse. As the day wore on, the weather grew hotter and the GIs were thirsty. Lack of water became an important issue for the men. "You come to realize how important water is when you're without it for three or four days," Asai said. "We'd come to a water hole and try to take a drink. We'd drink through a handkerchief in case it was contaminated. You'd get just a gulp before the next guy was on top of you to get his."

"It was very hot and I was very thirsty," Don Seki of Company L said with a laugh. "There was a stream, so I drank a lot of water. I walked up the stream and holy smokes, there's a big dead ox. I walked further upstream, and there's a dead German! I drank that water, but somehow I never got sick."

Hiro Asai recalls how they spotted a spring near the trail and how the platoon took turns filling their canteens. Asai filled his canteen without difficulty, but the next man wasn't so lucky. "A mortar shell hit the spring, and wounded the guy," Asai said. "Two of us had to take him back down the mountain on a stretcher. It was so steep that we wound up having to slide on our butts most of the way. Finally, we were relieved by some stretcher bearers who took him to an aid station. Then we had to work our way *back up* the mountain. Company E was moving so fast by then that it took two days to catch up again."

By now the GIs were moving too quickly, and pushing so deep into German territory that they ran the risk of becoming overextended. "Our patrol was moving from hill to hill, when all hell broke loose," Hiro Asai explained. "They were shooting at us from the side, and there was no place to take shelter. Half of us got wounded with shrapnel."

Meanwhile, on the left flank, the 100th Infantry Battalion, spearheaded by Company A, attacked the Germans along the ridge line which ran southwest from Monte Folgorito toward the coast. Here the GIs found themselves facing mine fields in addition to the interlocking fields of fire from the entrenched German machine gunners up on the slopes of the ridge.

Pinned down, the Company A men began taking heavy casualties. When his squad leader was hit and severely wounded, Private First Class Sadao Munemori rose to the occasion. He took command of the squad and led them through the German mine field to a point just thirty yards from one of the machine-gun positions.

Many of those around him were new men, replacements who had never tasted combat before, but Munemori was a veteran. He had arrived in Italy nearly a year earlier and had joined the 100th Infantry Battalion as a replacement during the fighting at Anzio. He had seen action in Italy, then France, and now he was back in the sights of the German machine gunners on a lonely hill in the Apennines.

It was a long way from Los Angeles, California, where Sadao Munemori was born twenty-two years earlier, and where his Japanese immigrant parents had raised their three sons and two daughters. They had grown up against the backdrop of old country lore, and an age-old culture from across the Pacific, but they had grown up American, more Californian than Japanese.

When he was eighteen, Sadao's father passed away, and as would have been the case whether or not he was the eldest son of a Japanese immigrant, or of a fifth-generation European American, Sadao had to take on the role of head of the family. He was working as an auto mechanic in December 1941 when the United States suddenly found itself at war. As with other young men his age, Sadao Munemori felt that it was *his* country that had been attacked at Pearl Harbor and he tried to enlist in the armed forces. However, unlike the other young men his age, the recruiter looked at him and saw the face of the nation that had attacked at Pearl Harbor.

In February 1942, not long after Sadao had been rejected by the recruiter and classified 4-C as an enemy alien, Executive Order 9066 went into effect, and the Munemori family found themselves abruptly uprooted. As with thousands of Southern California Japanese Americans, they were ordered to surrender for internment. After a five-hour bus ride, they arrived at the Manzanar relocation camp in the high desert country of California's desolate Owens Valley.

Within a few months, things had begun to turn. The patriotic young man who had tried to enlist now found himself recruited by the Military Intelligence Service. However, he yearned to be part of the real action, and he applied for a transfer to the infantry. After training at Camp Shelby, Mississippi, he headed overseas with an assignment to the 100th Infantry Battalion.

Now it was Thursday, April 5, 1945, and here he was on an Italian hillside with machine-gun rounds whistling all around his head, and fellow Nisei soldiers—many of them with families still at Manzanar or the other camps—lying wounded and bleeding in the dirt. Everyone was frightened. He could see it in their eyes. Munemori knew that he had to act. He had a couple of hand grenades, and he gathered up a few more from the men around him. Armed with half a dozen, he left his position and crawled forward, toward the two machine-gun nests that were sweeping the hillside with their deadly fusillades.

He managed to reach a point about halfway to the enemy. He stood, tossed a grenade, and ducked down. He tossed another, and another. The first machine-gun nest exploded in a dirty orange fireball, but gunfire from the other poured down on Munemori. He lobbed another grenade, and then another. With the sixth grenade, the second machine-gun nest erupted with an ugly explosion, then fell silent. For a moment, this slope of ridgeline was quiet.

Other German gunners from farther away took up the slack, but Munemori managed to reach the relative safety of a shell crater where two fellow Company A Nisei GIs had taken refuge. Just as he hunkered down, he felt something hit his helmet and bounce into the crater between the two other soldiers.

A German hand grenade!

Munemori reacted instinctively. It was too far away for him to reach down, grab it, and throw it away, so he made the only other choice. He jumped onto the grenade, covering it with his body. The explosion literally blew him apart, but his body absorbed enough of the blast that he was the only casualty. The other two men survived. Within an hour, the 100th Infantry Battalion had taken the top of the ridge west of Monte Folgorito, and the surviving defenders had surrendered. It was because of what had happened here that Sadao Munemori became the first son of Japanese immigrants to be written up for the Medal of Honor.

Back in California's Owens Valley, Sadao Munemori's family would remain incarcerated at Manzanar until September 21, 1945, three weeks after the surrender of the Japanese Empire, but they were living in San Pedro, California by the time his posthumous Medal of Honor was awarded in March 1946.

As the 100th Infantry Battalion moved forward, the 3rd Battalion was ensconced on the peak of Monte Folgorito, but they were taking a beating. They faced not only machine-gun fire, but heavy artillery fire from the large coastal fortifications at nearby La Spezia, and from mortar positions in the adjacent hills. By the end of Thursday, supported by artillery and a well-placed air strike, the 3rd Battalion had taken and held their objective against vicious German resistance. It had cost them seventeen men killed in action and eighty-three wounded. By this same time, elements of all three Nisei battalions had linked upon Monte Cerreto.

On Friday, April 6, the battle resumed, with the 442nd Regimental Combat Team continuing to push the Germans back, and the Germans continuing to make them pay for every yard. By noon, most of the ridge west of Monte Folgorito was in Nisei hands, except for a few isolated pockets where the German defenders were surrounded. Company F of the 100th Infantry Battalion had teamed up with Company I of the 3rd Battalion to capture Monte Carchio, while Company L of the 3rd secured Monte Cerreto. Most of the smaller hills code-named for American states were also in Nisei hands.

On the morning of April 6, the 2nd Battalion had followed the 3rd Battalion's earlier route through the steep pass east of Seravezza and circled north of Monte Folgorito toward the heavily defended Monte Belvedere, the pivotal high ground that controlled access to Massa. By Saturday, only Monte Altissimo and Monte Belvedere, among the 442nd's objectives, remained in German hands.

With the 3rd Battalion and the 100th Battalion having borne the brunt of the 442nd Regimental Combat Team action early in the week, it would be the 2nd Battalion that would be tasked with the capture of Monte Belvedere. After some initial actions on Friday aimed at probing enemy defenses, the main assault would jump off Saturday morning. Utilizing high ground that was already in American hands, the Nisei GIs of the 2nd Infantry Battalion would launch their attack from Monte Folgorito.

If the German resistance had been ferocious on Thursday on Friday, it was doubly so on Saturday. The Gothic Line defenders had been surprised on Thursday, but by Saturday, those on Belvedere had had two days of watching the action on the adjacent peaks to prepare for the Nisei.

As the first men of the 2nd Infantry Battalion moved forward at dawn, German mortar and machine gun fire cut them to ribbons. The air was filled with a hail of bullets, shrapnel, and fire. As the Americans took cover from the tracers, mortar shells churned up the rocks and dirt around them. In a particularly precarious place were the men of Company F. The interlocking fire from three machine-gun nests was so intense that nobody dared to raise his head. Nobody, that is, except Technical Sergeant Yukio Okutsu. He could see that the fire from the machine-gun nest just thirty yards up the hill could eventually wipe out the entire company unless something was done quickly.

Okutsu raised his head, and then his arm. In rapid succession, he heaved two hand grenades at the German gunners, and suddenly the three machine-gun nests raking the Nisei had been reduced to just two. Using the boulders littering the hillside as cover, he dashed up the hill, tossing another grenade into the second machine-gun nest, wounding two enemy soldiers. He then turned his attention to the third enemy strongpoint, advancing through withering fire.

A bullet was heard to strike his helmet, and the serious young man who had grown up on the Hawaii Island of Kauai crumpled into the dry, gravelly soil of Tuscany.

He was down, but he wasn't out.

Moments later, Yukio Okutsu miraculously staggered to his feet. The bullet had not penetrated his helmet, but merely glanced off it. He had been stunned and knocked down, but nothing more. The sergeant stood up and resumed his single-handed assault, his Thompson submachine gun blazing. Okutsu captured the machine-gun nest and its entire crew of four. Many, if not most, of the men of Company F owed their lives to him.

By the end of the day on Saturday, the 442nd Regimental Combat Team had captured Belvedere and had succeeded in not only piercing, but *breaking through*, the allegedly impregnable Gothic Line.

For his heroism, Yukio Okutsu was awarded one of the fifty-two Distinguished Service Crosses that were earned by men of the 442nd Regimental Combat Team in World War II. He received his medal in December 1945, but he donated it to the Kauai Museum. "My father was like that—a real generous man," his son Wayne Okutsu said in an interview with the *Honolulu Star-Bulletin* many years later. "He just wanted to give Kauai something to be proud of."

Born on November 3, 1921, Yukio had grown up in Koloa, on Kauai's eastern shore. He had enlisted in the 442nd Regimental Combat Team, and had arrived in Italy at the end of 1943. "I guess because we were under suspicion, we had to prove ourselves," he later recalled. "I guess most of us got pretty good, and we went all-out and got the job done. Most of us were volunteers, so we knew what we were getting into."

After the war, he trained as a watchmaker in Kansas, but later returned to Hawaii, where he and his wife Elaine settled on the Big Island of Hawaii. He worked for many years as a mechanic for the county of Hawaii, and he retired in 1985 as superintendent of the county parking meters branch. The hero of Monte Belvedere was recalled as a quiet man who enjoyed tinkering with watches and tending his two acres of anthuriums.

Several of the other men from the 442nd Regimental Combat Team also retired to the Big Island, where they continued to spend time with one another. Every Tuesday and Thursday morning for years, Okutsu would take his old friend Toshio "Hoxie" Nagami on a walk. Wounded in combat, Nagami later suffered a stroke, which left him a quadriplegic.

"They never lost sight of Hoxie. As more of them retired, more [of the men from the old wartime unit] joined the walk," his son, Wayne Okutsu recalled. "He told me he'd never forget his buddies from the war."

In June 2000, Okutsu's Distinguished Service Cross was among those that was upgraded to the Medal of Honor. However, he was one of just a half dozen men so honored who would actually to live to see the day.

"I knew they were going to upgrade some of the medals, but I didn't know if I was going to be in there," he told the *Honolulu Star-Bulletin*. "I never thought about it. What the heck, we're too damned old already."

On August 24, 2003, stomach cancer did what dozens of German gunners had failed to do fifty-eight years earlier, and Yukio Okutsu passed away at the Hilo Medical Center at the age of eighty-one.

"He's bigger than life already," said Wayne Okutsu. "He's bigger than all of us. He always was."

The same could be said of the hundreds of men from his wartime outfit, who volunteered under the most difficult of circumstances, and who distinguished themselves bravely in situations that most of us cannot imagine.

CHAPTER 19

The Irony of Dachau

As the infantry and engineer units of the 442nd Regimental Combat Team were battling their way through the Gothic Line in the mountains above Massa and Carrara, the Nisei artillerymen of the 522nd Field Artillery Battalion were three hundred miles north, across the Alps, fighting their way through the Siegfried Line into the Third Reich itself.

Nearly seven years in the making, the Siegfried Line, also known as the Westwall, was a complex network of barriers and fortifications supported by artillery and machine guns that covered Germany's entire western approach. Though most of it was not in the extremely rugged sort of terrain that made the Gothic Line so forbidding, the Westwall was manned by zealous German troops defending not just ground in a foreign country, but the border of their own homeland.

For the U.S. Army divisions that would be pounding their way through the Siegfried Line, artillery support would be essential, and the 63rd Infantry Division would be the first of several divisions to have the benefit of the 522nd, an outfit with one of the best reputations in the Seventh Army. The Nisei gunners were well known for being one of the most efficient battalions on the Western Front, and General Sandy Patch wanted to have *their* 105mm howitzers backing *his* march into Hitler's heartland.

For the next several weeks, the 522nd would function as a sort of fire brigade, being attached to various divisions within the Seventh Army as they needed extra artillery support for a specific objective. Detached from the 442nd on March 9, 1945, the 522nd caught up with the 63rd Infantry Division three days later. The division had just completed its difficult actions at Gudingen, a town on the Franco-German border south of Saarbrücken, and was now tasked with operations against the Siegfried Line.

The 522nd supported the 63rd as it captured Ormesheim on March 15, and as it finally broke through the Siegfried Line near Sankt Ingbert five days later. On March 21, with the 63rd through the Westwall, the 522nd was reassigned to support the crossing of the Rhine River by the 45th "Thunderbird" Infantry Division between Worms and Hamm, which occurred on March 26.

The next short assignment for the 522nd was to aid the 44th Infantry Division in its battle to capture Mannheim. The Nisei gunners followed the division across the Neckar River to attack and capture Mannheim in a two-day battle on March 28 and 29. The Nisei men then dashed back to rejoin the 63rd Infantry Division about fifteen miles southeast of Mannheim. On March 30, the 522nd aided in the capture of Heidelberg and in the crossing of the Neckar by the 63rd near Mosbach.

The Nisei artillery was next dispatched nearly a hundred miles east to support the 4th Infantry Division in capturing the crossroads village of Aub, near Würzburg. The battalion would remain with the 4th until the fighting in Germany came to a close. Known as the "Ivy Division," which is a pun on the Roman numeral "IV," the division had been one of the first U.S. Army units ashore at Normandy in June 1944 and it had seen action in the Battle of the Bulge in December. It was transferred from General George Patton's Third Army to Patch's Seventh Army in early March.

The 4th Infantry Division pressed on toward Würzburg, and by April 3, the Nisei gunners of the 522nd helped the division establish a bridgehead across the Main River. As they turned south toward the great city of Munich, capital of Bavaria, the reputation of the 522nd was growing. Perhaps it was the fact that they bounced around from assignment to assignment so often, but it was said that the 522nd could pull into an area, set up their howitzers, and complete their appointed barrage before gunners from the adjacent battalion could get off their first shot. By the time that the war ended, the 522nd had fired in excess of 11,000 artillery shells while serving under the command of at least seven divisions.

On April 29, three days after crossing the Danube River, the 522nd Field Artillery Battalion was among the many army units operating throughout Bavaria, facing little opposition and sensing that the end of the war was close at hand. Indeed, Adolf Hitler was, at that very moment, cringing in his Berlin bunker and twenty-four hours from committing suicide.

Among the detachments on the move that morning was a jeepful of forward observers from the 522nd's Battery C. They were reconnoitering the terrain, looking for possible targets for the battalion's howitzers. Among this team was a young staff sergeant from Montana named George Oiye.

The story of George's early years in Montana was a tale straight out of the Old West that could not have been farther from those of his fellow Nisei who grew up in places like Hawaii or California. He was born in 1922 in a log cabin on the continental divide on a February day when it was 40 degrees below zero outside. The nearest settlement was several miles away on homemade snowshoes. George's Issei father later worked in the Northern Pacific Railway roundhouse in Helena before taking a job at a cement plant in Trident, Montana, where George grew up. When George was in high school, his parents bought a twenty-three-acre truck farm near Logan, where members of the family would reside for the next five decades. Like anyone else growing up around these parts in the 1930s, George attended high school at Three Forks. By Montana standards, Three Forks was a major population center, boasting nine hundred people in 1940, the year that George graduated. He went on to attend Montana State College (now

Montana State University) in nearby Bozeman, majoring in mechanical and aeronautical engineering, subjects which would one day set him on his path to a future career. However, before he could realize that career, World War II intervened.

Oiye was in his second year at Bozeman when Pearl Harbor was attacked. A day earlier, he had been just another guy from a hick town north of Three Forks, but suddenly he was the enemy. Montana was a very lonely place for a person with a Japanese face. The landlord at the rooming house where George lived told him to leave, and he was nearly expelled from Montana State. Two months later, Executive Order 9066 was signed on George's twentieth birthday. It affected only Japanese Americans living in the coastal states, so Montana Nisei were safe from its draconian provisions. However, George's sister Peggy was living in California at the time, and she was interned.

In order to prove his loyalty, George Oiye, like so many other Nisei his age, tried to enlist in the U.S. Army Air Forces, but his 4-C draft classification made that impossible. A couple of his professors at Montana State wrote letters on his behalf, and finally he was accepted—not as an airman but as an artilleryman. After training at Camp Shelby, he was sent overseas to join the 522nd.

That morning in April 1945, as Hitler was contemplating suicide, Sergeant George Oiye was on the road about seventy-five miles as the crow flies from the Nazi leader's alpine retreat in the mountains above the Bavarian village of Berchtesgaden. The American GIs, and their leaders as well, had been speculating that Hitler might be hiding *here* rather than in Berlin. A lot of the GIs, and probably their leaders, too, were discussing what they would do if they were the ones to actually catch Hitler.

Even though it was the end of April, there was still snow on the ground, and the 522nd gunners in the jeep noticed some curious mounds along the road. They pulled over to investigate, and beneath the snow, the Nisei men were startled to discover human bodies. They were the remains of people who appeared to have starved to death.

"We didn't know who they were, or why they were there," Oiye told journalist Tara Shioya in an interview five decades later. "It was pretty horrifying, and bewildering, and disgusting."

Before long, the Nisei GIs started seeing something even more horrifying than the bodies. They started seeing people who were *standing and walking* and who appeared to have starved to death!

These people, more dead than alive, were the unfortunate former inmates of one of the large number of satellite camps associated with the large Nazi Konzentrationslager, or concentration camp, at Dachau, a few miles northwest of Munich. It was extremely cold, and the people were emaciated and sick. Some had no shoes. As Oiye and his comrades pulled over to share their food and give them their extra gloves, the starving camp survivors were startled to see Asian men in American uniforms.

The first of the infamous Nazi concentration camps to have been built, the facility at Dachau had been constructed before World War II to house the Jews and undesirables that Hitler wished to have removed from German society. Starting in 1941, Dachau also became a death camp, with an estimated 30,000 persons being deliberately executed there and untold thousands allowed to die from starvation or other causes. In addition to the main camp at the town of Dachau, there were more than a hundred satellite camps in the region that had been established for various purposes, such as to supply slave labor to German factories around Munich.

The main Dachau camp was liberated on April 29 by elements of the United States 42nd and 45th Infantry Divisions, both components of the Seventh Army, but controversy still swirls around the question of which unit actually had the *first* troops through the gates of the hideous place. On the same day, the Nisei GIs of the 522nd stumbled across the satellite camp known as Kaufering IV at Hurlach, near Landsberg, about fifty miles west of the center of Munich, and about forty miles southwest of Dachau.

"Our families were in concentration camps in the States," George Oiye told Frank Buckley of the Cable News Network in a

2004 interview. "Being the ones that liberated concentration camps, the real ones, in Europe . . . seemed so strange."

After the war, George Oiye went back to Montana State, earned his engineering degree in 1948, and went on to a distinguished career in the field. He worked with Bill Lear, the creator of the Learjet, designing aircraft engines. Later, he was involved in laser research, and he helped to develop what was at the time the third largest laser in the world, for the British government. An extensive number of photographs that he took during World War II, including those of the liberation of Holocaust survivors, are in the collection of the Montana Historical Society. Oiye eventually retired in California, but he continued to return to his old haunts in the Big Sky country to, as he told Andy Malby of the *Belgrade* [Montana] *News* in a 2004 interview, "visit old friends and do a little fishing."

At the same time that the men in Oiye's jeep made their gruesome discovery along the road, other men from the 522nd found the camp itself. They shot off the lock and came face-to-face with the Jewish victims of one of the twentieth century's worst outrages. One of these men was Donald Shimazu, who enlisted in the 442nd Regimental Combat Team at the age of nineteen. "We knew the Germans were exterminating the Jews," Shimazu told journalist Gregg Kakesako in a 1998 interview with the *Honolulu Star-Bulletin*. "But we didn't know where these camps were located. . . . Snow was still on the ground when the 522nd ran into wandering prisoners freshly freed from the prisons of Dachau."

Another GI, Ed Ichiyama, of the 522nd's C Battery, recalled in a Go For Broke Educational Foundation's Hanashi Oral History Program interview that "all of a sudden, we came across hundreds and hundreds and hundreds of so-called prisoners . . . in their black-and-white prison garb . . . shaved heads, sunken eyes, hollow cheeks. Bare skeletons, roaming aimlessly around the countryside. . . . We saw several guys shred either a dead horse or a dead cow and [they were] just eating the raw flesh."

Ichiyama told journalist Gregg Kakesako in another interview,

"It's impossible to describe. . . . I went in for a few moments and ran out to vomit."

Yukio Hibino, from Berkeley, California, recalled that a lot of the former concentration camp inmates were "in such bad shape that they couldn't take any food. We started to give them food, but we had to stop because they couldn't digest the rations. They were just skin and bones. They were just wandering around because they didn't know which way to go."

Joseph Ichiuji, who was born in the farming community of Salinas, California, and who grew up in Pacific Grove, was in a deuce-and-a-half truck that was pulling one of the battalion's 105 mm howitzers when they came across a group of survivors of Hitler's Holocaust. He had been attached to Battery A of the 522nd when the artillerymen supported the infantry who rescued the Lost Battalion in the Vosges in October 1944. It had been snowing in the Vosges and it was still snowing in Bavaria. Ichiuji recalled that the GIs shared their K and C rations with the concentration camp survivors around a fire that they had built toward evening on that providential day.

The irony of these sons of internees liberating the concentration camp survivors was obvious to all of the Nisei soldiers on that cold week in April 1945 and it remains so today. Ichiuji's own family was behind a barbed wire fence in Poston, Arizona, simply because they were Japanese. Joseph's father, Kulcijiro Ichiuji, had come to Hawaii in 1906 from Izumo, in the eastern part of Shimane prefecture. When the United States entered the war, he and his wife, Katsuno, and their family were living in Pacific Grove, California. In March 1942, Kulcijiro gave up his shoe repair shop and moved the family farther inland, across the state to a farm near the small Fresno County community of Reedley, where they lived with five other families, picking fruit to sell.

Joseph, meanwhile, had been drafted in 1941, and had finished his basic training just days before Pearl Harbor. He was at Camp Murray, Washington, when the U.S. Army suddenly began to discharge its Japanese American soldiers. He was back with his family near Reedley in August when they were all rounded up and put on a train bound for the Arizona relocation camp.

"Soldiers were at the [train] station guarding us," Ichiuji recalled in a 1999 interview with the *Jerusalem Post*. "They had goddam helmets on. Geez! We hadn't done anything to warrant such treatment."

When given an opportunity to reenlist to serve with the 442nd Regimental Combat Team, he told his mother, "This is my second opportunity to serve my country and prove that I'm a loyal American citizen. . . . By our showing that we're good fighters and loyal Americans the government may rescind [Executive Order 9066] and give [our family] an opportunity to be sent back home."

He arrived overseas in June 1944, and was involved in the advance of the 442nd through Livorno and against the Arno Line before playing his part in the rescue of the Lost Battalion.

After the war, Joseph Ichiuji had a long career with the United States government, both in the Veterans Administration and the Agency for International Development, and eventually retired in Rockville, Maryland. Active with a number of Japanese American veterans organizations, he often recalled his wartime experiences as a public speaker. His perspective on the unique experience of the men of the 522nd was a topic that came up frequently.

"The scope and the reason and the purpose was vastly different," he said, comparing the American internment camps with the German concentration camps in an interview with the Go For Broke Educational Foundation. "The American camp was for the duration of the war. Whereas the German camp was for the extermination of the Jewish race. . . . But the reason is the same. . . . In each case, an ethnic group was singled out for mass incarceration. . . . We [Japanese Americans] were singled out for mass incarceration despite the fact that [the United States was] at war with Japan, Germany, and Italy. We were the only ones singled out for that. So it was based on racial prejudice. That's what it was. And that's why when I give a talk, I make sure that people understand what we had gone through in the United States and because discrimination still exists in this country, we have to tell the story so it won't happen again. . . . I am proud to be of my heritage and my country. Because this country recognized the mistake they made and they vowed to never let it happen again. That makes a good country."

CHAPTER 20

To Genoa and Victory

As the 522nd Field Artillery Battalion was aiding four separate divisions in their crossings of the Siegfried Line and Germany's great rivers, the 92nd Infantry Division, to which the 442nd Regimental Combat Team was assigned, spearheaded the Fifth Army drive through the Gothic Line in the Apennines. Beginning with their dawn assault on April 5, the men of the 442nd had achieved the objective of capturing the ridgeline above Massa and the coastal road in three days of intense combat.

However, there was to be no respite. In the early hours of Sunday, April 8, two of the battalions were again on the move. Leaving the 100th Battalion to hold the hard-won positions on Monte Folgorito, Monte Belvedere, and the adjacent peaks, the other two battalions moved forward into the ridges and valleys to the north. The next major objective would be crossing the Frigido River, which flowed down out of the mountains near Carrara and Massa.

On the left flank, the 3rd Battalion jumped off Sunday morning and quickly captured the village of Montignoso, which lay below the ridgeline. From here, the 3rd Battalion fought its way through a German strongpoint on Tecchione Hill and managed to reach a point two miles from the Frigido.

Meanwhile, the 2nd Battalion dropped down from Belvedere and swung to the right to occupy the village of Altagnana, a few miles due

north of Montignoso. As the 2nd Battalion turned west from Altagnana toward Massa, Company F, Sergeant Yukio Okutsu's outfit, was in
the lead. The Germans had not considered Altagnana worth fighting
for, but as Company F reached nearby Paiana, they were met by a wall
of heavy automatic weapons fire.

The Nisei men pulled back, dug in, and resumed the attack on
Monday with mortar support. Under cover of a mortar barrage, Company F decimated the German heavy weapons battalion that had
stopped them the day before and secured the town. With this obstacle
out of the way, the bulk of the 2nd Battalion was able to make its way
to the banks of the Frigido by day's end.

For "outstanding performance of duty in action," actions between April 6 and 10, as well as for actions the previous October before and during the Lost Battalion rescue, the 2nd Battalion of the
442nd would be awarded a Presidential Unit Citation.

As the 442nd advanced briskly toward the river along the narrow
mountain roads, the unit's 232nd Engineer Combat Company was
working overtime to make the route passible for the regiment's deuce-
and-a-half supply trucks—and for vehicles evacuating the wounded to
field hospitals. The 232nd's bulldozer worked overtime, filling shell
craters in the road and building bypasses. On April 10, for example, the
regiment was stymied by a thirty-yard-long crater in the road near
Massa that had been dug and heavily mined by the retreating Germans. Most of the antitank and antipersonnel mines had been buried
too deep for electric mine detectors to locate, so the engineers used
careful hand probing to locate them.

The engineers worked in shifts overnight, despite the frequent
German artillery barrages, and got the road cleared by the following
afternoon. Among the conventional mines, they found twenty twelve-
inch artillery shells rigged as mines that had to be carefully lifted out
with truck winches. When one of their Caterpillar D7 bulldozers became hopelessly stuck as they were working on a bypass in a gully, the
ingenious Nisei engineers simply left it in place and used it as a pier to
build a temporary trestle bridge across the ravine.

The mines and the difficulty of detecting them made the work of the bulldozer operators a hazardous proposition. Four of those who braved this danger in order to get the road open promptly were wounded when undetected mines blew up their machinery. Despite incessant shelling, four heavy equipment operators and two other enlisted men—who were injured in four mine explosions—continued the work without interruption. The engineers were right in the thick of the fight, and a number of them, including company commander Captain Pershing Nakada, were among the wounded.

On Wednesday, April 11, the 3rd Battalion of the 442nd finally entered the great marble-cutting city of Carrara, where they found that partisans of the Italian resistance had already taken parts of the town from the retreating Germans.

With the city occupied and most of the American forces at or near the southern banks of the Frigido River, the advance was interrupted for forty-eight hours in order to permit supplies to catch up with the tactical units. During this short breather, the 100th Battalion, dug in near Belvedere since Sunday, officially rejoined the 442nd. They took over the place of the 3rd Battalion in the coming advance, giving the 3rd a well-deserved respite. The 2nd Battalion, meanwhile, marched north out of Carrara to Gragnana, a distance of about eight miles.

As the 442nd was reaching the banks of the Frigido and positioning themselves to enter Carrara, the 473rd Infantry Regiment was moving northwest along the coastal plain to their left. The 473rd entered the city of Massa on April 10 and made contact with German forces on the Frigido River west of the coastal highway. Though they had managed to occupy the city, crossing the river was problematic because the flat terrain approaching the river afforded no cover and German artillery was zeroed in on potential crossing points.

A plan was adopted under which the 442nd would capture the high ground overlooking Frigido—including Monte Pizzacuto—that was being used by German artillery and artillery spotters. With the pressure thus relieved by the Nisei GIs, the 473rd would then cross the river and push north.

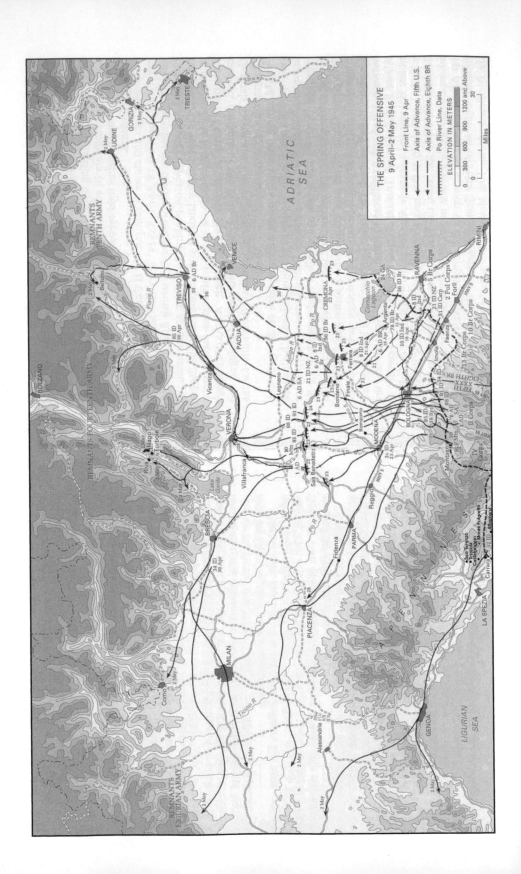

THE SPRING OFFENSIVE
9 April–2 May 1945

Front Line, 9 Apr
Axis of Advance, Fifth U.S.
Axis of Advance, Eighth BR
Po River Line, Date

ELEVATION IN METERS
0   300   600   900   1200 and Above
Miles

On Friday the thirteenth, the 442nd's 2nd Battalion moved farther north to Castelpoggio, which became the staging base for an assault on German positions on Monte Pizzacuto. Sending a contingent, including Company C, west to make contact with the 473rd Infantry Regiment, the 3rd Battalion of the 442nd moved its main force up to Gragnana to serve as backup for the 2nd Battalion's attack at Monte Pizzacuto. The 3rd Battalion patrol on the west ran into serious pockets of resistance, but Company C gained the upper hand, and had the area cleared by midday Saturday.

Farther north, the 2nd Battalion resumed their attack up Monte Pizzacuto at dawn on April 14, and by 9:00 A.M., they were able to report that it had been captured.

Even as the Germans on Monte Pizzacuto gave up, other enemy troops were in the process of counterattacking against Castelpoggio. However, they had greatly underestimated the number of Nisei GIs that were in the town. Company B soldiers who had taken up positions in buildings around the small village returned fire, forcing the Germans to retreat after a savage shootout.

With the men of the 442nd having cleared the surrounding hills of Germans, the 473rd Infantry Regiment was able to make their push out of Massa and across the Frigido River on April 14. With their Frigido Line now breached, the Germans fell back to La Spezia. In its previous role as a naval base, La Spezia had ceased to be of any importance to the Germans because Allied air and naval power had long since relieved them of a naval presence in the Mediterranean. However, the Allies still expected it to be a major German strongpoint and an obstacle in their march north.

Of perhaps greater importance was the smaller city of Aulla, which was located about 15 miles inland. Aulla was significant because it was an important crossroads city that lay astride the main highway leading across the Apennines from the coast near La Spezia into the Po River Valley, which was the ultimate objective of the ongoing offensive. As we have seen, the Germans needed desperately to prevent the Allies from getting through the mountainous terrain and into the Po

Valley. Therefore, the Germans needed to protect Aulla and the main highway that passed though it. To do this, both sides understood that the Germans must control the high ground overlooking Aulla and the highway. This high ground lay directly ahead of the advancing battalions of the 442nd Regimental Combat Team.

Rather than simply reinforcing defensive positions, the Germans proactively launched offensive operations of their own, intending to recapture ground lost to the Japanese American GIs. Saturday's abortive attack on Castelpoggio was merely one example of this, and for the next several days, the hills were alive with the gunfire of numerous small-unit actions as German patrols attempted to outflank positions held by the 442nd men.

There was so much action that Colonel Miller, the 442nd's commander, ordered the 232nd Engineering Combat Company to stop work on a supply road project and take up rifles to guard a ridge that the combat troops had captured. The idea was to use the engineer platoons to take over the defensive positions, thus permitting the infantry companies to go over to the offensive and counterattack against the Germans. Between April 15 and 17, the 232nd simply discontinued all their construction work and operated as infantry in defense of the regiment's positions in and around the village of Gragnana, about three miles southeast of Castelpoggio. The 1st Platoon of the 232nd relieved Company I, while the engineer company's 2nd and 3rd Platoons took over Company K's defensive positions.

In turn, Company K could now press forward, taking the fight across the ridgetops to the Germans. On April 20, the company finally reached the tiny village of Tendola, about eight miles northwest of Castelpoggio, and about halfway from Carrara to Aulla on the twisting mountain road that ran through the rugged high country between the two towns. There was a German position on the hillside above Tendola, and Joe Hayashi, a twenty-five-year-old private from Pasadena, California, was ordered to lead a small patrol tasked with taking it out. The soldiers managed to get to within seventy-five yards of the German machine guns before the enemy saw them and opened fire. Several GIs were wounded, but Hayashi managed to drag them to safety. He then crawled to an exposed location where he could direct Company K mortar fire against the Germans. Finally, he led a bold frontal assault on the machine-gun nests, overwhelming three of these positions and killing twenty-seven Germans.

Two days later, the Germans were still putting up a spirited opposition to the 442nd's advance across the hills near Tendola. Once again, Joe Hayashi's platoon came into the crosshairs of several enemy machine-gun nests. This time he led a squad up the hillside under heavy fire. He methodically destroyed two German positions with hand grenades and managed to kill four of the enemy troops in a third strongpoint. As he was chasing some retreating Germans, he was shot and killed. For his heroism during those days in April 1945, Joe Hayashi was awarded a Distinguished Service Cross, which was subsequently upgraded to the Medal of Honor fifty-five years later.

On April 21, the day between the two actions that earned the ultimate honor for Joe Hayashi's ultimate sacrifice, another GI of the 442nd Regimental Combat Team earned a Distinguished Service Cross that would be upgraded to the Medal of Honor. It was only a couple of miles northeast of Tendola, at another tiny village that is ignored on most maps, called San Terenzo. Second Lieutenant Daniel Inouye was leading a Company E platoon toward an important road junction near San Terenzo. Suddenly, they came under fire from German positions on the ridge overlooking the crossroads.

Though they were taking heavy incoming fire, Inouye rallied the men and led them to capture the German artillery and mortar post. "Everything worked," he recalled in his memoirs. "What little opposition we met, we outflanked or pinned down until someone could get close enough to finish them off with a grenade. We wiped out a patrol and a mortar observation post without really slowing down."

Inouye's platoon reached the main line of resistance ahead of the central assault force, finding themselves directly beneath the enemy guns, and just forty yards from the German bunkers. When the German machine guns opened fire on them again, Inouye made his way to within fifteen feet of the enemy gunners in a log bunker. He tossed in a hand grenade and it exploded in a shower of dirt. When the gun crew staggered up, he cut them down. As his platoon approached, he waved them toward the other two gun emplacements.

By now, Inouye had been hit by a sniper and was badly injured, although he recalled that it felt like he had merely been punched. It was not until someone pointed out that he was bleeding that he realized a German bullet had hit him in the side. Running on adrenaline, he refused to seek first aid and continued to lead the platoon.

"I wanted to keep moving," he recalled. "We were pinned down again and, unless we did something quickly they'd pick us off one at a time. I lurched up the hill again, and lobbed two grenades into the second emplacement before the gunners saw me. Then I fell to my knees. Somehow they wouldn't lock and I couldn't stand. I had to pull myself forward with one hand."

The Nisei GIs were still being raked by the last German machine-gun emplacement on the hill, and something had to be done. Inouye realized that he was close enough to pull the pin on the only hand grenade that he had left. As he raised his arm to toss it, he could see a German stand up, aim a rifle grenade at him from a range of ten yards and fire. The German grenade exploded into Inouye's right elbow just as he was about to throw his own grenade.

"I looked at my hand, stunned," he recalled. "It dangled there by a few bloody shreds of tissue, my grenade still clenched in a fist that suddenly didn't belong to me anymore. . . . Then I tried to pry the grenade out of that dead fist with my other hand. At last I had it free. The German was reloading his rifle, but my grenade blew up in his face."

Inouye then stumbled to his feet and ran toward the German bunker, firing his Thompson submachine gun with his left hand. The last German standing returned fire just before a Nisei bullet took him down. This German fusillade caught Inouye in the right leg and threw him to the ground.

Dan Inouye lost his right arm that day at San Terenzo, but became the highest-ranking member of the 442nd Regimental Combat

Team, and the only officer, to earn a Distinguished Service Cross that was later upgraded to the Medal of Honor.

On April 23, as Inouye being taken back to the field hospital, the men of his 2nd Battalion succeeded in outflanking the Germans and capturing San Terenzo. Meanwhile, the 3rd Battalion took the enemy garrison defending nearby Monte Nebbione. At San Terenzo, the Nisei GIs captured 115 enemy prisoners, many of whom turned out to be Italian Fascists. This was an indication that the Germans were finally beginning to abandon the front line in Italy.

By this time, the Nisei GIs were also starting to see Asian faces among the German prisoners. These turned out to be men from the Russian Far East who had been in the Red Army. They had either been appropriated by the Germans as slave labor, or, like many Soviet troops, they had changed sides when captured by the Germans. Now they had been captured by Japanese Americans. Many of the Nisei veterans recall that they would say hello to them in Japanese, but they didn't understand.

Frank Michico Fukuzawa from Santa Barbara, who was with Company F, recalls that these sons of Japanese immigrants would kid one another, shouting "Hey, there's your brother," when they passed the Asian prisoners.

The Japanese American soldiers also crossed paths with ethnic Japanese among the Cobras Fumantes—smoking snakes—the 25,000-man Brazilian Expeditionary Force that fought with the Allies in Italy for the last eight months of the war. These men spoke Portuguese and couldn't understand English, but they could communicate with the Japanese Americans in Japanese.

As the last week of April arrived, an almost sudden collapse of the German armies in Italy began to happen all across the country. Just as the Allied planners had hoped, once the Gothic Line was breached, the enemy would have no remaining defensive lines behind which to put up another fight. On the II Corps front, Bologna was captured on April 21 by the American 34th Infantry Division, the division to which the 442nd had been assigned during its first tour of duty in

Italy. By the time that the Nisei solders had secured San Terenzo in the west, the Fifth Army was flooding into the Po Valley and beginning to cross the river itself at many points.

With evidence of an impending enemy collapse, and with the momentum gained from the breakthroughs around San Terenzo, the 442nd moved quickly. Spearheaded by a task force comprising Companies B and F, led by Major Mitsuyoshi "Mits" Fukuda, the Nisei troops outflanked Aulla and captured the city on April 25.

Meanwhile, on the night of April 23–24, the 473rd Infantry Regiment had broken through the last German resistance at La Spezia and captured that city. The Americans were now about one hundred miles from Genoa, the hometown of Christopher Columbus, and the largest port on Italy's west coast north of Naples.

At the rate that they had been progressing since the beginning of April, it might have been said that it would take about two months for the 442nd and its fellow regiments within the 92nd Infantry Division to reach Genoa, but the enemy opposition was withering. The 92nd's commander, General Almond, wagered with Brigadier General Donald Brann, the 15th Army Group operations officer, that his division could make this two-month advance in four days. In fact, it took just *sixty hours!*

"Everyone realized that the war was over, but we couldn't stop," Lawson Sakai recalled. "The Germans were retreating, and we had to go after them. We didn't do much firing, but we were chasing them. They were in vehicles and going like hell on the coastal highway, and we were in vehicles chasing them. It was like a car chase."

The lead elements of the 473rd Infantry Regiment entered Genoa at around 9:30 A.M. on April 27, only to discover that most of the 4,000-man Axis garrison had already surrendered to Italian resistance fighters the day before. On the afternoon of the same day, across Italy near Lake Como, former Italian Fascist dictator Benito Mussolini and his mistress Claretta Petacci were captured by Italian partisans while in the process of trying to escape to Switzerland. They were executed the following day.

Happily loading themselves into deuce-and-a-half trucks, the footsore men of the 442nd followed the rapid advance of the 473rd up the coast. As the lead elements of the 100th Battalion reached the suburbs of Genoa late on April 27, they were ordered to move inland to capture the city of Busalla, about fifteen miles to the north. The idea was to seal the mountain pass at Isola del Cantone and cut off possible enemy escape routes in the direction of Turin. Dismounting from the trucks because of damaged highway bridges, the 100th Battalion hiked most of the way to Busalla, capturing the city with minimal fuss by 10:00 A.M. on April 28. By this time, the 442nd's 3rd Battalion had reached Genoa, impeded only by having to stop to process an estimated one thousand German troops who wanted to surrender.

By April 28, the Fifth Army had occupied an vast area north of the once problematic Gothic Line that stretched from the French border near Menton across the Po Valley to Verona. On that same day, representatives of the German army approached the 15th Army Group headquarters in Caserta to orchestrate a cease-fire and the unconditional surrender of all remaining Axis forces south of the Alps.

On April 29, with the fighting in Italy all but over, the 100th Battalion was relieved at Busalla and moved into regimental reserve at Boizaneto on the northwestern periphery of Genoa. The 2nd Battalion, meanwhile, was ordered to Alessandria, about forty-five miles north of Genoa, mainly to coordinate the surrender of a German contingent in that area. Eventually, the unit moved farther east to round up the huge numbers of Germans wishing to surrender.

"We chased the Germans all the way to Brescia," Lawson Sakai explained. "That's where they finally gave up. That was the end. They gave up. There were only a couple hundred of us, but there were *thousands* of them!"

On April 30, the last operation by the 442nd Regimental Combat Team in World War II saw the regimental intelligence and recon platoon, together with the Company H machine-gun teams, make a fast dash to the big industrial city of Turin, about seventy miles west of

Alessandria. Again, their only actions involved processing prisoners. On this same day Adolf Hitler committed suicide.

On May 2, the formal cease-fire order was broadcast, and troops on both sides in Italy lay down their arms. On that day, the Soviet armies had entered Berlin, and the final collapse of the German armies occurred five days later as the German high command formally agreed to unconditional surrender of all of their forces on all the remaining fronts. World War II was finally over in Europe.

With the war finished, most of the 442nd moved into a bivouac area at Ghedi, near Brescia and Lake Garda in northern Italy, to await transportation home. The 522nd Field Artillery Battalion remained in Germany, occupying the town of Donauwörth on the Danube River until the end of 1945. The 232nd Engineering Company, like many engineering units, was kept occupied with road and bridge survey and repair work along the coast of the Ligurian Sea from the vicinity of Massa in the south to past the French border in the vicinity of Menton, where the regiment had spent the previous winter.

With the war over in Europe, the U.S. Army made plans for the men of the 442nd to return to the United States as a unit. This pleased the troops, for whom their unit identity, forged in battle, was very strong. "Six of us went AWOL from the field hospital at Pisa to rejoin the unit," laughed Shig Kizuka of Company L, who had suffered a severe shrapnel wound to his chest near Carrara.

It was near Carrara that Robert Ichikawa of Company E came in contact with one of the lesser heralded perils faced by the GIs in Italy. Ichikawa, who had been wounded near Pieve di San Luce in July 1944, had spent much of the latter half of the year in field hospitals, but he had returned to the 442nd before the regiment returned to Italy in March 1945.

"I went to sleep on a straw mattress in an Italian house, and woke up covered head to toe with bedbugs," he said with a grin. "I went to the medic, and the medic said, 'Get away from me!' They sent me to Pisa to get deloused, and by the time I was deloused, the war had ended."

CHAPTER 21

Final Actions
in the Pacific

As the men of the 442nd Regimental Combat Team were rounding up the last of Hitler's surrendering legions in Italy, other sons of Japanese immigrants in the Military Intelligence Service (MIS) were involved in the final battles in the war against Japan. After having played an important role in gathering and interpreting enemy intelligence in the campaigns in the Marianas and the Philippines, about fifty Nisei linguists went ashore with the Marines at Iwo Jima in February 1945, and another large contingent accompanied the big American invasion of Okinawa two months later.

In the bloody battle to capture heavily defended Iwo Jima, there were few moments of levity, but the laughter occurred only when situations that could have been so much worse turned out for the better. One such story involved Hideto Kono, who served at the Joint Intelligence Center for the Pacific Ocean Area in Hawaii, and with the MIS on Saipan before landing on Iwo Jima. As had been the case on Saipan, one of the tasks undertaken by the MIS linguists on Iwo Jima was "cave flushing," the process of persuading the Japanese troops or civilians hiding in caves to surrender. According to an interview with Kono conducted by the Go For Broke Educational Foundation Hanashi Oral History Program, he and a shorter fellow from Kagoshima in Japan were called to "flush" a well.

"War is over," shouted the man from Kagoshima. "I'm here. I was with the 145th [Infantry Regiment of the Imperial Japanese Army] and I'm taken good care of by the [American military]. . . . So why don't you guys come out?"

They refused the other man's call for them to leave the cave, so Kono took off his helmet and looked down into the well.

"Why are you staying there?" Kono asked. "No point in staying."

They came out.

In a postsurrender interview, Kono asked the enemy soldiers why they didn't come out when the other fellow was asking. They explained that because he was dark and short, he must have been a Korean whom the Americans were using to deceive them. They expected that they were being tricked and that they would be shot.

"But when we saw you," they told Kono, "here is a true Japanese. He looks like Japanese. We felt safe and came out."

As Kono said later, "We all had a big laugh."

There had been some Japanese civilians on Saipan and other islands, but beginning on April 1, 1945, the landings on Okinawa put American forces in direct contact with very large numbers of Japanese civilians. Indeed, the island had been a prefecture of Japan proper since the 1870s.

Communicating with the Japanese civilians on Okinawa was difficult for the Nisei linguists. It was not that there was a language barrier, it was that after years of official propaganda, there was a credibility barrier. The Imperial Japanese authorities had convinced the civilians that the Americans meant to rape and torture them, and this perception was hard to overcome, especially under circumstances wherein the civilians were huddled in dank, dark caves listening to someone from an invading army shouting at them from the distance.

One of the MIS men, Hawaiian-born Technician Third Grade Takejiro Higa, was especially well suited for the task. He had spent fourteen of his first sixteen years on Okinawa, although he had returned to Hawaii in 1939. Not only his ability to speak Japanese, but to do so in the Okinawan dialect, was naturally a huge advantage for Higa in his work. In one case, Higa was able to prevent a mass suicide involving hundreds of civilians hiding in a cave by speaking to them in Okinawan-accented Japanese. As with language, Higa's knowledge of Okinawan culture proved useful. For example, prior to the American landings, he helped aerial photointerpreters distinguish between fortifications and traditional mausoleums, and between machine-gun nests and compost pits.

Just as most MIS men spoke Japanese without an Okinawan accent, so, too, did most Imperial Japanese troops. Thus, Higa was later able to ferret out captured Japanese soldiers—including a colonel—who were attempting to pass as civilians.

Higa's having grown up on Okinawa also led to a strange encounter. As he was questioning some Japanese personnel captured during the battle, Higa recognized that two of them were people with whom he had attended the Japanese equivalent of junior high school. They were stunned to see him in an American uniform. As he related the story in a 1993 interview published by the MIS Veterans Club of Hawaii, the unexpected reunion greatly relieved the Japanese prisoners, who had been briefed to fear capture by the American forces.

"They looked up at me in total disbelief and then started crying . . . in happiness and relief," Higa said. "That hit me very hard and I, too, could not help but shed some tears."

In an interview with the Go For Broke Educational Foundation, Takejiro Higa admitted that he had had some reservations about going to the Pacific, but that he was glad for what he was able to accomplish there. "At the beginning, I was afraid . . . to go into service as an interpreter," he said. "I was afraid I might be sent to somewhere that I might run into somebody I know—relatives or a classmate or whatever. But to think about it now, I'm glad I was sent to the Pacific. . . . Without firing a single shot of my carbine I was able to discharge my obligation as an American soldier. And at the same time, to help the people I grew up with. [For] this, I am grateful. . . . I wish I could [have done] more. . . . but we tried our best, our very best to save them. Too bad they [all] didn't believe us."

Because many details of MIS activities remained classified for so long after World War II, the contributions that Takejiro Higa and others made to the success of the Okinawa operations never received the attention that they deserved in the years immediately after the war, when the exploits of the troops were being etched into the collective American memory.

Colonel Sidney F. Mashbir, who headed the Allied Translator and Interpreter Section (ATIS), said, "The United States of America owes a debt to these men and to their families which it can never fully repay. . . . They were worthy, as individuals and as a group, of the highest praise for their invaluable contributions to the success of Allied arms."

Major General C. A. Willoughby, assistant chief of staff for intelligence in the U.S. Army's Far East Command under General Douglas MacArthur, quantified the contributions of the MIS men when he wrote that the Nisei linguists had "saved over one million American lives and shortened the war by two years. . . . they collected information on the battlefield, they shared death in battle . . . in all they handled between two and three million [enemy] documents. The information received through their special skills proved invaluable to our battle forces."

In his 1994 paper *Nisei Linguists and New Perspectives on the Pacific War*, Dr. James McNaughton, the command historian for the Defense Language Institute, eloquently summarized the contributions of these men, writing, "The majority served in non-combat assignments in JICPOA and ATIS. But several hundred were sent forward to serve in combat operations in New Guinea, Burma, the island-hopping campaigns, and the Philippines. They served with the Army, Navy, Marines, and Army Air Forces. Over a dozen were killed in action. Like their fellow soldiers, they suffered the fear and stress of combat. The Nisei experienced all this and more. In the typhoon of steel, they were in the eye, grappling with the enemy, not with bayonet and bullet, but with their eyes and ears and hearts."

CHAPTER 22

Frank Fujita and the Other Lost Battalion

Over time, certain stories become part of the collective memory of history, and others fade into obscurity. As the collective memory of the war recedes, many stories of Americans in action during World War II have been forgotten to all but a handful of military historians. Today, more than half a century later, this is understandable, but one such story was forgotten by many even *before* the war ended. It involves the *other* Lost Battalion of the 36th Infantry Division.

In October 1944, the men of the 442nd Regimental Combat Team rescued the men of the division's 1st Battalion, 141st Infantry Regiment, in a Lost Battalion rescue that is an integral part of the history of both the 442nd and of the 36th Division. What is largely forgotten is that the Texas Division lost another battalion, one that was not rescued, and one whose roster included the first Japanese American captured during World War II.

As noted earlier in this book, Sergeant Frank Fujita and the other Texans assigned to the 2nd Field Artillery Battalion of the 131st Field Artillery Regiment had shipped out of San Francisco sixteen days before the Pearl Harbor attack as part of a top-secret effort to bolster the defenses of the Philippines in anticipation of a possible Imperial Japanese Army invasion. When the war began, they were diverted to Australia and then sent to the Netherlands East Indies in January 1942. When the Indies fell during the second week of March, Fujita and his comrades were captured. The 2nd Field Artillery Battalion had become the 36th Infantry Division's first Lost Battalion.

As far as families back in Texas knew, the men of the battalion had disappeared without a trace. One of the first mentions of the unit in the media appeared in the *Fort Worth Star-Telegram* on June 1942. At that time, no one even knew whether they had been killed or captured: "Somewhere in the rugged terrain of Java there is a bunch of Texas men who are members of the Second Battalion, 131st Field Artillery, which until last November was a unit of the Lone Star State's own 36th Division.

"The fate of these men, who comprised one of the first American contingents to face the overpowering odds of the Japanese in the Pacific, is unknown. The War Department has simply said that the soldiers are considered 'missing in action.' There have been rumors that the Texans may still be fighting in the mountain vastness of the Netherlands East Indies island but the general assumption is that they are prisoners of war. But wherever they are and whatever they are doing, Texas is certain that they will uphold all the glorious traditions of America. Just as certain of this are the hundreds of bereaved fathers and mothers of the boys of the 'Lost Battalion.'"

In fact, by that time, the men of the Lost Battalion were incarcerated, along with Dutch, Australian, and other Allied prisoners, at a prison camp near Batavia (now Jakarta) on Java prior to being moved to Singapore in October. Strangely, the Imperial Japanese troops had not yet determined that Fujita was of Japanese ancestry, although this fact had circulated among the other prisoners. At first, he was regarded with suspicion by the Allied prisoners, who feared that he might be an enemy "plant." However, when they saw him being treated with high regard by his fellow Texans, they gradually accepted him.

During their brief stay in Singapore, the Lost Battalion and other Allied prisoners were held at a prison camp where they were guarded not by Japanese troops, but by Sikh troops who had apparently defected from the British army. As with other prisons they would experience as "guests" of Imperial Japan, rations left a great deal to be desired, so much so that the men resorted to killing fruit bats with slingshots in order to add protein to their diet. At one point, Foo and several other Texans incurred the wrath of the British POWs when they killed and ate the dog that had been the Royal Air Force mascot. After Singapore, the Texans of the Lost Battalion were moved again, this time to Japan itself, where they arrived around the first anniversary of Pearl Harbor.

"As we came nearer to land, the harbor traffic increased, and it became evident that this was a fair-sized city," Fujita later wrote in his memoirs. "I was experiencing strange feelings as I gazed about, and as had happened so many times in our travels, I had this strange feeling that I had been here before. A wave of excitement came over me when someone announced that this was Nagasaki, Japan. My mind was awhirl with the incredible odds of my having arrived at the very place from which Dad had left back in 1914. I wondered if any of those on shore watching our arrival might be distant relatives."

Amazingly, the Japanese authorities had still not figured out that Fujita was of Japanese ancestry. Apparently the guards with whom he had come in contact were unfamiliar with the Japanese surname being written in the Roman alphabet. As for his Asian features, they probably thought he was Filipino, as there was a sizable number of Filipinos serving with American forces who had been captured in the Philippines. Though he lived in constant dread that they would execute him as a traitor if they found out about his ethnic origin, Fujita resisted the advice of his fellow Texans to change his name. If a list of Lost Battalion prisoners was ever released—as it finally was early in 1943—he wanted his real name on the list so that his family would know that he was still alive.

In Japan, Fujita and the other prisoners were assigned to Fukuoka POW Camp Number 2 on Koyagi Shima, a small island a few miles from Nagasaki. His life for the next ten months would consist of backbreaking work in the nearby shipyard, building transport vessels for delivering Japanese troops and supplies to the war zone. Life in the prison camp was awful, as the men suffered from the cold, inadequate rations, and vermin, as well as diseases from pneumonia to beriberi. Conditions were so bad that some men asked fellow prisoners to break their arms in order to get them excused from work detail—but this backfired. Anyone who was too ill or infirm to work had his already meager rations cut.

In June 1943, when his captors finally discovered that Fujita had a Japanese surname, he came to be treated more as a curiosity than as a traitor. For a few weeks, his work detail changed, and he briefly became a servant to the camp commandant, who showed him off almost as a souvenir. When he was interrogated and found to be unable to speak or read Japanese, they attempted to force him to learn the language. Finally, as the novelty wore off, they sent Fujita back to the shipyard.

When his identity was discovered, the Japanese had made several attempts to convince him to join the Imperial Japanese Army. He steadfastly resisted their offers and went out of his way to assure the other Americans at Fukuoka that he had no intention of becoming a turncoat. In October 1943, his battle seemed lost when his captors announced that they were transferring him to a prison in Tokyo.

"Since my capture I had felt that my real war with the Japanese started the day I was captured," Fujita wrote in his autobiography. "If they could not sway me, being part Japanese, over to their side, then perhaps they would not be too eager to attempt the same thing with others who were not Japanese. I had to prove to all the POWs I was thrown in with that I was 100 percent American, and meant to thwart the Japanese in any way that I could and still keep my head on my shoulders where it belonged. It now seemed that my success in this was soon to cease."

After he was captured in Java, Fujita had kept a diary filled with sketches and narrative about the experiences of the Lost Battalion in captivity. He entrusted this sketch book to Sergeant David Williams, a fellow Texan when he was pulled out of Fukuoka and transferred to the Omori Prisoner of War Camp, located on an island in Tokyo Bay. On the first of December he was moved again, this time to a prison located in a former girls school in central Tokyo that was known as Bunka Gakuin. The Americans referred to it as "Bunker Hill."

As Fujita ascertained, the inmates at Bunker Hill had been brought together to be used for propaganda broadcasts via the Japan Broadcasting Corporation to Allied troops in the Pacific. The inmates, of which Fujita was the only man of Japanese ancestry, were mainly British and American, but one each was Australian and Dutch. Some had prewar experience in broadcasting. Each of the prisoners was asked to write scripts which they would later read over Radio Tokyo on mixed music and commentary programs with names that roughly translated as "The Circle of the Sun Hour," "The Zero Hour," and "Humanity Calls." Some of the broadcasts were simply messages to friends and family, but the men were also asked to read propaganda statements. They were reminded that failure to cooperate would be punished by execution.

Some of the men tried to use the inflection in their voices to discredit the propaganda, but as Fujita observed, "The Japanese would, at times, inject their own verbiage into someone's writing, and in that case there was nothing the writer could do except object."

At least one of the Americans appeared to be enthusiastic about the project. The enigmatic Sergeant John David Provoo was a Caucasian Californian who had spoken Japanese and who had studied Buddhism— Fujita remembered it as Shintoism—in Japan before the war. He had been on Corregidor at the time of the American surrender, and had later been observed by many Americans to be cooperating with the Imperial Japanese Army. Known as the "Traitor of Corregidor," Provoo had begun acting as an interpreter for the Japanese occupiers immediately after they landed, and according to a description of Provoo, read into the *Congressional Record* by Senator Daniel Akaka in 1996, he had been directly responsible for the death of a U.S. Army Medical Corps officer named Thompson. After the war, Provoo was tried and convicted of treason, but the conviction was overturned on a technicality.

Also reading more overt propaganda over other Radio Tokyo programs during this time were about a dozen Nisei women who had been trapped in Japan at the beginning of the war and who were called upon to broadcast to American troops in American-accented English. Because they featured popular American music, these broadcasts had a large audience among American troops, who referred to the women collectively by the nickname "Tokyo Rose." The most famous of these women was Los Angeles-born Iva Toguri, who was tried and convicted of treason after the war in a trial tainted by admissions of perjury by some prosecution witnesses. She served six years in prison, but she ultimately received a presidential pardon from Gerald Ford.

Because he was an accomplished artist and cartoonist, Fujita's role was to sketch pictures of the others making the broadcasts, although he was eventually permitted to make a monthly broadcast addressed to his parents. "The attitude of the front office toward me," Fujita wrote later of his experience at Bunker Hill and Radio Tokyo, "ranged from benign tolerance, to ignoring me completely, to hateful and threatening."

Occasionally, he had a bit part in a skit that was broadcast. By the spring of 1944, the Americans had been given wide latitude to develop soap operas that were rich in double entendre and off-color dialogue.

In November 1944, the U.S. Army Air Forces staged the first air raid on Tokyo since the Doolittle mission of April 1942, but this time the attack was not an isolated anomaly, but the beginning of a bombing campaign of gradually increasing intensity that would see American bombers over the Japanese capital on a routine basis through the end of the war. The biggest of these attacks came on March 9, 1945, when the USAAF launched 325 B-29 bombers in a massive incendiary raid on Tokyo. Amazingly, the Bunker Hill compound, despite being located in the heart of Tokyo, was unscathed in a raid that destroyed at least a quarter of the city.

The air raids did often interrupt the water supply into Bunker Hill, which made Fujita's duties as *benjo honcho* (toilet cleanup man) especially distasteful.

In August 1945, the prisoners at Bunker Hill heard about the nuclear strikes on Hiroshima and Nagasaki soon after they occurred, and a sense of foreboding settled over the place. On the one hand, their captors had told them repeatedly that the closer American forces got to Tokyo, the closer they came to death. On the other hand, they feared they would be killed if a nuclear weapon were used against Tokyo.

On August 15, Emperor Hirohito read a statement over the radio in which he announced that Japan would surrender, and, the following day, the prisoners were told that they would be moved to another camp for repatriation. Unsure where to go or what to do, they remained at Bunker Hill for a week before a truck came to transport them back to Omori prison, where there were hundreds of other Allied troops, all of whom were in the limbo between being prisoners of war and being liberated. On August 29, they first caught sight of American ships in Tokyo Bay. As U.S. Navy landing craft carrying medical personnel approached Omori, Frank Fujita became so excited that he foolishly jumped into the bay and tried to swim toward them. In his weakened condition, he nearly drowned before being pulled to safety.

Fujita and his fellow Omori residents were taken aboard American transports and hospital ships, where they were fed, deloused, and given medical checkups. Several days after the formal surrender ceremonies, which took place on September 2 aboard the USS *Missouri*, anchored nearby in Tokyo Bay, Foo Fujita started his journey home. His first stop was on Okinawa, where he was reunited with a number of the Texans from the Lost Battalion, including Sergeant David Williams, to whom he had entrusted his sketchbook almost two years before.

From Okinawa, Fujita and the others were transferred to Alabang in the Philippines, where former prisoners of war from all across the Far East were being consolidated for assignment to available transportation back to the United States. It was here that he discovered that his Lost Battalion truly had been *lost*.

Each of the prisoners was being interviewed by a U.S. Army clerk, who was tasked with identifying the man's unit and the place and date of his being captured. When the clerk asked where Fujita had been captured, he told him Java. The clerk that accused him of "trying to be funny," asserting that the United States didn't have any troops in Java.

"Damned if that's not a fine howdy do!" Fujita recalled later. "We go fight a war for our country with a bunch of secondhand stuff, left over from World War I, get captured and spend three and one-half years of being starved, tortured, and overworked, and you mean to tell me that the army didn't even know we were there?"

The 2nd Field Artillery Battalion had become lost not only to the enemy, but to the U.S. Army, and to history!

The misplaced nature of the Lost Battalion from Texas continued to dog Frank Fujita even after he returned to the Lone Star State. Around Abilene, the story of the 2nd Field Artillery Battalion was well known, but several months after the war, Fujita crossed paths with a 36th Infantry Division colonel who didn't know the story. He was at the military hospital at Fort Sam Houston in San Antonio when the colonel noticed his uniform. Sergeant Fujita wore the "T-Patch" insignia of the division, as well as his Asiatic-Pacific Theater ribbons and Presidential Unit Citations. The colonel demanded that Fujita remove either the T-Patch or the ribbons, because the 36th Infantry Division had been operational in the *European* Theater, not in the Far East. This was, of course, almost entirely true—but only *almost*. Fujita refused, and the enraged colonel issued a direct order, but a doctor intervened to calm the situation. After a whispered explanation, the colonel turned white, then beet red, and told Fujita to "carry on."

Today, the "other" Lost Battalion is remembered in an exhibit in the Wise County Museum in Decatur, Texas, that includes the sketchbooks and some drawings that were the work of Frank "Foo" Fujita a long time ago.

CHAPTER 23

The Last Man In

T he story of the Japanese American GIs in the service of the United States in World War II ended dramatically on September 20, 1945. Less than three weeks earlier, as Frank Fujita watched from a nearby transport ship, the government of Imperial Japan had formally surrendered to the Allies on the *Missouri* in Tokyo Bay, but there was still one last Nisei soldier in the field—literally.

"Don't shoot!" this dirty, bedraggled man shouted when he was challenged by a pair of GIs in a field on the island of Luzon. "I'm an American! Can't you see? An American!"

However, they couldn't see that. The notion that this man was an American was not at all obvious to the two American soldiers. The disheveled fellow didn't look like an American. He did speak like an American, but he looked Japanese, and he dressed like someone who had been living for a very long time in the Philippine jungles. In fact, he was all three.

These two soldiers were part of a U.S. Army medical evacuation team operating in the Philippines, when the man approached them to say that he was an American who had been captured by the Japanese at the beginning of the war. He identified himself as Master Sergeant Richard Sakakida and gave them his army serial number, 10100022.

The incredulous GIs agreed to take him to their commanding

officer, where Sakakida repeated his story. Again, he was met with disbelief, but the officer finally agreed to contact the Combat Information Center (CIC) field office to report the incident. Within a few hours, a team from the CIC arrived to collect the scraggly man who spoke like an American and looked Japanese. They confirmed the amazing tale. It was true. Sakakida was on a watch list of agents that was issued by General Douglas MacArthur's headquarters. Sakakida was a wanted man, but he was wanted because he was one of *ours*.

Richard Motoso Sakakida was born in the village of Puunene, on the Hawaiian island of Maui on November 19, 1920, the son of Japanese immigrants. Three years later, his parents packed up their three sons and two daughters and moved to the big city—Honolulu. At that time, the territorial capital was the only major population center in the Islands, and the land of opportunity.

Unfortunately, Richard's father passed away in 1927, and his widowed mother was compelled to shoulder the full responsibility for raising the five children. As he was growing up, Richard's mother instilled in him a sense of honor and loyalty that would guide him through his most difficult years during World War II.

Richard Sakakida attended McKinley High School in Honolulu, as well as the Hongwanji Japanese language school, and graduated from both in June 1939. At McKinley, Richard had been part of the school's ROTC program, and the U.S. Army took a special interest in him because of his Japanese language skills.

By this time, relations between Japan and the United States were already strained. In the Philippines, an American Commonwealth scheduled for independence in 1946, the Japanese were known to have a network of espionage and subversion agents operating within the Japanese expatriate community. General MacArthur's headquarters in the Philippines had requested that Japanese American counterespionage agents fluent in Japanese should be sent to the Philippines to counter this threat. The army picked Richard Sakakida and Arthur Komori, a fellow Nisei ROTC cadet from Lihue on the island of Kauai.

They went on active duty as sergeants in March 1941, and were given a crash course in codes and ciphers. After less than a month of training, they embarked on their secret mission. The two young Nisei men reached Manila on April 21 after two weeks at sea. Posing as a traveling salesman, Sakakida worked his way into the local Japanese business community. Komori got a job as an English teacher at the Japanese Cultural Center in Manila, where he befriended the Japanese consul general and many other important people. Soon the two were able to start passing along useful information to U.S. Army intelligence.

On December 8, 1941, everything changed abruptly. Across the International Dateline, where it was December 7 in Sakakida's home state, the Imperial Japanese Navy launched their attack on Pearl Harbor. Japanese air raids against the Philippines began the same day. Both Sakakida and Komori found themselves in the uncomfortable position of toasting the Pearl Harbor attack with their Japanese contacts, who were strongly supportive of the expansion of the Japanese Empire in the Far East.

Sakakida remained undercover and continued to pass information along to U.S. Army intelligence. When the Japanese invaded the Philippines, however, Sakakida began to suffer the resentment of the Filipinos, who took out their anger with the Imperial Japanese Army by rock throwing and name-calling aimed at any and all Japanese seen in Manila.

When the Philippine Constabulary began to round up suspected Japanese spies, Sakakida and Komori agreed to maintain their cover and to be taken into custody along with them. As the Japanese began their full-scale assault on Manila at Christmas 1941, their usefulness as spies appeared to have come to an end, so General MacArthur arranged for their release and they went back into uniform.

They served as translators and interrogators over the next few months as things went from bad to worse for the Americans and the Filipinos in and around Manila. Japanese bombers roamed at will over the city, bombing and strafing. Soon, as Japanese tanks approached the city, the United States forces abandoned Manila and retreated into the

Bataan peninsula. When that, too, was threatened, MacArthur ordered a further withdrawal to the fortress island of Corregidor.

After Bataan fell to the Japanese on April 9, 1942, General MacArthur was ordered to evacuate his Corregidor headquarters to Australia. He also wanted Sakakida and Komori evacuated because he knew that they would not be treated kindly if captured.

On the fateful morning of on April 13, the two men boarded the evacuation plane on Corregidor, but at the last minute, Sakakida gave up his seat to Clarence Yamagata, a Hawaiian-born local civilian with a family. Yamagata had been one of Sakakida's primary contacts while he was undercover, and Sakakida feared for his life.

Komori made it to Australia, but Richard Sakakida remained behind. On May 6, as the Japanese landed on Corregidor, General Jonathan Wainwright decided that the Americans should surrender to avoid annihilation. When a group of American officers took a small harbor craft to Bataan to contact the Japanese commanders, Sakakida went along as a translator. When they landed, Imperial Japanese Army troops took them into custody and separated Sakakida from the Caucasian Americans.

After Corregidor surrendered, all of the Caucasian Americans were taken back to Bataan, where they joined the former defenders of that peninsula in the infamous Bataan Death March. Denied food, water, and medical attention as they were marched to prison camps, many of the Americans died. Many others were simply gunned down by the Japanese en route to the camps.

Meanwhile, Richard Sakakida was imprisoned on Corregidor for interrogation by the dreaded Kempei Tai, Japan's equivalent of the Nazi Gestapo. He attempted to resume his previous cover story, telling them that he had been interned by the American forces after Pearl Harbor and had been forced to cooperate. Unfortunately, some of the Japanese whom he had interrogated while in U.S. Army uniform testified against him. It has also been suggested that Sergeant John David Provoo, the "Traitor of Corregidor," who would cross paths with Frank Fujita in Tokyo nineteen months later, had a role in Sakakida's becoming of special interest to the Kempei Tai. Many reports, including that which Senator Daniel Akaka read into the *Congressional Record* in 1996, assert that Provoo informed on Sakakida, as well as on fellow American intelligence agent James Rubard.

Despite months of brutal torture, Sakakida stuck to his story. He maintained his claim that he was a Japanese American who was in sympathy with the Japanese, and that he had collaborated with the U.S. Army only under pressure.

Amazingly, Richard Sakakida avoided a trial for treason—and almost certain execution—through a strange legal loophole. In August 1941, four months before the United States entered the war, his mother had gone to the Japanese consulate in Honolulu and had his Japanese citizenship revoked. Legally, he was no longer Japanese, so he couldn't be considered a traitor!

Instead of being killed, Sakakida was thrown into Bilibid Prison in December 1942. Though his life had been spared, another twist of fate awaited him. His fellow prisoners included Japanese soldiers who had surrendered to U.S. Army forces during the battles earlier in the year, and many were men whom Sakakida had interrogated. They were now serving life sentences for the crime of having surrendered to the Americans. When they recognized Sakakida, they took out their frustrations on him and made his life miserable.

In February 1943, another strange thing happened to Sakakida. The judge advocate general of the Imperial Japanese Fourteenth Army, the force occupying the Philippines, reviewed his case and decided that the story that he had been telling the Kempei Tai for the past nine months was *true!*

Suddenly Sakakida found himself out of prison and working as an official translator in the Fourteenth Army Headquarters in Manila. He traded his jail cell for a billet in the former English Club, which was being used to intern foreign nationals.

Among the routine work that Sakakida did at the headquarters was translating for Filipinos who came in to request the official paperwork that the Japanese occupation forces required for nearly everything. One day, a woman came in to request a pass to visit her husband, who was in prison. He turned out to be Ernest Tupas, a resistance leader who was serving a fifteen-year sentence in Muntinglupa prison for anti-Japanese activities. Sakakida quietly revealed his identity to her, and soon he was passing information to the resistance from inside the Fourteenth Army Headquarters.

Gradually, Sakakida developed an ambitious plan to break the resistance members out of Muntinglupa. The scheme called for Tupas and other prisoners to work their way into jobs with access to the prison's electrical system. Resistance leaders on the outside would arrange to pilfer Japanese uniforms and to monitor the prison and the schedules of the comings and goings of official Japanese inspections and visits to the prison. For his part, Sakakida would wear one of the stolen uniforms and impersonate a Japanese officer.

By October 1943, everything was in place, and one night, Sakakida sneaked out of the English Club in the dead of night. He and several Filipino resistance men who looked as though they could pass as Japanese donned the uniforms and walked into the prison according to a typical nighttime inspection visit by Fourteenth Army personnel. Taking on the arrogant swagger of the Imperial Japanese Army officers that he encountered on a daily basis, Sakakida played the role to the hilt. He ordered the guards to stand aside, and as they bowed in deference to his supposed superior rank, the resistance men clobbered them.

Next, right on schedule, the imprisoned men with access to the electrical system plunged the prison into darkness. Other partisans waiting outside sprang into action, quickly overpowering the guards and taking control of the prison. Almost five hundred prisoners were set free in the biggest prison break to occur under Japanese occupation. Before daybreak, Ernest Tupas and the freed men had disappeared into the civilian population, and Richard Sakakida was back at the English Club as though nothing had happened. The prison break was the hot topic at work that day, but Sakakida pretended to be just as shocked as everyone else.

Tupas managed to set up a clandestine radio link with American forces outside the Philippines, and the intelligence information that Richard Sakakida continued to glean from his unique place in the inner sanctum of the Japanese occupation was now going directly to General MacArthur. He conveyed important information about troop movements and shipping schedules, as well as Japanese strategic planning.

When MacArthur's armies began the long-awaited liberation of the Philippines in October 1944, Manila once again became a target. In a role reversal from 1941, it was now the Americans who had control of the skies, and the targets were Japanese military facilities within the city. General Tomoyuki Yamashita, who had commanded the Imperial Japanese Army's capture of Singapore in 1942, was brought in to organize the Japanese defense of the Philippines. In December, he made the decision to relocate the Fourteenth Army Headquarters from Manila to Baguio in the mountains to the north.

United States and Filipino troops recaptured Manila from the Japanese in March 1945, and up in Baguio Richard Sakakida began making his plans to leave his employers. In June he walked out of the Fourteenth Army Headquarters for the last time. He escaped into the mountains, where he joined the partisans.

While he was with the resistance, Sakakida was badly injured in a Japanese attack. The shrapnel wounds that he suffered in the attack would dog him for the rest of his life. Because these wounds slowed him down, the guerrilla band that he had joined left him behind, and he would spend the remainder of the war alone. He lived off the land for the next several months, subsisting on wild fruit and battling malaria, dysentery, clouds of insects, and the effects of the shrapnel embedded in his body.

Though he had no way of knowing about the course of the war, he did eventually notice that the distant sounds of artillery faded away and he no longer saw American aircraft making bombing runs on Japanese targets. He decided to leave the mountains and follow a river downstream and investigate what might be going on in the Philippines and in the world beyond.

When he saw the American GIs on September 20, he did not recognize their uniforms because U.S. Army gear had changed so much since 1941. In fact, until he heard them speak, he thought they might be Germans.

Richard Sakakida was taken to the 441st Combat Information Center Detachment, and welcomed with open arms. The Americans treated him to fried chicken, white bread, and beer, all things that he had not tasted for a very long time. Though he was happy, his stomach was not, and the rich food left him hospitalized for a week.

He was debriefed in Manila, where many Army intelligence people still found his amazing tale hard to believe. Had he been a Japanese collaborator? Had he been a double agent or a *triple* agent?

Having finally proven his bona fides, Sergeant Sakakida found himself back in uniform. After a two-week leave to visit Hawaii and to celebrate Christmas 1945 with his family, he returned to the Philippines. His new assignment was to serve as a translator and investigator in the war crimes trials of Japanese officers who had committed atrocities against civilians in the Philippines during the war. One of these was the feared General Yamashita, who was convicted and executed in 1946.

In 1947, Richard Sakakida received his commission as a lieutenant in the Army Counter Intelligence Corps. At the same time, under the United States Defense Department reorganization, the U.S. Army Air Forces were divorced from the U.S. Army to become the independent U.S. Air Force. When this occurred, Richard Sakakida chose to transfer to the air force. In 1948, he was assigned to the Air Force Office of Special Investigations (AFOSI) in Japan. Also in 1948, Richard Sakakida married fellow Maui native, Cherry Kiyosaki.

Promoted to lieutenant colonel, Sakakida eventually became the commanding officer of AFOSI in Japan, responsible for four detachments with 250 agents throughout the country. Under the United States occupation of Japan, Lieutenant Colonel Sakakida inaugurated a procedure to coordinate all of the Japanese investigative agencies in the Tokyo metropolitan area, including customs, national police, and

Tokyo police, in an effort to stop black market activities. For these activities, he received the praise of the Japanese government. He also returned to the United States to testify against John David Provoo when he was on trial for treason.

Meanwhile, Arthur Komori also rose though the ranks. Having reached Australia in 1942, he was assigned to the newly formed Allied Translation and Interrogation Section (ATIS) under Colonel Sidney Mashbir, a unit tasked with translating captured enemy documents and interrogating captured Japanese soldiers. He later served under General Elliott Thorpe, the chief of military counterintelligence in General MacArthur's headquarters. He was one of the first U.S. intelligence officers to arrive in Japan as the war came to an end in September 1945. After his retirement, he went on to a career as an attorney and as a district court judge in Kauai.

Richard Sakakida retired from the U.S. Air Force in September 1975, and he and his wife moved to Fremont, California. For the next two decades, the man with one of the most amazing wartime experiences of all quietly indulged such hobbies as gardening, carpentry, photography, and cooking with his wife. In 1994, he received the Philippines Legion of Honor for "exceptional meritorious conduct in performance of outstanding service to the Filipino American Freedom Fighters."

He passed away on January 23, 1996, after a lengthy illness compounded by his wartime wounds. In 1998, he was posthumously awarded the Distinguished Service Medal which was accepted by his widow at a ceremony at Fort Shafter in Hawaii on February 12, 1999. Sakakida's old comrade, Arthur Komori, died a year later, on February 17, 2000.

The Military Intelligence
Service in Japan

B
y the time World War II officially came to a close on
September 2, 1945, the Military Intelligence Service
Language School (MISLS) had graduated more than
4,800 linguists, and had about a thousand more enrolled. The school,
which had moved from Camp Savage to Fort Snelling in Minneapolis
in August 1944, moved again in June 1946, reopening at the Presidio
of Monterey in California as the U.S. Army Language School. Many
of the faculty members from Minnesota, including Shig Kihara, who
had been with program practically from day one, relocated to Monterey and stayed with the school. In 1963, the school became the Defense Language Institute, and it remains today one of the world's
leading language schools.

With the end of the war, American veterans from around the
world began flooding back to the United States, but the Nisei linguists
were only just beginning a new phase in their important work. In the
administration of General Douglas MacArthur's American military
government of Occupied Japan, interpreters and translators were very
much in demand. Both their language skills and their understanding
of Japanese customs and culture were significant. The Allied Translator
and Interpreter Section, which had employed such a large number of
Nisei linguists during the war, moved from Brisbane to Manila in

1945, where its hardworking staff prepared the Japanese-language translation of the surrender documents that were signed in Tokyo Bay on September 2, 1945. It was relocated to Tokyo in 1946 to aid in the occupation activities.

Some of the linguists remained in uniform, while others were discharged and rehired as civil service employees of MacArthur's military government. In Japan, the linguists worked as the liaisons between the occupation personnel and Japanese local government and interviewed the millions of former Japanese troops and civilians returning home from the vast areas of Asia that had previously been conquered and occupied by Japan. They operated with the United States Counter Intelligence Corps, ferreting out saboteurs and insurgents, and with the Civil Censorship Detachment, which had the more mundane task of censoring the Japanese radio and print media.

Other MIS linguists aided in the repatriation of the millions of Japanese troops and civilians from the vast areas of the Far East, especially China, that had been occupied as the Japanese Empire aggressively expanded, beginning in the 1930s. Milton Murayama recalls having accompanied Generalissimo Chiang Kai-shek's Nationalist Chinese Army when it reoccupied Taiwan after the war.

"Chiang Kai-shek had asked for a U.S. Army division to accompany his troops to Taiwan, but the United States said we'll send you one hundred support troops," he said. "We landed with the Nationalist Chinese in Chilung, a port in northern Taiwan. We were supposed to stay for a month, but an order came for us to stay there to repatriate the Japanese. . . . I was the interpreter for the American quarantine officer." Murayama would later recall the complexities of shipping ten thousand people back to Japan at one time. The mass exodus of millions of Japanese occupation troops and support personnel from Taiwan, and especially from mainland China, was a staggering logistical undertaking. So, too, was the process of integrating these large numbers of people into war-torn Japan, where the transportation infrastructure had been systematically disrupted by American air attacks. The fact that the process succeeded with no major problems is a testament both to American organization and to the rigid internal discipline that was maintained, even in defeat, within the Japanese military units.

John Fujito Aiso, the Harvard Law School grad whom the army assigned to motor pool duty until he was discovered by Kai Rasmussen on the eve of the war, was promoted to major, and later lieutenant colonel, the highest rank attained by a Japanese American in World War II. After serving as chief instructor at the MISLS, he was sent to Japan, where he served on General MacArthur's intelligence staff during preparations for the war crimes trials. After leaving the service he was the first Japanese American to serve as a judge on the Los Angeles Municipal Court, and he went on to sit as a California Court of Appeals associate justice.

George Katagiri, who was just fifteen years old when his family was shoved into the Pacific International Livestock Exposition Pavilion in Portland, had experienced the strangeness of being incarcerated in his hometown. Now he experienced the strangeness of being a Japanese American conqueror walking the streets of a defeated Japan. In an interview with the Go For Broke Educational Foundation, he told of visiting a small town where his family had relatives. Not many American soldiers had yet been into this remote corner of rural Japan, so it was especially strange for the townspeople when one of the first Americans they saw had a Japanese face.

"When I walked down the road, they would stand to the side and bow until I'd passed," he explained. "I think it was the showing of respect to somebody much higher. I guess I was the conqueror, so they were showing me that respect. At first, I couldn't understand what was going on, and I had to ask my cousin, why he did that. He said, 'Because you are a GI, a conquering GI soldier.' And I said, 'That's nice.' I thought it was an odd custom."

He went on to tell about passing a small factory where a group of workers were on their lunch break. "They were quite noisy when they were eating lunch, but the minute I came into view, there was silence," he recalled. "Without looking at them, I could just tell they were all staring at me, at this American soldier. And I think they were surprised that, gosh, he looks just like one of us. . . . If I took my cap off, no one would pay any attention to me. The minute I put the cap on I became an American soldier."

Henry Ikemoto from Stockton, California, had served in the antitank company of the 442nd Regimental Combat Team before transferring to the language school. He was then sent to Japan to analyze the Imperial Japanese Army chemical weapons program at Oji, north of Tokyo. He recalls an amusing story about the interaction between the Nisei and the locals.

"They knew about the Nisei because a lot of Nisei guys were involved with the occupation, but a lot of them didn't realize that I was Japanese American because I was so tall," Ikemoto laughed. "I was standing with some Caucasian guys on the platform at a train station, and there were some Japanese girls talking about us. I listened for a while, and finally I told them that I was a Nisei and I understood everything they were saying. They were so embarrassed!"

Over the next several years, the linguists examined and translated wartime documents recovered from military installations in Japan, as well as at the Japanese embassy in Berlin. They did translation and interpreter duty at the war crimes trials and participated in the repatriation of Japanese returning from China. They aided in the reorganization of the Japanese postwar government, and Japanese Americans helped to draft Japan's first democratic constitution.

Grant Hirabayashi, the Nisei linguist who had nearly starved to death while operating behind enemy lines in Burma with Merrill's Marauders, had an especially memorable perspective on his return home at the end of 1945. After his discharge Hirabayashi would serve as an instructor at the MISLS, and later as an interpreter, interrogator, and court interpreter with the Supreme Command Allied Powers Legal Section for war crimes trials in Yokohama, Japan. He went on to serve for three decades with the United States Department of State, the Library of Congress, and the National Security Agency. Hirabayashi told an interviewer with the Go For Broke Educational

Foundation oral history project, "I left Calcutta and I returned to New York via the Suez Canal." He said, "As the Liberty ship approached the Statue of Liberty we all hugged each other in joy. . . . As we sailed into the harbor, I could see the crowd waving the Stars and Stripes. And as we were about to dock the band struck up the song 'Sentimental Journey.' I said to myself, it *was* a journey. It was a journey that took me around the world in twenty-six months at government expense. . . . I wished they had told me that I had a round-trip ticket, but it was a great feeling. It was a journey that I took on my own volition, serving my country as an American, exercising my right and duty."

Grant Hirabayashi summarized the feelings of a generation of these sons of Japanese immigrants when he spoke of his pride in serving his country *as an American*.

In the beginning, the Nisei GIs had fought the bureaucracy because they saw military service to be their *right* as Americans. The fact that they saw it as their *duty* confirmed that their loyalty as Americans should never have been called into question.

CHAPTER 25

After the War

When World War II ended in Europe on May 7, 1945, the men of the 442nd Regimental Combat Team and its battalions could lay down their arms. The work of some Military Intelligence Service linguists would continue, but for the vast number of Nisei veterans, it was time to return home to the United States. The Nisei GIs had gone overseas anxious to prove themselves both as soldiers and as Americans. As they began to make their way home to small towns from Watsonville to Waialua, they had plenty to be proud of on both accounts. Acknowledged as the most decorated regiment in the U.S. Army, the 442nd came home from Europe with six Presidential Unit Citations (originally Distinguished Unit Citations) and received a seventh from President Harry S Truman in person on the White House lawn.

In a War Department memo, dated August 1, 1945, it was noted officially that 20,861 Nisei enlisted men, 162 officers, and 79 WACs had served in the U.S. Army during World War II. Most of them had served within the 100th Infantry Battalion and the 442nd Regimental Combat Team.

Literally thousands of the men had been written up for individual medals, although it would take months, even years, for all of the medals to actually be awarded. As of April 30, 1946, 48 men would be awarded the Distinguished Service Cross, America's second highest award for valor, and four more would be awarded by the turn of the century. By the end of April 1946, 343 Silver Stars had been awarded—although this number would later be increased to more than 550—along with more than a dozen Oak Leaf Clusters in lieu of second Silver Stars. There were 807 Bronze Stars awarded through April 1946, but eventually, as the paperwork inched its way through the system, that number would more than quadruple. There were also a pair of Italian Crosses for Military Merit (Croce ai Merito di Guerra) and two Italian Medals for Military Valor (Medaglia di Bronzo ai Valor Militaire) as well as a dozen French Croix de Guerre.

Purple Hearts, awarded to men killed or wounded in battle, numbered 2,022 in April 1946, but that did not include wounded personnel who had been shipped to hospitals in the United States. The 100th Infantry Battalion had seen so many men killed or wounded in action that it came to be known as the "Purple Heart Battalion." The number of Purple Hearts awarded to men of the 442nd Regimental Combat Team and its battalions later increased to 9,486, although when one attends veteran reunions and get-togethers, one often hears stories about men who never received Purple Hearts to which they were entitled.

As for the Medal of Honor, the highest American tribute to its military personnel for heroism in wartime, Private First Class Sadao Munemori was the first (and for half a century the *only*) member of the 442nd to be awarded the medal. A member of Company A, he had earned it by sacrificing his life to save others at Seravezza on April 5, 1945. His mother, Nawa Munemori, was still in Manzanar when she got the news of Sadao's death, but she was back living in San Pedro when the medal was authorized. It was issued posthumously on March 7, 1946, and the actual medal was handed to Munemori's widowed mother a week later at her home.

Sadao Munemori's Medal of Honor is now on display at the Smithsonian Institution in Washington, D.C. On April 25, 2000 a monument was dedicated to Private First Class Munemori at Pietrasanta in Italy, not far from where he gave his life to save his comrades.

Four months after Nawa Munemori was handed her son's medal, men of the 442nd assembled in Washington, D.C., to be officially honored by the president with their seventh Presidential Unit Citation. On the rainy afternoon of July 15, 1946, a contingent of men from each of the regiment's three battalions marched down Constitution Avenue and stood in review on the Ellipse south of the White House grounds for the president, the secretary of war, and other dignitaries who wanted to be associated with the highly decorated unit.

"It is a very great pleasure to me today to be able to put the seventh regimental citation on your banners," Harry Truman told the men, aware no doubt of the irony that they were standing in the shadow of the building in which Truman's predecessor had signed Executive Order 9066 nearly five years earlier. "You are to be congratulated on what you have done for this great country of ours. I think it was my predecessor who said that Americanism is not a matter of race or creed, it is a matter of the heart.

"You fought for the free nations of the world along with the rest of us. I congratulate you on that, and I can't tell you how very much I appreciate the privilege of being able to show you just how much the United States of America thinks of what you have done.

"You are now on your way home. You fought not only the enemy, but you fought prejudice—and you have won. Keep up that fight, and we will continue to win—to make this great Republic stand for just what the Constitution says it stands for: the welfare of all the people all the time. Bring forward the colors."

The following day, *The New York Times* carried the story under a headline that read "The Commander-in-Chief Honors Nisei Heroes." The men had gone to war eager to prove themselves, and they had. A long, long time before, in the scheme of things, the Nisei men had gone to boot camp as pariahs, as representatives of an ethnic group that was despised by the angry voice of the American media, which often referred to Japanese Americans simply as "Japs." Now *The New York Times* was calling these sons of Japanese immigrants heroes.

The parade down Constitution Avenue involved merely a contingent from the battalions of the 442nd, because the majority of the men had dispersed across the United States by then. By now, another exodus had taken place across the West, as Issei and Nisei members of families who had been interned in 1942 left the camps to pick up the pieces of their former lives. With the end of the war and the release of the internees, the internment camps were closed between September and December 1945, and the War Relocation Authority went out of business.

By the time President Truman honored the unit in Washington, the war in Europe had been over for a year. Depending on how many points they had—the "point system" governed the order in which GIs were sent home—many of the men had already come home. However, not all those who returned to the States came home right away. For many, there would be long periods of recuperation in military hospitals. Don Seki, who had lost his arm near Biffontaine, was sent to the army hospital at Brigham City, Utah, about fifty miles north of Salt Lake City for about nineteen months.

"The nurses treated the Buddhaheads real nice because we didn't yell and complain," he observed. "Down in Salt Lake, all the Japanese community—from the Buddhist Church to the Girls Club—would throw the Nisei boys a party every weekend. There were Italian prisoners working on the ward, and they went on strike because they didn't like the food. They got rid of the Italians and brought in the German prisoners of war. They were good soldiers."

Seki was fitted with a prosthesis and discharged in December 1946. He then took a civil service job, doing construction work at Tachikawa in Japan. It was here that he was reunited with his parents, whom he had not seen since October 1941, when they had decided to go back to Fukushima. They had wanted to take their sons, but the boys had remained in Hawaii. So much had happened in the intervening years—in both places.

Most of the veterans and former internees returned to the homes they had known before December 7, 1941. Many were lucky. Neighbors had cared for their homes and property while they were gone.

Others were not. They went back to the homes in which they had welcomed the year 1942 only to discover that they had lost everything. In many cases, their former homes were now occupied by someone else. Apartments held new tenants, and many of those who had owned property had felt compelled to sell it in 1942. Now they had to start over. Those who had lost their homes found themselves scrambling for shelter amid the worst housing shortage in decades. Many of the Japanese Americans, including a sizable number of the returning Nisei GIs, wound up in federal housing projects.

Some of those who had managed to take refuge in inland states to avoid the camps remained, but others returned to the West Coast. Lawson Sakai's family had returned to Montebello, California, from Delta, Colorado, during the summer of 1945. When they got home, they discovered that the man to whom they had entrusted their house and acreage had just moved in, and they had to call the sheriff to have him evicted. By the time Lawson got home from Italy, the family was back in the house. Lawson himself married Mineko Hirasaki, whom he met in Colorado, and moved north to Gilroy, California.

"It took quite a while before Japanese Americans were fully integrated back into West Coast society," he recalled. "The American Legion was opposed to having the Nisei back. They even had Japanese American names taken off the unit honor rolls. The Caucasian officers who had been with the 442nd were sent out to the West Coast by the army to speak to the American Legion posts, and other groups. It took a very long time."

The July 15, 1946, "homecoming" parade in Washington, D.C., was the one that had gotten the attention of the commander in chief and *The New York Times,* but the most enthusiastic parade came exactly one month later and 4,800 miles to the west. On March 28, 1943, the city of Honolulu had turned out to give the Nisei GIs of the 442nd Regimental Combat Team a massive send-off. Now, they would turn out to welcome them *home.* The two boisterous civic parties forty-one months apart were like a pair of bookends bracketing the heroic service of the men of the 442nd.

The fun began on August 9, 1946, as the USS *Waterbury Victory* entered the harbor at Honolulu carrying the Nisei veterans. A myriad of smaller vessels steamed or sailed out to meet the ship and to escort it to its berth near the famous Aloha Tower. What a far cry this home-coming was from June 5, 1942, the day that the men of the 100th Infantry Battalion had sailed secretly from this same harbor aboard the SS *Maui* so long ago!

Accompanied by Lieutenant Colonel Alfred Pursall, the 3rd Battalion commander, they disembarked, carrying the regimental colors, which now included the Presidential Unit Citation presented by Truman at the White House. From dockside, the colors were carried to Iolani Palace, the former royal palace of King Kamehameha that later served as the territorial capitol building. Here officers and men of the 442nd were formally greeted by Governor Ingram Stainback. On August 15, it was the turn of the people of Honolulu to welcome the men home as they marched in the Veterans Day Parade, headed by the regimental color guard.

They had gone overseas wanting only to be considered Americans, and they had come back American heroes. Captain Young Oak Kim, the determined and skilled Korean American officer who commanded Company B and later became the operations officer for the 100th Infantry Battalion, said in an interview with the Go For Broke Educational Foundation, "I think the actual success of the 100th and later the 442nd exceeded our fondest hopes. . . . I don't think there was doubt in anyone's mind that they had a goal and they had to do well."

Kim remained in the U.S. Army after World War II, and during the Korean War, he became the first Asian American to command a regular combat battalion. He retired as a colonel in 1972, and was later a principal cofounder of the Japanese American National Museum and the Korean American Museum, both in Los Angeles.

Gradually, Japanese Americans overcame the stigma of the wartime discrimination. A large number of the Nisei veterans attended college on the GI Bill, and a large number became doctors, dentists, architects, scientists, and engineers and took a prominent place in American society. It is hard to sit down with a group of former members of the 442nd or the MIS without meeting retired professionals. Some entered politics, and two became United States Senators. Japanese Americans benefitted greatly from the winds of political and social change that began to blow through the American landscape in the 1950s. It was in 1952 when first-generation Japanese Americans—the parents of the Nisei—were *finally* given the right to become naturalized United States citizens.

Recognition of the accomplishments of the 442nd Regimental Combat Team went a long way toward altering the perception and stereotypes. In 1951, MGM even released a Hollywood feature film. Written and directed by Robert Pirosh, it was called *Go For Broke*, borrowing the regimental slogan of the 442nd. It stars veteran leading man Van Johnson as Lieutenant Mike Grayson, who becomes a metaphor for all the army officers who were skeptical and displeased with having Japanese Americans in uniform. When the newly minted lieutenant is transferred from the 36th Infantry Division to the 442nd to lead a platoon, he is angry and stunned to see a barracks full of Japanese faces. He tries and fails to be transferred out, and goes overseas to Italy, and then France, with his men. Gradually, he becomes a convert, becoming impressed with the skill and bravery of the Nisei GIs.

Receiving second billing in *Go For Broke* was Lane Nakano, a Nisei man who grew up in the Boyle Heights area of Los Angeles, and who actually saw service overseas with Company E of the 442nd while his family was interned at Heart Mountain in Wyoming. After World War II, he began a career as a singer, and he was "discovered" by Robert Pirosh, who saw him perform. He later appeared in King Vidor's 1952 film *Japanese War Bride*, and in episodes of television series such as *Hawaiian Eye* and *Route 66*.

Nowhere were the political and social changes more evident than in Hawaii, where a third of the population was ethnic Japanese. In 1954, two years after the Issei got the right of citizenship, Japanese Americans became a majority in the territorial legislature. Captain

Sakae Takahashi, who commanded the 100th Infantry Battalion's Company B, entered politics, and served as Hawaii's first Japanese American treasurer. It was also in Hawaii that two veterans of the 442nd Regimental Combat Team started out in local politics and went all the way to the United States Senate. Both Daniel Inouye of Company E and Spark Masayuki Matsunaga of Company F, left the U.S. Army with the rank of captain, and attended law school on the mainland—George Washington and Harvard respectively—before returning to the Islands to run for office on the Democratic ticket. They both became members of the Japanese American majority in the territorial legislature in 1954, where they were both major proponents of statehood.

In 1959, Hawaii finally became the fiftieth state, and Daniel Inouye went to Washington as Hawaii's first member of the United States House of Representatives. It was an abbreviated term because Hawaii was not yet a state during the 1958 congressional elections, but Inouye was reelected to a full term in 1960.

In September 1960, shortly before the election, Daniel Inouye had the opportunity to visit the land of his ancestors as an American delegate to the Interparliamentary Union, which was meeting that year in Tokyo. While he was in Japan, he took the opportunity to visit Kyushu and the little village of Yokoyama from which Asakichi Inouye had begun the transpacific odyssey that landed a spur of the Inouye family in what was to become one of the United States. While there, he met his uncle at the thatched-roof Inouye ancestral home. The congressman was invited to remain in Yokoyama and was offered his choice of housing. He declined, having worked too hard to become an American, both in World War II and in his quest for Hawaii statehood.

In 1962, Inouye ran for the U.S. Senate, and his old 2nd Battalion comrade Spark Matsunaga ran for his congressional seat. Both men won. Matsunaga had been nicknamed "Spark," after a cartoon character in the old *Barney Google* comic strip, by his classmates when he was growing up on Kauai. He would later adopt the name officially. He served in the House of Representatives until 1976, when he ran for

Hawaii's other Senate seat and won. He went on to serve as chief deputy whip for twelve of his fourteen years in the Senate, where he also was a member of the Finance Committee and the Energy and Natural Resources Committee. There were two veterans of the 442nd Regimental Combat Team in the United States Senate for fourteen years, until Matsunaga died in 1990 at the age of seventy-three while still in office.

Having achieved a national reputation while serving on the Senate Watergate Committee in the early 1970s, Inouye went on to chair the Select Committee on Intelligence from 1975 until 1979. He was chairman of the Committee on Indian Affairs from 1987 to 1995, and from 2001 to 2003. By the turn of the century he had won seven consecutive senatorial contests, and he was reelected in 2004.

Beginning in 1988, several Nisei men who had served with the MIS during World War II were inducted into the Military Intelligence Corps Hall of Fame at Fort Huachuca, Arizona. Richard Sakakida and Arthur Komori were among the first inductees, as was Hisashi "Johnny" Masuda, the MIS translator whose team intercepted the first evidence of the collapse of the war cabinet of dictatorial Japanese premier Hideki Tojo. Harry Akune, the MIS translator who parachuted under fire into Corregidor in 1945, made the list, as did John Aiso, the brilliant MISLS chief instructor, and Roy Matsumoto, of Frank Merrill's famous "Marauder Samurai."

The roster of the Military Intelligence Corps Hall of Fame also includes the names of Kan Tagami, who served behind enemy lines in Burma with the 124th Cavalry Regiment's Mars Task Force and later as General MacArthur's personal translator from 1946 to 1951, as well as Gero Iwai, whose top-secret 1941 report allowed General Delos Emmons to know that he could trust the Japanese Americans in Hawaii. More important, indeed monumentally more important, was the fact that Iwai's report opened Emmons's mind so far that he suddenly decided to champion the idea of the Nisei battalion that became the 100th Infantry Battalion, which ultimately led to the creation of the 442nd Regimental Combat Team. Without Iwai's little-known report back in the dark days just after Pearl Harbor, the chain of events that culminated in the story behind this book might not have unfolded at it did.

Also in 1988, after years of lobbying, especially by Hawaii's two senators, Congress passed, and President Ronald Reagan signed, the Civil Liberties Act ordering reparations of up to $20,000—and an apology—to be given to Japanese Americans who had been incarcerated in the relocation centers during World War II.

In 1994, the California State Assembly officially honored the Nisei veterans with its Concurrent Resolution 62, which created a "triad" of memorial highways. As mentioned in the beginning of this book, the section of California Highway 99 between the cities of Salida and Manteca became the "442nd Regimental Combat Team Memorial Highway." A portion of the same thoroughfare between Fresno and Madera became the "100th Infantry Battalion Memorial Highway" and farther south, the segment of California Highway 23 between US Highway 101 and Route 118 in Ventura County was named as the "Military Intelligence Service Memorial Highway."

In the meantime, in 1989, a group of Nisei veterans formed the 100th/442nd/MIS World War II Memorial Foundation with the objective of raising the funds to build a permanent monument in the Little Tokyo district of downtown Los Angeles. Captain Young Oak Kim, the 442nd's well-liked Korean American officer, is remembered within the Japanese American and Nisei veteran communities for being instrumental in the establishment of the monument. Designed by Los Angeles architect Roger Yanagita, and dedicated on June 5, 1999, the Go For Broke Monument is a forty-foot-in-diameter black granite circle, rising nine feet at its highest point. Located near the intersection of Temple and Alameda streets, it is engraved with the names of 16,126 Nisei officers and soldiers who served overseas during World War II, as well as those of 37 Nisei women who also served in the armed forces.

The inscription on the monument, written by Ben Tamashiro of the 100th Infantry Battalion and entitled "An American Story," reads:

"Rising to the defense of their country, by the thousands they came—these young Japanese American soldiers from Hawaii, the States, America's concentration camps—to fight in Europe and the Pacific during World War II. Looked upon with suspicion, set apart and deprived of their constitutional rights, they nevertheless remained steadfast and served with indomitable spirit and uncommon valor, for theirs was a fight to prove loyalty. This legacy will serve as a sobering reminder that never again shall any group be denied liberty and the rights of citizenship."

In 2000, the Memorial Foundation formed the Go For Broke Educational Foundation as its operating organization dedicated to carry out its educational mission to teach the story of the Nisei soldiers of World War II, as well as the story of the internment of Japanese Americans during World War II. When the state of California mandated that the story of Nisei veterans be part of the state school curriculum, a grant was awarded to Go For Broke to develop a program to define that story for schoolchildren within the Golden State.

Gradually, the Nisei veterans were getting the recognition that they were due, and at the same time certain veterans were being specifically acknowledged for their wartime actions. When Spark Matsunaga died in 1990, he was replaced by Daniel Kahikina Akaka, the first native Hawaiian to serve in the United States Senate. Four years later, Akaka, who had served with the U.S. Army Corps of Engineers during World War II, won election to a full term in the Senate.

Akaka soon became a very outspoken proponent of the Nisei veterans. Thanks to Akaka and several MIS veterans, especially Harry Fukuhara, Secretary of the Army Louis Caldera arranged for the awarding of a long overdue Presidential Unit Citation to the Military Intelligence Service for "extraordinary heroism in military operations against an armed enemy, 1 May 1942 to 2 September 1945." The two dates are those of the first graduating class of the MIS Language School, and the signing of the surrender documents in Tokyo Bay.

In 1996, Senator Akaka sponsored a bill which initiated a review of the combat records of all Asian American World War II veterans—

including Japanese Americans—to determine whether any of them had been awarded Distinguished Service Crosses or Silver Stars for actions that might have deserved the Medal of Honor, America's highest decoration for wartime valor.

At the time Akaka's bill initiated the review, only four Medals of Honor had ever been awarded to Japanese Americans, and just one to a World War II veteran. This single medal was that which was awarded posthumously to Sadao Munemori for his actions at Seravezza on April 5, 1945. The second Medal of Honor awarded to a Japanese American GI was earned by Sergeant Hiroshi Miyamura of the 7th Infantry Regiment, 3rd Infantry Division, in 1951, during the Korean War. He was captured the day after his Medal of Honor action, and he spent nearly twenty-eight months as a prisoner of war and did not receive his medal until 1953. Miyamura had joined the 442nd Regimental Combat Team as a replacement during World War II, but the war had ended before he went overseas. During the Vietnam War, two Japanese American soldiers, Sergeant Rodney James Takashi Yano and Sergeant Terry Teruo Kawamura, both of the 11th Air Cavalry, were posthumously awarded the Medal of Honor for actions during 1969.

The review of Asian-American World War II records would take four years and add twenty names to the list of Japanese American Medal of Honor awardees, as well as those of a Chinese American GI and a Filipino American of Spanish descent. Captain Francis Wai was killed in action in the Philippines, while Lieutenant Rudolph Davila, who earned his Distinguished Service Cross during the fighting at Anzio, would survive the war.

Said Ed Ichiyama, a 442nd Regimental Combat Team veteran who was instrumental in researching the records for the information that led to the awarding of these medals, "It is absolutely fantastic that after four years, it has finally born fruit. The awardees and their families are excited about these events. That's what makes it all worthwhile—to see the families and the awardees so enthused."

As Secretary of the Army Louis Caldera later pointed out, "It was time to correct the record and render proper recognition. . . . we didn't go out to say whether there was racism or prejudice. We went out to say, 'Are their actions deserving of the Medal of Honor?'"

On June 21, 2000, the Medals of Honor were awarded by President Bill Clinton in a formal ceremony at the White House. Only six of the awardees from the 442nd Regimental Combat Team had lived to see the day. By the summer of 2000, George Sakato was living in Denver, and the others were all living in Hawaii: In addition to Senator Inouye, they were Barney Hajiro of Waipahu, Yukio Okutsu of Hilo, Shizuya Hayashi of Pearl City, and Yeiki "Lefty" Kobashigawa of Waianae. Rudolph Davila, who was then living in Vista, California, was also present.

Senator Akaka, speaking on the floor of the Senate the same day, said that during World War II, the United States "refused to appropriately recognize that these men distinguished themselves by gallantry and audacious courage, risking their lives in service above and beyond the call of duty. . . . It may have taken half a century, but the passage of time has not diminished the magnificence of their courage."

Having pinned the medals on these aging members of America's Greatest Generation at the White House, President Bill Clinton observed, "As sons set off to war, so many mothers and fathers told them, live if you can, die if you must, but fight always with honor, and never ever bring shame on your family or your country. Rarely has a nation been so well served by a people it so ill-treated."

These sons of Japanese immigrants had finally received the recognition that they had earned in the battlefields of Europe more than half a century before.

Epilogue

Two months after the former Nisei GIs received their long, long overdue Medals of Honor, they attended a luncheon at the Hawaii Convention Center in Honolulu, where the choice of keynote speaker was a clear confirmation of how times had changed for Japanese Americans in the U.S. Army since World War II. Back then, there were few Japanese Americans in the army, and virtually no officers above the rank of captain. At the time the medals were awarded in 2000, the U.S. Army's chief of staff was Japanese American.

General Eric "Ric" Shinseki, who spoke at the veterans' luncheon, was the highest-ranking Japanese American ever to serve in the U.S. Army. He had a special connection to the men because he had been inspired to pursue his military career by the stories told by two of his uncles who had served in the 442nd Regimental Combat Team during World War II. A 1965 West Point graduate, Shinseki had lost part of a foot to a land mine in Vietnam, and had been awarded the Distinguished Service Medal, among other decorations.

Shinseki said of the Medal of Honor awardees, "It has been very humbling and gratifying to have these men as our role models. . . . Your generation enabled America to close out the twentieth century as the greatest nation in the history of mankind, the only remaining superpower, the world's leading economy and the world's most respected and feared military force in the world—respected by our friends and allies, feared by our adversaries."

In speaking about the careers of these sons of Japanese immigrants after the war, Shinseki said, "It was the leadership you assumed and provided to us in government, in business, in education, and in many other ways you made your marks. It was the sense of service that you brought back with you—of sacrifice and having served something bigger than yourselves."

Shinseki's own career was a testament to how far Japanese Americans had come in the decades since World War II, but perhaps an even more important testament came at the end of the war, when the contribution of the Nisei GIs was still vividly apparent to the leadership of the U.S. Army. When the war began, the service had questioned whether Japanese Americans should serve at all. Even those who agreed that units such as the 100th Infantry Battalion and 442nd Regimental Combat Team were an experiment worth trying remained skeptical of the potential of Japanese American GIs. However, in just a few short years back then, heads were turned and minds were changed by the courageous example set by the Nisei troops.

At war's end, General Joseph Stilwell, the commander of United States forces in the Asiatic Theater in World War II, was called upon to present the Distinguished Service Cross to Mary Masuda, the sister of Kazuo Masuda, who was killed in action in Italy. In so doing, Stillwell said, "They bought an awful hunk of America with their blood. . . . You're damn right those Nisei boys have a place in the American heart, now and forever. We cannot allow a single injustice to be done to the Nisei without defeating the purposes for which we fought."

Through the decades since the war, many of the veterans traveled back to France and Italy to see the places where they had become heros. Some made several trips, participating in tours organized by 442nd veteran organizations. Others made just one trip back.

More than six decades after the war ended, Shig Kizuka, the third man on top of Monte Folgorito, and one of the three men to create the first hairline crack in the Germans' once-invincible Gothic Line, prepared to make his second trip to the hills above Carrara.

"I want to go back," he told this author with a twinkle in his eye, and a great deal of significance in his choice of words. "I want to see the mountain that we climbed."

APPENDIX 1

Japanese American Recipients of the Medal of Honor During World War II

Awarded at the home of Nawa Munemori in San Pedro, California, on March 7, 1946:

Munemori, Sadao (Private First Class, 100th Infantry Battalion)
For sacrificing his life to save others at Seravezza, Italy on April 5, 1945. (Posthumous)

Awarded at the White House in Washington, D.C., on June 21, 2000:

Hajiro, Barney F. (Private, 442nd Regimental Combat Team)
For actions at Bruyères and Biffontaine, France, during October 1944.

Hasemoto, Mikio (Private, 100th Infantry Battalion)
For actions at Cerasuolo, Italy on November 29, 1943. (Posthumous)

Hayashi, Joe (Private, 442nd Regimental Combat Team)
For actions at Tendola, Italy, during April 1945.

Hayashi, Shizuya (Private, 100th Infantry Battalion)
For actions at Cerasuolo, Italy, on November 29, 1943.

Inouye, Daniel K. (2nd Lieutenant, 442nd Regimental Combat Team)
For actions at San Terenzo, Italy, on April 21, 1945.

Kobashigawa, Yeiki "Lefty" (Technical Sergeant, 100th Infantry Battalion)
For actions at Lanuvio, Italy, on June 2, 1944.

Kuroda, Robert T. (Sergeant, 442nd Regimental Combat Team)
For actions at Bruyères, France on October 20, 1944. (Posthumous)

Moto, Kaoru (Private First Class, 100th Infantry Battalion)
For actions at Castellina, Italy, on July 7, 1944. (Posthumous)

Muranaga, Kiyoshi K. (Private First Class, 442nd Regimental Combat Team)
For actions at Suvereto, Italy, on June 26, 1944. (Posthumous)

Nakae, Masato "Curly" (Private, 100th Infantry Battalion/442nd Regimental Combat Team)
For actions near Pisa, Italy, on August 19, 1944. (Posthumous)

Nakamine, Shinyei (Private, 100th Infantry Battalion)
For actions at La Torreto, Italy, on June 2, 1944. (Posthumous)

Nakamura, William K. (Private First Class, 442nd Regimental Combat Team)
For actions at Castellina, Italy, on July 4, 1944. (Posthumous)

Nishimoto, Joe M. (Private First Class, 442nd Regimental Combat Team)
For actions at La Houssière, France, on November 7, 1944. (Posthumous)

Ohata, Allan M. (Sergeant, later Captain, 100th Infantry Battalion)
For actions at Cerasuolo, Italy, during November 1943.

Okubo, James K. (Technical Sergeant)
For actions near Biffontaine, France, on October 28 and 29, and November 4, 1944. (Posthumous)

Okutsu, Yukio (Technical Sergeant, 442nd Regimental Combat Team)
For actions at Monte Belvedere, Italy, on April 7, 1945.

Ono, Frank H. (Private First Class, 442nd Regimental Combat Team)
For actions at Castellina, Italy, on July 4, 1944. (Posthumous)

Otani, Kazuo (Staff Sergeant, 442nd Regimental Combat Team)
For actions at Pieve di San Luce, Italy, on July 15, 1944. (Posthumous)

Sakato, George T. (Private, 442nd Regimental Combat Team)
For actions in Biffontaine, France, on October 29, 1944.

Tanouye, Ted T. (Technical Sergeant, 442nd Regimental Combat Team)
For actions at Molina, Italy, on July 7, 1944. (Posthumous)

List of Internment Camps

This list is included for the sake of general reference. A full discussion of the internment of Japanese Americans during World War II is beyond the scope of this work (although only barely) and has been dealt with more extensively elsewhere.

The War Relocation Authority oversaw the construction of ten incarceration camps in sparsely populated and isolated areas, mostly on unused desert or swampland under federal control. Between June and October 1942, internees were transferred from assembly centers to the larger camps. Housing approximately 120,000 people, the internment camps were designed to be self-contained communities, complete with residential areas, factories, hospitals, offices, post offices, schools, and warehouses. Some were near existing towns, others in remote locations.

Gila River (Arizona)
Granada (Amache, Colorado)
Heart Mountain (Wyoming)
Jerome (Denson, Arkansas)
Manzanar (California)
Minidoka (Hunt, Idaho)
Poston, a.k.a. Colorado River (Parker, Arizona)
Rohwer (McGehee, Arkansas)
Topaz, a.k.a. Central Utah (Delta, Utah)
Tule Lake (Newell, California)

Prior to being sent to these camps, most Japanese American internees were held briefly in temporary assembly centers located in facilities such as horse racing tracks. In addition to those interned at the large camps, a small number of Japanese Americans were held for varying lengths of time at such locations as Department of Justice facilities, army camps, citizen isolation centers, federal prisons, and immigration detention stations.

Text of the Presidential Unit Citations awarded to the
100th Infantry Battalion and the 442nd Regimental
Combat Team

The 100th Infantry Battalion (Separate)
Cited in War Department General Orders 66, 15 August 1944:

The 100th Infantry Battalion (Separate) is cited for outstanding performance of duty in action on 26 and 27 June 1944 in the vicinity of Belvedere and Sassetta, Italy. The 100th Infantry Battalion was assigned the mission of neutralizing a strongly defended German center of resistance at Belvedere, Italy, which dominated a vital highway and seriously impeded an American infantry division's northward advance. With insufficient time for a proper physical reconnaissance but with a determined desire to fulfill its important mission, the battalion quickly formulated its plan and launched the operation. The battalion maneuvered to a point one mile northwest of Belvedere where a large and determined force of German infantry and field artillery, including self-propelled guns and tanks, was encountered. Initially one company of the 100th Infantry Battalion was committed toward the west to engage the enemy reserves and field artillery batteries. A second company passed through the leading company to continue the attack southward to cut the road leading to Sassetta, Italy. All three companies went into action, boldly facing murderous fire from all types of weapons and tanks and at times fighting without artillery support. Doggedly the members of the 100th Infantry Battalion fought their way into the strongly defended positions. The stubborn desire of the men to close with a numerically superior enemy and the rapidity with which they fought enabled the 100th Infantry Battalion to destroy completely the right flank positions of a German army, killing at least 178 Germans, wounding approximately 20, capturing 73, and forcing the remainder of a completely disrupted battalion to surrender approximately 10 kilometers of ground. In addition, large quantities of enemy weapons, vehicles, and equipment were either captured or destroyed, while the American infantry division operating in the sector was able to continue its rapid advance. The fortitude and intrepidity displayed by the officers and men of the 100th Infantry Battalion reflect the finest traditions of the Army of the United States.

The 100th Battalion, 442nd Regimental Team
Cited in War Department General Orders 78, 12 September 1945:

The 100th Battalion, 442nd Regimental Team, is cited for outstanding accomplishment in combat during the period 15 to 30 October 1944, near Bruyères, Biffontaine, and in the Forêt Domaniale de Champ, France. During a series of actions that played a telling part in the 442nd Regimental Team's operation which spearheaded a divisional attack on the Seventh Army front, this unit displayed extraordinary courage, endurance, and soldierly skill. Jumping off in the attack on the morning of 15 October 1944, the 100th Battalion fought an almost continuous four-day fire fight in freezing and rainy weather, through jungle-like forests, to wrest the strongly fortified Hill A, dominating Bruyères, from a fanatically resisting enemy. When, during the course of the attack, the progress of an assault company was delayed by a strong point consisting of 50 enemy riflemen and an SP [self-propelled] gun, a second company of the battalion swept in on the enemy force from the flank and completely routed it. To attack Hill A proper, the battalion was forced to cross 150 yards of open terrain covered by seven enemy machine guns and heavy automatic weapon fire. Following an artillery barrage, limited because a draw lay between the two high hills, the battalion, with one company acting as a base of fire, launched a frontal attack. Covered by friendly tank fire, waves of platoon after platoon zigzagged across the open field into a hail of hostile fire. So skillfully coordinated was the attack that the strongly fortified hostile positions were completely overrun, numerous casualties were inflicted on the enemy, and the capture of the town was assured. During the three-day operation, beginning on 21 October 1944, that resulted in the capture of Biffontaine, the 100th Battalion fought two miles into enemy territory as a self-contained task force. On the third day of the attack, the battalion launched an assault to capture the isolated town. In the first surprise onslaught the battalion captured large quantities of supplies and ammunition which it turned against the enemy. Counterattacking enemy troops and tanks approached and fired point-blank into their positions. Shouting defiance in the face of demands for surrender, the men of the 100th Battalion fired their rifles and threw captured hand grenades at the enemy tanks. Bitter fighting at close range resulted in the capture of the entire town. During this action the battalion captured 40 prisoners, killed or wounded 40 of the enemy, and destroyed or captured large quantities of ammunition and enemy materiel. On 27 October 1944 the 100th Battalion was again committed to the attack. Going to the rescue of the "Lost Battalion," 141st Infantry Regiment, it fought without respite for four days against a fanatical enemy that was determined to keep the "Lost Battalion" isolated and force its surrender. Impelled by the urgency of its mission, the battalion fought forward, risking encirclement as slower moving units left its flanks exposed. Fighting yard by yard through a mine field the battalion was stopped by an enemy strong point on the high ground which he had made the key to his defense. As the terrain precluded a flanking movement, the battalion was forced to the only alternative of a frontal attack against a strongly entrenched enemy. Attacking in waves of squads and platoons, and firing from the hip as they closed in to grenade range, the valiant men of the 100th Battalion reduced the enemy defense lines within a few hours. Between 50 and 60 enemy dead were found at their automatic weapon emplacements and dugouts. On the fourth day, although exhausted and reduced through casualties to about half its normal strength, the battalion fought doggedly forward against strong enemy small-arms and mortar fire until it contacted the isolated unit. The extraordinary heroism, daring determination, and esprit de corps displayed by the men of the 100th Battalion, 442nd Regimental Team, during these actions live as an inspiration and add glory to the highest traditions of the armed forces of the United States. (General Orders 360, Headquarters Seventh Army, 3 August 1945, as approved by the Commanding General European Theater.)

The 442nd Regimental Combat Team
(less the 2nd Battalion and the 522nd Field Artillery Battalion)
Cited in War Department General Orders 34, 10 April 1946, as amended by
War Department General Orders 106, 20 September 1946:

The 442nd Regimental Combat Team (less the 2nd Battalion and the 522nd Field Artillery Battalion) composed of the following elements: [442nd Infantry Regiment; 232nd Combat Engineer Company] is cited for outstanding accomplishment in combat for the period 5 to 14 April 1945 in the vicinity of Serravezza, Carrara, and Fosdinovo, Italy. When the 92nd Infantry Division with the 442nd Regimental Combat Team attached was ordered to open the Fifth Army offensive by executing a diversionary attack on the Ligurian Coast of Italy, the combat team was ordered to make the main effort of the attack. It was done by executing a daring and skillful flanking attack on the positions which formed the western anchor of the formidable Gothic Line. In four days, the attack destroyed positions which had withstood the efforts of friendly troops for five months. This was accomplished in the face of skilled enemy forces nearly equal in strength to the attacking forces and who had at least five months in which to improve their position. The 442nd Regimental Combat Team drove forward, despite heavy casualties. Allowing the enemy no time for rest or reorganization, the combat team liberated the city of

Carrara, seized the heights beyond, and opened the way for further advances on the way to the key road center and port of La Spezia and to Genoa. It accomplished the mission of creating a diversion along the Ligurian Coast, which served as a feint for the subsequent breakthrough of the Fifth Army forces into Bologna and the Po Valley. The successful accomplishment of this mission turned a diversionary action into a full scale and victorious offensive, which played an important part in the dual destruction of the German armies in Italy. The gallantry and esprit de corps displayed by the officers and men of the 442nd Regimental Combat Team in bitter action against a formidable enemy exemplify the finest tradition of the armed forces of the United States.

The 2nd Battalion, 442nd Regimental Combat Team
Cited in War Department General Orders 83, 6 August 1946:

The 2nd Battalion, 442nd Regimental Combat Team, is cited for outstanding performance of duty in action on 19 October 1944 near Bruyères, France, on 28 and 29 October 1944 near Biffontaine, France, and from 6 to 10 April 1945, near Massa, Italy. The 2nd Battalion executed a brilliant tactical operation in capturing Hill 503, to expedite the forward movement beyond Bruyères, France and to erase the German threat from the rear. While two companies pressed forward against a formidable enemy main line of resistance, other elements of the battalion struck the enemy paralyzing blows from all directions, practically eliminating an entire German company and destroying numerous enemy automatic weapons. Attacking the strategic heights of Hill 617 near Biffontaine, France, on 28 October 1944, the 2nd Battalion secured its objective in a two-day operation, which eliminated a threat to the flanks of two American divisions. In the face of intense enemy barrages and numerous counterattacks, the infantrymen of this battalion fought their way through difficult jungle-like terrain in freezing weather and completely encircled the enemy. Methodically, the members of the 2nd Battalion hammered the enemy, inflicting heavy casualties upon the defenders and wresting this vital feature from the surviving Germans. Maintaining its admirable record of achievement in the vicinity of Massa, Italy, the 2nd Battalion smashed through and exploited the strong Green Line on the Ligurian Coast. Surging over formidable heights through strong resistance, the 2nd Battalion, in five days of continuous, heavy fighting, captured a series of objectives to pave the way for the entry into the important communications centers of Massa and Carrara, Italy, without opposition. In this operation, the 2nd Battalion accounted for more than 200 Germans and captured or destroyed large quantities of enemy materiel. The courage, determination, and esprit de corps evidenced by the officers and men of the 2nd Battalion, 442nd Regimental Combat Team, exemplify the highest traditions of the armed forces of the United States. (General Orders 89, Headquarters Fifth Army, 17 July 1945.)

The 3rd Battalion, 442nd Regimental Combat Team Cited in War Department General Orders 68, 14 August 1945:

The 3rd Battalion, 442nd Regimental Combat Team, is cited for outstanding accomplishment in combat during the period 27 to 30 October 1944, near Biffontaine, France. On 27 October the 3rd Battalion, 442nd Regimental Combat Team, was committed to battle after 1½ days in a divisional reserve. One of the battalions of another unit which had been advancing deep into enemy territory beyond the town of Biffontaine was suddenly surrounded by the enemy, and separated from all friendly units by an enemy force estimated at 700 men. The mission of the 3rd Battalion was to attack abreast with the 100th Battalion and four other battalions and relieve the entrapped unit. The mission was more difficult than it first appeared for the enemy had reoccupied the thickly wooded hills situated within the 2½ miles separating the "Lost Battalion" from our front lines. For four days the battalion fought the stubborn enemy who was determined to stop all attempts to rescue the besieged battalion. Several roadblocks skillfully reinforced by machine guns had to be destroyed while under heavy artillery fire. On 29 October the battalion encountered a well-defended hill where the enemy, 100 strong, held well-dug-in positions on the hill and would not be dislodged. After repeated frontal assaults had failed to drive the enemy from the hill, Companies I and K, then leading the attack, fixed bayonets and charged up the slope, shouting at the enemy and firing from their hips, while the enemy fired point-blank into their ranks. Despite effective enemy fire the determined men pressed the assault and closed in with the enemy nearing the enemy machine-gun and machine-pistol positions; some of the men charged the gun emplacements with Thompson submachine guns or BAR's, killing or seriously wounding the enemy gun crew, but themselves sprawling dead over the enemy positions they had just neutralized. Completely unnerved by the vicious bayonet charge, the enemy fled in confusion after making a desperate stand. Though seriously depleted in manpower, the battalion hurled back two determined enemy counterattacks, and after reducing a heavily mined roadblock finally established contact with the besieged battalion. The intrepidity, fearless courage, and complete disregard for personal safety displayed by the officers and enlisted men of the 3rd Battalion, 442nd Regimental Combat Team, exemplify the finest traditions of the armed forces of the United States. (General Orders 317, Headquarters Seventh Army, 16 July 1945, as approved by the Commanding General, European Theater of Operations.)

Companies F and L, 442nd Regimental Combat Team Cited in War Department General Orders 14, 4 March 1945:

Companies F and L, 442nd Regimental Combat Team, are cited for outstanding performance of duty in action on 21 October 1944, in the vicinity of Belmont, France. Assigned the mission of assaulting the flank and rear of the resistance which had stopped two frontal attacks by the combat team, Companies F and L, 442nd Regimental Combat Team, designated the O'Connor Task Force, launched an attack down the north slope of the wooded ridge, Forêt de Belmont. Company L, leading the assault, defeated a security group in a short, sharp action, capturing several prisoners. Then, by the prompt use of hand grenades and mortars, the garrisoned houses just outside the woods were quickly reduced. The capture of these houses was an important factor in the success of the mission as it gave the task force observation on the ground to the enemy rear. To complete its work the task force now had to interdict enemy movement, drive a wedge through the forces resisting the combat team, and effect a junction with the main force. Heavy casualties were inflicted by artillery fire directed by the task force's forward observer on the enemy positions. Then assault groups began to clear the defenders from houses to the north of La Broquine. The capture of these houses not only divided the enemy forces, but made certain that large numbers of the enemy would be trapped between the task force and the advancing combat team. By midafternoon the task force and the combat team made contact and what enemy troops were not surrounded were completely routed, thus bringing to a close a plan brilliantly conceived and expertly executed. By the next day the combat team had secured the high ridge which dominates Belmont. In destroying the enemy main line of resistance and advancing the divisional front lines by approximately 2,000 meters, the task force captured 56 prisoners, killed 80 of the enemy, and captured considerable quantifies of enemy materiel and equipment. The fearless determination, daring, and intrepidity displayed by the officers and enlisted men of the O'Connor Task Force exemplify the finest traditions of the armed forces of the United States.

The 232nd Engineer Combat Company
(then attached to the 111th Engineer Combat Battalion)
Cited in War Department General Orders 56, 17 June 1946:

111th Engineer Combat Battalion with 232nd Engineer Combat Company (attached), for heroism, esprit de corps, and extraordinary achievement in combat from 23 October to 11 November 1944 near Bruyères, France. When it was decided to attack through the Forêt

Domaniale de Champ and outflank the German forces in the Laveline-Corcieux Valley, this unit was called upon to build a supply road out of a mountain trail which rose 1,000 feet above the valley floor and progress through a dense forest to the division objective. Working directly behind the assault elements, the men of this unit labored unceasingly to build and maintain this road. Artillery fire crashed into the trees, showering shrapnel on the engineers, who had no protection as they worked. Enemy snipers infiltrating behind our lines caused casualties and some of the engineers engaged these Germans in a fire fight while the others continued to work. Tanks were called up and, though these heavy vehicles tore the bottom from the trail, the engineers were able to keep it open so that the constant flow of supplies to the nine infantry battalions engaged in the action and the constant evacuation of dead and wounded was never interrupted. Corduroy and planking were used, hundreds of enemy mines were removed, and gravel and paving stones were hauled from the surrounding country side. At no time during the 19 days of this action did the work cease. Even though the engineers sustained 57 casualties in dead and wounded, they captured 27 German prisoners and killed many more as they worked. Almost continuous rain and snow made their task more difficult, and yet by sheer determination and grit, these men accomplished this magnificent feat of engineering. Without this road, the division operation could not have succeeded and it is due to the extraordinary achievement of the 11th Engineer Combat Battalion with the 232nd Engineer Combat Company (attached) that the 36th Division was able to outflank the enemy forces in the Laveline-Corcieux Valley and pursue a disorganized enemy to the banks of the Meurthe River. (General Orders 425, Headquarters 36th Infantry Division, 1 October 1945, as approved by the Commanding General, 36th Infantry Division.)

BIBLIOGRAPHY

BOOKS AND PUBLICATIONS

Allen, Gwenfread. *Hawaii's War Years, 1941–1945.* Greenwood. 1971. Originally published 1950.

Ankrum, Homer R. *Dogfaces Who Sailed Through Tears: The 34th Red Bull Infantry Division and Attached 100th (Hawaiian) Battalion and 442nd Go for Broke Regimental Combat Team in World War II: A Chronicle of the Heartbreaks, Hardships, Heroics, and Humor of the North African and Italian Campaigns.* Graphic. 1987.

Armor, John; Hersey, John; and Wright, Peter. *A Mistake of Terrifically Horrible Proportions.* With commentary by John Hersey, photographs by Ansel Adams. Times Books. 1988.

Blumenson, Martin. *Salerno to Cassino.* U.S. Army Center of Military History. 1969.

Burton, J.; Farrell, M.; Lord, F.; and Lord, R. *Confinement and Ethnicity: An Overview of World War II Japanese American Relocation Sites.* Western Archeological and Conservation Center. National Park Service. U.S. Department of the Interior. 1999.

Burton, Jeffery F. *Three Farewells to Manzanar: The Archeology of Manzanar National Historic Site, California.* Western Archeological and Conservation Center Publication in Anthropology 67. National Park Service. 1996.

Chang, Thelma. *I Can Never Forget: Men of the 100th/442nd.* Sigi. 1991.

Chuman, Frank. *The Bamboo People: The Law and Japanese Americans.* Japanese American Research Project. 1976.

Clinton Foundation. *Fact Sheet on Historic Patriotism of Japanese Americans.* March 19, 2001.

Cohen, Irene J. *Manzanar: A Japanese American Relocation Center Memorial.* Master's thesis, School of Architecture, University of Illinois. 1994.

Coles, Harry L., and Weinberg, Albert K. *Civil Affairs: Soldiers Become Governors.* U.S. Army Center of Military History. 1992.

Commission on Wartime Relocation and Internment of Civilians. *Personal Justice Denied.* Government Printing Office. 1982.

Crost, Lyn. *Honor by Fire: Japanese Americans at War in Europe and the Pacific.* Presidio Press. 1994.

Crowl, Philip A. *Campaign in the Marianas, The United States Army in World War II: The War in the Pacific.* Office of the Chief of Military History. 1960.

Daniels, Roger. *Concentration Camps, North America: Japanese in the United States and Canada During World War II.* Robert E. Krieger, Malabar, Florida. 1989.

Daniels, Roger; Taylor, Sandra C.; and Kitano, Harry H. L., eds. *Japanese Americans from Relocation to Redress,* rev. ed. University of Washington Press. 1991.

Davis, Daniel S. *Behind Barbed Wire: The Imprisonment of Japanese Americans During World War II.* E. P. Dutton. 1982.

Dower, John W. *War Without Mercy: Race and Power in the Pacific War.* Pantheon. 1986.

Drea, Edward J. *MacArthur's Ultra: Codebreaking and the War Against Japan, 1942–1945.* University Press of Kansas. 1992.

Drinnon, Richard. *Keeper of Concentration Camps: Dillon S. Myer and American Racism.* University of California Press. 1987.

Duus, Masayo Umezawa. *Unlikely Liberators: The Men of the 100th and 442nd.* University of Hawaii Press. 1987.

Embrey, Sue Kunitomi; Hansen, Arthur A.; and Mitson, Betty Kulberg. *Manzanar Martyr: An Interview with Harry Y. Ueno.* Japanese American Oral History Project. California State University, Fullerton. 1986.

Felt, Marion F. *The Operations of the 2nd Platoon, Company A, 100th Battalion, 442nd Combat Team in the Attack on Hill Georgia, North of Serravesza* [sic] *Italy, 6 April 1945 (Po Valley Campaign).* Personal Experience of a Platoon Leader. Fort Benning Infantry School. 1949.

Finnegan, John P., and Gilbert, James L. *U.S. Army Signals Intelligence in World War II: A Documentary History.* U.S. Army Center of Military History. 1993.

Finnegan, John Patrick. *Military Intelligence.* U.S. Army Center of Military History. 1998.

Fisher, Ernest F., Jr. *Cassino to the Alps.* U.S. Army in World War II. U.S. Army Center of Military History. 1977.

Fujita, Frank. *Foo: A Japanese American Prisoner of the Rising Sun: The Secret Prison Diary of Frank "Foo" Fujita.* University of North Texas Press. 1993.

Gardiner, C. Harvey. "The Latin American Japanese and World War II." In *Japanese Americans: From Relocation to Redress,* edited by Roger Daniels, Sandra C. Taylor, and Harry H. L. Kitano. Rev. ed. University of Washington Press. 1991.

Garrett, Jessie A., and Larson, Ronald C. *Camp and Community: Manzanar and the Owens Valley.* Japanese American Oral History Project. California State University. 1977.

General Headquarters, Far East Command, Military Intelligence Section, General Staff. *A Brief History of the G-2 Section, GHQ, SWPA, and Affiliated Units.* U.S. Army. 1947–1948.

Girdner, Audrie, and Loftis, Anne. *The Great Betrayal: The Evacuation of the Japanese-Americans During World War II.* Macmillan. 1969.

Goto, George. *History of the 232nd Engineer Combat Company.* 232nd Engineer Company, U.S. Army. No date.

Halloran, Richard. *Sparky: Warrior, Peacemaker, Poet, Patriot.* Honolulu. Watermark Publishing. 2002.

Hansen, Arthur A. *Transforming Barbed Wire,* edited by Rick Noguchi. Arizona Humanities Council. 1977.

Harrington, Joseph D. *Yankee Samurai: The Secret Role of Nisei in America's Pacific Victory.* Pettigrew Enterprises. 1979.

Hirabayashi, Gordon K. "The Japanese Canadians and World War II." In *Japanese Americans from Relocation to Redress,* edited by Roger Daniels, Sandra C. Taylor, and Harry H. L. Kitano. Rev. ed. University of Washington Press. 1991.

Ichinokuchi, Tad, ed. *John Aiso and the MIS: Japanese-American Soldiers in the Military Intelligence Service, World War II.* Military Intelligence Service Club of Southern California. 1988.

Ichioka, Yuji. *Views from Within: The Japanese American Evacuation and Resettlement Study.* Asian American Studies Center. University of California. 1989.

Inouye, Daniel K., with Lawrence Elliot. *Journey to Washington.* Prentice Hall. 1967.

Inouye, Mamoru. *The Heart Mountain Story: Photographs by Hansel and Otto Hagel of the World War II Internment of Japanese Americans.* Privately published, Mamoru Inouye. 1997.

Iriye, Akira. *Power and Culture: The Japanese-American War, 1941–1945.* Harvard University Press. 1981.

Irons, Peter. *Justice at War: The Story of the Japanese American Internment Cases.* Oxford University Press. 1983.

Japanese American Curriculum Project. *Wartime Hysteria: The Role of the Press in the Removal of 110,000 Persons of Japanese Ancestry During World War II.* Japanese American Curriculum Project. 1973.

Keegan, Christopher R. *The Operations of the 2nd Battalion, 442nd Infantry (Attached to the 34th Infantry Division) in the Pursuit to the Arno in the Vicinity of Suvere, Italy, 26th June 1944 (Rome-Arno Campaign).* Personal Experience of a Heavy Weapons Company Commander. Fort Benning Infantry School. 1949.

Kikuchi, Charles. *The Kikuchi Diary: Chronicle from an American Concentration Camp: The Tanforan Journals of Charles Kikuchi,* edited by John Modell. University of Illinois Press. 1973.

Leighton, Alexander H. *The Governing of Men: General Principles and Recommendations Based on Experience at a Japanese Relocation Camp.* Princeton University Press. 1945.

Lindstrom, Lamont, and White, Geoffrey M. *Island Encounters: Black and White Memories of the Pacific War.* Smithsonian Institution Press. 1990.

Marshall, Lieutenant Colonel Carley, and Stephenson, Captain Roy L. *History, 133rd Infantry Regiment, 34th Infantry Division From 22 September 1943 to 31 October 1943.* U.S. Army. 1943.

McNaughton, Dr. James C. *Nisei Linguists and New Perspectives on the Pacific War: Intelligence, Race, and Continuity.* Presented at the Conference of Army Historians. 1994.

MIS Association of Northern California and National Japanese American Historical Society. *The Pacific War and Peace: Americans of Japanese Ancestry in Military Intelligence Service 1941 to 1952.* MIS Association of Northern California and National Japanese American Historical Society. 1991.

MIS Veterans Club of Hawaii. *Secret Valor: MIS Personnel, World War II, Pacific Theater, Pre-Pearl Harbor to September 8, 1951.* MIS Veterans Club of Hawaii. 1993.

Mitson, Betty E., and Hansen, Arthur A. *Voices Long Silent: An Oral Inquiry into the Japanese American Excavation.* California State University. Japanese American Project. 1974.

Morita, Hiroaki. *The Nation's Most Decorated Military Unit: The 100th/442nd Regimental Combat Team.* Army War College. 1992.

Murphy, Thomas D. *Ambassadors in Arms: The Story of Hawaii's 100th Battalion.* University of Hawaii Press. 1954.

Myer, Dillon S. *Uprooted Americans: The Japanese Americans and the War Relocation Authority During World War II.* University of Arizona Press. 1971.

Nakamura, Robert A. *Something Strong Within.* Japanese American National Museum. 1994.

Nakano, Takano Ujo, and Nakano, Leatrice. *Within the Barbed Wire Fence: A Japanese Man's Account of His Internment in Canada.* University of Toronto Press. 1980.

Nakatsuka, Lawrence. *Hawaii's Own: Picture Story of 442nd Regiment, 100th Battalion.* L. H. Sakamoto. 1946.

National Japanese American Historical Society. *Due Process: Americans of Japanese Ancestry and the United States Constitution.* National Japanese American Historical Society. 1995.

Ogaawa, Dennis M., and Fox, Evarts C., Jr. "Japanese Internment and Relocation: The Hawaii Experience," in *Japanese Americans from Relocation to Redress.* (Revised edition, edited by Roger Daniels, Sandra C. Taylor, and Harry H. L. Kitano.) University of Washington Press. 1991.

Oiye, George. *Footprints in My Rearview Mirror.* Xulon Press. 2003.

Rademaker, John A. *These Are Americans: The Japanese Americans in Hawaii in World War II.* Pacific Books. 1951.

Saiki, Patsy Sumie. *Ganbare! An Example of Japanese Spirit.* University of Hawaii Press. 1982.

Santos, Robert LeRoy. *The Army Needs Men: An Account of the U.S. Army Rehabilitation Center at Turlock, California 1942–1945.* University Library, California State University, Stanislaus. No date.

Sayer, Ian, and Botting, Douglas. *America's Secret Army: The Untold Story of the Counter Intelligence Corps.* Franklin Watts. 1989.

Spector, Ronald, ed. *Listening to the Enemy: Key Documents on the Role of Communications Intelligence in the War with Japan.* Scholarly Resources. 1988.

Stanley, Jerry. *I Am an American: A True Story of Japanese Internment.* Crown Publishers. 1994.

Takaki, Ronald. *Strangers from a Different Shore: A History of Asian Americans.* Little, Brown. 1989.

Tanaka, Chester. *Go For Broke: A Pictorial History of the Japanese American 100th Infantry Battalion and the 442nd Regimental Combat Team.* Go For Broke, Inc. 1982.

Tateishi, John. *And Justice for All: An Oral History of the Japanese-American Detention Camps.* Random House. 1984.

Thomas, Gerald W.; Billington, Monroe L.; and Walker, Roger D. *Victory in World War II: The New Mexico Story.* Rio Grande Historical Collections. New Mexico State University Library, Las Cruces. 1994.

Unrau, Harlan D. *Manzanar: Historic Resource Study / Special History Study,* vol. 1 and 2. Manzanar National Historic Site. U.S. Department of the Interior, National Park Service. 1996.

U.S. Army Center of Military History. *Anzio Beachhead (22 January–25 May 1944).* American Forces in Action. U.S. Army Center of Military History. 1947.

U.S. Army Center of Military History. *Anzio: 22 January–24 May 1944.* U.S. Army Campaigns of World War II. U.S. Army Center of Military History. 1945.

U.S. Army Center of Military History. *Fifth Army at the Winter Line (15 November 1943–15 January 1944).* American Forces in Action. U.S. Army Center of Military History. 1945.

U.S. Army Center of Military History. *Naples-Foggia: 9 September 1943–21 January 1944.* U.S. Army Campaigns of World War II. U.S. Army Center of Military History. 1945.

U.S. Army Center of Military History. *North Apennines: 10 September 1944–4 April 1945.* U.S. Army Campaigns of World War II. U.S. Army Center of Military History. 1945.

U.S. Army Center of Military History. *Po Valley: 5 April–8 May 1945.* U.S. Army Campaigns of World War II. U.S. Army Center of Military History. 1945.

U.S. Army Center of Military History. *Rome-Arno: 22 January–9 September 1944.* U.S. Army Campaigns of World War II. U.S. Army Center of Military History. 1945.

U.S. Army Center of Military History. *Salerno: American Operations from the Beaches to the Volturno (9 September–6 October 1943).* American Forces in Action. U.S. Army Center of Military History. 1944.

U.S. Army Center of Military History. *Training History of the Military Intelligence Service Language School, Fort Snelling, Minnesota.* U.S. Army Center of Military History. 1945–1946.

U.S. Army Center of Military History. *Volturno: From the Volturno to the Winter Line (6 October–15 November 1943).* American Forces in Action. U.S. Army Center of Military History. 1945.

U.S. Army Mediterranean Theater of Operations. *The Story of the 442nd Combat Team Composed of 442nd Infantry Regiment, 522nd Field Artillery Battalion, 232nd Combat Engineer Company.* U.S. Army Mediterranean Theater of Operations. 1945.

U.S. Army Military History Reference Branch. *442nd Combat Team, World War II: A Working Bibliography of Military History Sources.* 1999.

U.S. Army. *Combat Chronicles of U.S. Army Divisions.* U.S. Government Printing Office. 1950.

U.S. Army. *Go For Broke.* Brochure of exhibit. Presidio Museum. 1981.

U.S. Army. Information and Education Section, Mediterranean Theater. *The Story of the 34th Infantry Division, Book I, Louisiana to Pisa.* Compiled by Members of 34th Infantry Division. 1945.

U.S. Army. *The Army Almanac: A Book of Facts Concerning the Army of the United States.* Government Printing Office. 1950.

U.S. Army. *The Story of the 36th Infantry Division.* Division booklet compiled from *T-Patch,* the Division Newspaper. Printed by Desfossés-Néogravure, Paris. 1945.

U.S. Department of the Army. Office, Chief of Military History. *Army Lineage Book.* U.S. Army Center of Military History. Government Printing Office. 1953.

U.S. Department of the Interior. War Relocation Authority. *Nisei in Uniform.* Government Printing Office. 1944.

U.S. War Department. Military Intelligence Division. *Salerno: American Operations from the Beaches to the Volturno, 9 September–6 October 1943.* U.S. Army Center of Military History. 1990. Originally published 1944.

Uyeda, Clifford. *The Meaning of Citizenship to Americans of Japanese Ancestry.* Presented before the Organization of American Historians. San Francisco. April 18, 1997.

Wakamatsu, Jack K. *Silent Warriors: A Memoir of America's 442nd Regimental Combat Team.* JKW. 1992.

Weglyn, Michi. *Years of Infamy: The Untold Story of America's Concentration Camps.* Morrow Quill. 1976.

PERIODICALS

Alvarez, Gayle. "Japanese-American War Heroes Honored." *Seattle Times,* March 26, 2001.

Akaka, Senator Daniel. "Tribute to the Late Lieutenant Colonel Richard Sakakida." *Congressional Record,* January 30, 1996.

"American-Born Japs Enjoy War on Nazis." *St. Paul Pioneer Press,* October 20, 1943.

"American Born Japs Fight with 5th Army." *Washington News,* October 4, 1943.

Ano, Masaharu. "Loyal Linguists: Nisei of World War II Learned Japanese in Minnesota." *Minnesota History.* Fall 1977.

"Ben Kuroki, American." *Time,* February 7, 1944.

Blakeman, Karen. "Yeiki Kobashigawa, World War II Hero." *Honolulu Advertiser,* May 13, 2005.

Bradsher, Greg. "The Z Plan Story: Japan's 1944 Naval Battle Strategy Drifts into U.S. Hands." *Prologue Magazine.* Fall 2005.

Burress, Charles. "Shigeya Kihara Taught Japanese to U.S. Soldiers in World War II." *San Francisco Chronicle,* January 24, 2005.

"The Commander-in-Chief Honors Nisei Heroes." *New York Times,* July 16, 1946.

Denver Post. "Editorial: Camp Amache Historic, Indeed." May 17, 2006.

Durdin, Tillman. "Merrill's Raiders Make War Record, Men in

North Burma Have Marched Farther, Fought More Than Any Other of U.S." By Wireless to *The New York Times,* Myitkyina, Burma. May 17, 1944.

Eisele, Albert. "Daniel Inouye's Forty-Year Climb to Power in the Senate." *The Hill, the Capitol Newspaper,* August 4, 1999.

Embree, John F. "The Relocation of Persons of Japanese Ancestry in the United States: Some Causes and Effects." *Journal of the Washington Academy of Science.* 1943.

Erickson, Jim. "World War II Internees' Lives in Catalinas Examined: Renowned Japanese-American Looks Back." *Arizona Daily Star,* August 30, 1998.

Fong, Elizabeth. "Vet Put Priority on Family, War Buddies." *Honolulu Star-Bulletin,* September 7, 2003.

Fujimori, Leila. "Hero Kept World War II Deeds Quiet. A Chance Visit Revealed the Soldier's Heroism." *Honolulu Star-Bulletin,* April 24, 2005.

Fukuhara, Harry. "'America's Secret Weapon': MIS and the Occupation of Japan." *Nikkei Heritage.* Winter 2002.

Gillespie, James J., and McBride, Lauren E. "The 100th Battalion (Nisei) Against the Germans." *Infantry Journal,* December 1944.

Glasgow, Matt. "Go For Broke: The 442nd Combat Team Story." *Soldiers,* November 1978.

Hoshiko, Mike. "Putting Rohwer, Arkansas on the Map." *Pacific Citizen Holiday Issue,* December 23–30, 1988.

James D. Marchio. "Support to Military Operations: The Evolution and Relevance of Joint Intelligence Centers." *Studies in Intelligence: The Journal of the American Intelligence Professional.* Unclassified Edition. Central Intelligence Agency, 2005.

"Japanese-Americans: They Battle the Axis in Italy." *The New York Times,* October 3, 1943.

"Japanese Help Allies Take Benevento." *Washington Post,* October 12, 1943.

Kakesako, Gregg K. "522nd Vets Bear Witness to Dachau Horror." *Honolulu Star-Bulletin,* July 15, 1998.

————. "AJA Medic's Medal May Be Upgraded, The Late James K. Okubo of the 442nd Is on Track for the Medal of Honor." *Honolulu Star-Bulletin,* September 15, 1999.

————. "A Half-Century After Their Wartime Valor, 21 Receive the Nation's Highest Award." *Honolulu Star-Bulletin,* May 12, 2000.

————. "Twenty-two Asian Pacific Americans Finally Receive Their Medals of Honor." *Honolulu Star-Bulletin,* June 22, 2000.

————. "Medal Winners Honored at the Pentagon and on Floor of the U.S. Senate." *Honolulu Star-Bulletin,* June 22, 2000.

Kiuchi, Atsushi. "A Special Hero." *Army,* January 1999.

Lum, Steve. "Fort Shafter's Joe Takata Field." *Hawaii Herald,* July 4, 2003.

Malby, Andy. "War Hero, Accomplished Scientist Embraces Local Roots." *Belgrade [Montana] News,* October 26, 2004.

Masaoka, Mike. "The Japanese American Citizens League Creed, Written in 1940." *Congressional Record,* May 9, 1941.

"Medal of Honor Approved, Finally." *Detroit Free Press,* May 27, 2000.

Nakagawa, Martha. "DB Boys, an Untold World War II Story." *Pacific Citizen,* November 11, 1999.

O'Neill, James P. "The Battle of Belvedere." *Yank,* August 25, 1944.

Portner, Stuart. "The Japanese-American Combat Team." *Military Affairs,* Fall 1943.

Ramirez, Marc. "Japanese-American Vets Honored—56 Years Too Late." *Seattle Times,* March 26, 2001.

Shioya, Tara. "The Conflict Behind the Battle Lines: The Japanese Americans Who Fought in World War II Were Engaged in Another, Private Battle, Against Prejudice and Misunderstandings." *San Francisco Chronicle,* September 24, 1995.

Shirey, Orville C. "Americans: The Story of the 442nd Combat Team." *Infantry Journal,* 1946.

————. "Review of *Go For Broke*." *Combat Forces Journal,* July 1951.

Tizon, Alex. "From Medal of Honor to Courthouse Tribute?" *Seattle Times,* August 17, 2000.

————. "Medal of Honor for a Fallen Hero 56 Years Later." *Seattle Times,* May 28, 2000.

"The Victims Who Liberated Jews." *Jerusalem Post,* July 26, 1999.

Watson, Emmett. "Medal of Honor List Recalls Valor of Japanese American Battalion." *Seattle Times,* May 24, 2000.

DOCUMENTS

American Red Cross. *1942 Report of the American Red Cross Survey of Assembly Centers in California, Oregon, and Washington.* U.S. Commission on Wartime Relocation and Internment of Civilians. 1942.

Caoile, Joyce. *Interview with Colonel Young Oak Kim.* Asians in America Project. August 2003.

Conard, Joseph. *Japanese Evacuation Report Number 8.* Seattle Office of the American Friends Service Committee. Hoover Institution Archives, Joseph Conard Collection. April 2, 1942.

DeWitt, General John B. *Final Report, Japanese Evacuation from the West Coast, 1942.* Government Printing Office. 1943.

Dixon, Colonel Sherwood. *Letter to Reverend Masao Yamada.* Files of the 442nd Regimental Combat Team. National Archives. College Park, Maryland. November 22, 1944.

Merritt, Ralph P. *Project Director's Final Report.* War Relocation Authority, Manzanar Relocation Center. UCLA Special Collections. 1946.

Munson, Curtis B. *The Munson Report (on the Loyalty of Japanese Americans).* November 1941.

Roberts, Owen Josephus. *Roberts Commission Report on Pearl Harbor.* January 23, 1942.

U.S. Army, War Department General Orders 14. *Citation for Companies F and L, 442nd Regimental Combat Team.* March 4, 1945.

U.S. Army, War Department General Orders 34 (as amended by War Department General Orders 106). *Citation for the 442nd Regimental Combat Team (less the 2nd Battalion and the 522nd Field Artillery Battalion).* April 10, 1946 and September 20, 1946.

U.S. Army, War Department General Orders 56. *Citation for the 232nd Engineer Combat Company (then attached to the 111th Engineer Combat Battalion).* June 17, 1946.

U.S. Army, War Department General Orders 66. *Citation for the 100th Infantry Battalion (Separate).* August 15. 1944.

U.S. Army, War Department General Orders 68. *Citation for the 3rd Battalion, 442nd Regimental Combat Team.* August 14, 1945.

U.S. Army, War Department General Orders 78. *Citation for the 100th Battalion, 442nd Regimental Team.* September 12. 1945.

U.S. Army, War Department General Orders 83. *Citation for the 2nd Battalion, 442nd Regimental Combat Team.* August 6, 1946.

U.S. Army. *442nd Infantry Narrative of Events.* U.S. Army. October 1944.

U.S. Army. *442nd Infantry Regiment. The Album. 1943:The 442nd Combat Team.* U.S. Army. 1943.

U.S. Army. *442nd Infantry Regiment. History of 442nd Infantry. February 1943–June 1944.* Reports from 92nd Division Records. 1944.

Yamada, Reverend Masao. *Letter to Colonel Sherwood Dixon.* Files of the 442nd Regimental Combat Team, National Archives. College Park, Maryland. October 30, 1944.

ABOUT THE AUTHOR

Bill Yenne is the San Francisco–based author of more than two dozen books on military and historical topics. *The Wall Street Journal* said recently of his *Indian Wars: The Campaign for the American West* that it "has the rare quality of being both an excellent reference work and a pleasure to read... with cinematic vividness."

His other works include *Operation Cobra and the Great Offensive: Sixty Days that Changed the Course of World War II, Aces: True Stories of Victory and Valor in the Skies of World War II, Secret Weapons of the Cold War, Secret Weapons of World War II, Black '41: The West Point Class of 1941 and the American Triumph in World War II, The History of the U.S. Air Force,* and *SAC: A Primer of Strategic Air Power.* Of the latter, Major Michael Perini wrote in *Air Force Magazine*: "This book deserves a place on any airman's bookshelf and in the stacks of serious military libraries."

Mr. Yenne is a member of the American Aviation Historical Society and the American Society of Journalists and Authors, as well as a graduate of the Stanford University Professional Publishing Course. He is a regular contributor to *International Air Power Review,* and he has written corporate histories of America's greatest planemakers, specifically, Boeing, Convair, Lockheed, McDonnell Douglas, and North American Aviation.

He was also a contributor to the *Simon & Schuster D-Day Encyclopedia,* and penned all of the United States entries to *World War I, A Visual Encyclopedia.* He worked with the legendary U.S. Air Force commander General Curtis E. LeMay to produce *Superfortress: The B-29 and American Airpower in World War II,* which *Publishers Weekly* described as "an eloquent tribute."

INDEX

Bunker Hill, 229, 230, 231
burp gun, 101–2
Burress, Charles, 50

Cable News Network, 204
Caesar Line, 93, 95, 96
Caldera, Louis, 94, 257, 258–59
California (battleship), 4
California Highways, 256
Canada, Japan at war with, 31
Caoile, Joyce, 46
Carr, Ralph Lawrence, 32
Carrara, Italy, 189–90, 211, 220, 262, 272–74
Casablanca, 69–70
Castellina, Italy, 110, 114, 264, 265
Castelpoggio, 213–14
Castle Hill, 75
cave flushing, 221
CBI. *See* China-Burma-India Theater
Cerasuolo, Italy, 263, 265
Champagne Campaign, 182–83
Chiang Kai-Shek, 243
China, 37, 243
China-Burma-India (CBI) Theater, 143–44
Chinese Americans
  immigration of, 8–17
  Medal of Honor awardees, 258
Chinese Exclusion Act, 9, 11
Churchill, Winston, 69
CIC. *See* Combat Information Center
Civil Liberties Act, 256
Clark, Mark, 68, 71, 74, 79, 85, 86, 88, 114, 188
Clinton, Bill, vii, 94, 259
Clough, Caspar, 83, 88–89, 91
Combat Information Center (CIC), 234
Concentration camps. *See* Nazi concentration camps
Concurrent Resolution 62, 256
Congressional Record, 237
Conley, James, 186, 190
Corregidor, 134–36, 236, 255
  Traitor of, 229, 236
Croix de Guerre, 248
Crowley, Thomas, 107

Dachau, 200–208
Dahlquist, John, 152, 154, 158–60, 164–66, 168, 174, 176–77, 180
Davila, Rudolph, 258, 259
Davis, Edward, 169
Davis, Elmer, 57
Dawley, Ernest, 68

Defense Language Institute, 224, 242
Deutsch, Monroe, 139
DeWitt, John L, 23, 24, 26, 38, 42, 49
discrimination. *See* racism
Distinguished Flying Cross awards, 139
Distinguished Red Cross awards, 73, 80–81, 93–95, 107
Distinguished Service Cross (DSC) awards, 2, 80, 121, 197, 217, 247–48, 258
  Akahoshi, 92, 93
  Awakuni, 75
  Hajiro, 158, 170, 173
  Hasemoto, 80–81
  Hayashi, J., 81, 215
  Kim, 91–93
  Kobashigawa, Y., 94
  Kuroda, 158
  Kuroki, B., 139
  Masuda, K., 261
  Miyamoto, 173
  Moto, 112
  Muranaga, 104
  Nakae, 120–21
  Nakamine, 95
  Nakamura, 107–9
  Nishimoto, 179
  Ohata, 80–81
  Okutsu, Y., 197–98
  Ono, 108–9, 112
  Otani, 117–18
  Sakato, 169, 173
  Takata, 73
  Tanouye, 112
Distinguished Service Medal awards, 141
  Sakakida, 241
  Shinseki, 260
Distinguished Unit Citations. *See* Presidential Unit Citations
Dixon, Sherwood, 176–77
DSC. *See* Distinguished Service Cross awards
Durdin, Tillman, 146

Eisenhower, Dwight D., 27
Eisenhower, Milton, 27, 30, 57
Elmer Gantry (Lewis, S.), 168
Emmons, Delos, 38, 39, 40, 255
enemy aliens, draft of, 34–35, 100
English Club, 238
Enigma code, 126–27
Ensminger, Ralph Burnell, 63, 103
espionage, 39–40, 234–35
Executive Order 9066, 26, 32, 49, 55, 60, 194, 203, 207, 249